With my appreciation for their love and encouragement,
I dedicate this book to my parents,
Jack and Phyllis Burke Jovich.

REFLECTIONS ON JFK'S ASSASSINATION

250 Famous Americans Remember
November 22, 1963

TABLE OF CONTENTS

Alexander M. Haig
Daniel Patrick Moynihan
Mark Lane

Harry Reid
Michael N. Castle
Art Buchwald

James J. Blanchard
Geraldine A. Ferraro
Neil Goldschmidt
Joseph A. Califano, Jr.
Richard D. Lamm
Jessica Walter
Richard W. Riley
Larry Pressler
Rona Barrett
Julia Child
Rudy Boschwitz
Donald W. Riegle, Jr.

Charles S. Robb
Mike Sullivan
Barbara A. Mikulski
George S. Mickelson
Richard G. Lugar
Carl Levin
Robert W. Kasten, Jr.
Gary Hart
Stephen J. Cannell
Bill Clinton
Daniel L. Boren

James Abdnor
Lamar Alexander
Bill Allain
Victor Atiyeh
James A. Baker, III
Norman H. Bangerter
Abraham D. Beame
Henry Bellmon
Lloyd Bentsen
Jeff Bingaman
William F. Bolger
Chistopher S. Bond
Julian Bond
Bill Bradley
Terry E. Branstad
John Breaux
Edward W. Brooke
Richard H. Bryan
Yvonne Brathwaite Burke
George Bush
Carroll A. Campbell, Jr.

Jimmy Carter
William J. Casey
John H. Chaffee
Lawton Chiles
William S. Cohen
Martha Layne Collins
Kent Conrad
Steve Cowper
Mario M. Cuomo
Dennis DeConcini
George Deukmejian
Pete V. Domenici
Michael S. Dukakis
David Durenberger
Anthony S. Earl
James Exon
Jake Garn
John Glenn
Albert Gore, Jr.
Bob Graham
Fred Grandy

Charles E. Grassley

Joe Frank Harris

Orrin G. Hatch

Mark O. Hatfield

Mike Hayden

Chic Hecht

Howell Heflin

Jesse Helms

Ernest F. Hollings

Harry Hughes

Nancy Landon Kassebaum

Thomas H. Kean

Jack Kemp

Jeane J. Kirkpatrick

Paul Laxalt

James G. Martin

Ned McWherter

Howard M. Metzenbaum

William G. Milliken

Frank H. Murkowski

George Nigh

Sam Nunn

Robert D. Orr

Charles H. Percy

Pat Robertson

George Romney

Terry Sanford

Ted Schwinden

Paul Simon

Alan K. Simpson

George A. Sinner

Arlen Specter

Robert T. Stafford

James R. Thompson

Richard Thornburgh

Paul Trible

George Wallace

Caspar Weinberger

Mark White

Ronald L. Ziegler

Cleveland Amory

Jack Anderson

Isaac Asimov

Jules Bergman

Jim Bishop

Ed Bradley

James Brady

David Brinkley

Tom Brokaw

Helen Gurley Brown

Hugh Downs

Richard Eberhart

Ray Gandolf

Ellen Goodman

Alex Haley

Floyd Kalber

Jim Lehrer

James A. Michener

Norman Vincent Peale

Gayle Sierens

John Updike

Abigail Van Buren

Mike Wallace

Arthur Walworth

Edward Asner

Dan Aykroyd

Burt Bacharach

Joan Baez

Kaye Ballard

Gene Barry

Ralph Bellamy

Stephen Bishop

Erma Bombeck

Michael Caine

Dick Clark

Rosemary Clooney

Doris Day
Jimmy Dean
Phyllis Diller
Chad Everett
Douglas Fairbanks, Jr.
Tennessee Ernie Ford
Dick Gautier
Marla Gibbs
Robert Goulet
James Gregory
Pat Harrington
Helen Hayes
Florence Henderson
John Houseman
Billy Joel
Clare Kirkconnell
Kreskin
Michael Learned
Loretta Lynn
Barbara Mandrell

Lee Meriwether
Peter Nero
Buck Owens
Gary Owens
Patti Page
Cliff Robertson
Roy Rogers
Mark Russell
Susan Saint James
Neil Sedaka
Artie Shaw
Dinah Shore
Robert Stack
Elizabeth Taylor
John Travolta
Robert Vaughn
Lawrence Welk
Betty White
David L. Wolper

Mario Andretti
Arthur Ashe
Ben Crenshaw
Mike Ditka
Don Drysdale
Lee Elder
Franco Harris
Woody Hayes
Lou Holtz
Hale S. Irwin
Tom Landry
Tom Lasorda
Jack Nicklaus
Arnold Palmer

Joseph V. Paterno
Floyd Patterson
Ray Perkins
Brooks Robinson
Buddy Ryan
Marty Schottenheimer
Donald F. Shula
Sam Snead
Bart Starr
Roger Staubach
Johnny Unitas
Joe Walton
Jerry West

Garner Ted Armstrong
Mary Kay Ash
Jim Bakker
Melvin M. Belli. Sr.

Henry W. Bloch
Frank Borman
Cesar Chavez
Theodore M. Hesburgh

Sandra Day O'Connor
Oral Roberts
Jonas Salk
Donald K. Slayton

Mort Walker
John Weitz
Elmo R. Zumwalt, Jr.

Editor's Note

My memory of November 22, 1963 is probably not unique. But like everyone else old enough to remember that day, the tragedy is seared into my memory. I will always remember where I was, what I saw, and how I—and it seemed, the rest of my small world—felt.

On November 22, 1963 I was eight years old, and attending Bennett Elementary School in Youngstown, Ohio. Mrs. Barnett, my teacher, was at the chalkboard. Suddenly, the school's principal, Miss Wyman, entered our room and walked swiftly toward the teacher. Miss Wyman's face did not possess its customary stern expression; it displayed shock and pain. She whispered to her, "I've got bad news. President Kennedy was shot while riding in a car somewhere in Dallas. They say he was hit in the head." Mrs. Barnett's hand went to her mouth in disbelief.

Despite Miss Wyman's attempt to be discreet, a handful of us overheard her words. My first thought at that moment is still vivid: "I like President Kennedy. Why would anyone want to shoot him in the head?" My mind tried to grasp the news. I did not understand the workings of American Government or the policies of the Kennedy administration. But I knew who John F. Kennedy was, and both he and Ohio astronaut John Glenn were my heroes. More importantly, my parents admired JFK.

Miss Wyman rushed back to the school office and put NBC Radios's bulletins on the school's public address system. A few minutes later, I heard the voice I came to know later as Chet Huntley's say, "John Fitzgerald Kennedy, the thirty-fifth President of the United States, is dead." I glanced around me. There was complete silence. Then, a girl named Gayle began weeping. Mrs. Barnett's eyes, too, filled with tears and her lips trembled as she fought to keep her composure.

School was dismissed early. As I left, I saw the school custodian lowering the flag in the school courtyard to half-mast. I walked home. An elderly school crossing guard whom we all affectionately knew as "Pete" wept openly. I naively thought to myself, "Grown men don't cry, do they?" I then noticed the vast number of vehicles pulling off to the side of the road, the drivers listening in stunned horror to the news on their radios. Finally, running into my home, I saw my mother sobbing at the kitchen table, holding my younger sister in her arms. I began to cry, too.

The events of that terrible day are still clear in my memory, and I think they always will be.

It turned out, of course, that my reactions to John Kennedy's death were shared by millions of other Americans. And as I grew older, it became clear that every time President Kennedy's name was raised in conversation, the next natural point of discussion seemed to be everyone's whereabaouts when they heard the news of his death. Then I became curious, just where was everyone? So I decided simply to ask people, writing to hundreds of prominent citizens seeking information about their reactions to the President's death. And the responses I received painted a fascinating picture of America on that tragic day. Now I can share them with you.

But this book would not have been possible without the help of many people during various stages of its completion.

In Boston, Massachusetts, I am indebted to a number of people. David F. Powers, JFK's closest friend and now curator of the John Fitzgerald Kennedy Library, sat me down in one of the late President's rocking chairs and made the Library's resources available to me. Mr. Powers still possesses the wit, vigor and incredible memory which JFK valued so highly.

The majority of the photographs depicting President Kennedy with many of the respondents in this book were procured through the efforts of Allen Goodrich and Donna Hanlon, JFK Library archivists. Their continuous help to me in locating the appropriate photographs was immeasurable.

I would like to express my appreciation to Sally Coker and Mary Ruth Brannon, administrators at Draughon's Junior College of Business in Paducah, Kentucky, for their gracious assistance to me in preparing my initial questionnaire solicitation back in 1983.

Many thanks to Jerry Pam of the Guttman and Pam, Ltd. public relations firm in Beverly Hills, California, for his help in arranging my contacts with Michael Caine, Clare Kirkconnell, Burt Bacharach, and Robert Vaughn.

I would also like to extend my gratitude to Kelly Bishop, who responded on behalf of her then-ailing husband, the late Jim Bishop, and to Deborah Mary Higgins, Personal Assistant to Susan Saint James, for arranging my interview with the actress, and to my Administrative Assistant at Wilder-Manley Associates, Audrey Whitten, for her kindness in transcribing that conversation.

I also wish to thank my boss at Boston-based Wilder-Manley Associates, company President Stephen M. McParland, and his wife, Beth, for their wonderful hospitality during my journey to Boston.

No writer could have wished for more enthusiastic support than that which I received from Woodbine House. It was a pleasure to work with everyone there.

To my agent, Vicki Lansky, I extend my heartfelt thanks for her belief in my manuscript as a contribution to contemporary history.

If a posthumous note of appreciation can be considered appropriate, I extend one now to the late Congressman Michael J. Kirwan of Youngstown, Ohio. One of the most powerful members of the United States Congress in his day, Mike would host the largest St. Patrick's Day parties in Washington, which JFK regularly attended as congressman, senator, and president. Dave Powers has referred to Mike Kirwan as "One of President Kennedy's Congressional favorites." As a young and impressionable boy growing up in Youngstown, I would listen intently as Mr. Kirwan shared with me his personal recollections of our beloved 35th President. I am convinced that, to a large degree, my memory of Mike Kirwan's fondness of Kennedy inspired the idea for this book.

I am grateful to Charles and Pattie McAtee of Paducah, Kentucky, for their moral support. Thanks also to Gary Resek of Olmstead, Ohio; Sy Sussman, of Las Vegas, Nevada; and Laura Herman, of Tampa, Florida, for their assistance in making possible many of the portrait illustrations in this work.

Finally, my deepest appreciation of all is reserved for my wife, Lisa, for her assistance, patience and steadfast support. Her applause for this project means more to me than that which the most noted critic could possibly bestow.

JOHN B. JOVICH
Tampa, Florida

Introduction

On November 22, 1963, John Fitzgerald Kennedy–35th President of the United States–was assassinated in Dallas, Texas. The first reports, however, indicated only that he had been seriously wounded, and was still alive. As that news swept across the land, all of America held its breath. For nearly an hour, the nation huddled around its radios and television sets, anxiously awaiting any bit of good news. But at 1:30 P.M. CST, the official word came from Mac Kilduff, the assistant White House press secretary, "President John F. Kennedy died at approximately one o'clock."

The nation was stunned. No, not the *Nation* symbolized by the Government, but simply a nation of people–men, women, and children in every corner of the country. In classrooms and offices, in factories and on farms, in stores and at home, every American–perhaps as never before–shared the same overwhelming sorrow and grief. The sense of loss was universal. Everyone felt it, regardless of race or religion, political affiliation, or ideology.

Everyone old enough to remember that day knows exactly where they were when they first heard the tragic news. Now, twenty-five years after John Kennedy's death, two hundred fifty prominent Americans have been brought together to recall their own personal reactions, and to candidly reveal the hopes and fears they experienced on that fateful November day.

Taken together, these reflections of JFK's assassination capture the feelings of a nation on one memorable day. The recollections of former Presidents, journalists, Members of Congress, Governors, entertainers, sports legends, and religious leaders offer a rare look at a single moment in this nation's history when all Americans were united by our common loss.

For those readers who remember the events in Dallas, you can relate your own experiences to those recounted here. For anyone who does not remember November 22, 1963, this book will illustrate the enormous impact that the death of John Kennedy had on the lives of so many people, as well as on the life of this nation.

Hundreds of prominent people throughout the world were contacted, and were asked to respond to these three questions:

> Where were you when you first heard the news of President Kennedy's shooting?;

> How did you react to the news?; and

> On that date, what impact did you feel President Kennedy's death would have on the nation?

More than 250 persons responded, with their responses taking a variety of formats: a few short words or phrases, a letter, or in some instances, extensive reprints of memoirs published previously. To best portray the statements of the respondents, their original responses are reproduced here, except in those cases where handwritten letters became illegible when reduced. Those letters have been typeset. In each case, however, the response has been carefully edited to present those portions which deal directly with President Kennedy. Accompanying each response is a short biographical statement about the respondent, and in most cases, a photograph. And to offer a better perspective of each response, the repondent's age at the time of President Kennedy's assassination is found in brackets.

The respondents were genuinely anxious to share their personal feelings about that day in history, and about President Kennedy. Many specifically expressed their gratitude for being given that opportunity. Some even recalled how President Kennedy's death actually changed their lives.

John Kennedy was more than just the President of the United States. He was also a husband, a father, a son, a brother, and a friend. Of his forty-six years, less than three of them were spent in the White House. So it is important to review not only his Presidency, but his entire life. In Chapter I, historian and author James Edward Peters presents an informative profile of John Kennedy, one of nine children born into a wealthy family, who went on to become a naval hero, Pulitzer Prize-winning author, Congresssman, Senator, and then President.

It was this life—so filled with promise and hope—that ended so tragically in Dallas. Chapter II offers a recounting of the events that day from five eyewitnesses; two renowned journalists, a Kennedy insider, an LBJ confidant, and the Speaker of the House of Representatives. Although both are well-known journalists today, in 1963 Robert Mac-Neil and Douglas Kiker were young reporters on their first Presidential trip, sent to cover what was considered one of the first stops for President Kennedy's 1964 re-election campaign. They were with Kennedy when he landed in Dallas, and were part of the motorcade that wound its way through Dealey Plaza, and ended at Parkland Hospital. Larry O'Brien—one of JFK's closest friends and advisors—presents a behind-the-scenes look at the events at Parkland, aboard Air Force One, and later in the White House. Jack Valenti was a special assistant to Vice President—then suddenly President—Lyndon Johnson. He, too, was in the motorcade and recalls the Vice President's reaction; and Speaker Jim Wright, then a five-term Congressman, was part of the President's Texas entourage.

As the events in Dallas unfolded, the news wires sprang to life back in Washington. At 12:34 CST, just four minutes after the shots were fired, the UPI wire errupted: "THREE SHOTS WERE FIRED AT PRESIDENT KENNEDY'S MOTORCADE." Then, just moments later: "FLASH KENNEDY SERIOUSLY WOUNDED PERHAPS FATALLY BY ASSASSINS BULLET." By the time the President's death was confirmed, the news had spread across the capital like wildfire.

The first group of people forced to face the consequences of President Kennedy's assassination were those who were entrusted to share the responsibility of government with John Kennedy. Caught off guard by the events in Dallas, they were compelled to keep the wheels of government turning while dealing with the death of a friend and leader. Like President Kennedy, many were away from Washington that weekend. Dozens of Congressmen and Senators, Cabinet members, and military leaders scrambled to get back to the nation's capital.

The memoirs in Chapter III track the reaction in official Washington as it learned the news. Twenty-five years later, Senators, Congressmen, Cabinet members, Supreme Court justices and journalists vividly recall the events in Washington in November 1963. From their responses you learn that in the Senate, the President's brother Edward was presiding; that Members of the House fell to their knees in prayer; that Cabinet members enroute to the Far East returned immediately to the capital; and that some people in Washington suspected a far-reaching conspiracy. In an intimate and candid memoir, Senator Barry Goldwater discusses his relationship with Jack Kennedy and Lyndon Johnson. Then-Congressman Charles Mathias recounts the participation of the Congress in memorial services in the Capitol. Other Washington reactions include those of former President Gerald Ford, Congressman Robert Michel, Supreme Court Justice Arthur Goldberg, journalists, members of the Kennedy administration, and Warren Commission critic Mark Lane.

Many people in public life today were at the threshold of their careers in 1963. During his inaugural address, President Kennedy challenged young Americans to heed the call to public service. In Chapter IV, more than two dozen of today's public figures recall how John Kennedy first inspired their involvement in our political process.

The death of President Kennedy affected the lives of everyone, regardless of ideology or political affiliation. Chapter V brings together many of the nation's current political leaders to share their memories of JFK and his death. Former President Jimmy Carter, Vice President George Bush, Governor Michael Dukakis, and dozens of other current and former Senators, Congressmen, Governors, Cabinet Members, Mayors, Ambassadors, and presidential appointees recall their whereabouts when they first heard the tragic news.

The trip to Dallas was just another political trip; just another political news story, until Lee Harvey Oswald killed the President. Then Dallas became the story of a lifetime. Every facet of the media focused on the death of John Kennedy and the reaction to it. President Kennedy had enjoyed a good relationship with the press. He found their frequent encounters challenging as well as entertaining. Kennedy had also been a prize-winning author and an avid reader, and had empathized with writers and their work. In Chapter VI, two dozen of America's leading journalists and writers offer their reflections of the Kennedy Presidency.

Chapter VII presents the reactions of many of this nation's top entertainers. Even in Hollywood, where "the show must go on," sets faded to black as cameras and microphones fell silent. Even Hollywood could not escape the sorrow which JFK's death produced. All thoughts were diverted from performing and shifted to the fallen President and his family. Performances were cancelled throughout the country as members of the entertainment world joined the rest of America to watch the televised memorial services in Washington.

Sporting events were also cancelled as a tribute to John Kennedy, himself an avid, active sportsman. Kennedy promoted physical activity, and his youth and vigor attracted a great following among the sports figures of 1963 and today. Players and coaches from the worlds of golf, baseball, racing, boxing, football, tennis, and basketball have been brought together in Chapter VIII to remember JFK as President and sportsman.

But people who remember John Kennedy can be found in every profession, and Chapter IX presents the reflections of a variety of Americans, including national religious figures, military and business leaders, members of the legal commmunity, former astronauts, and others. Some of these people knew John Kennedy, and felt the loss personally. Others may have disagreed with his policies, but respected him as a leader.

As a final tribute to President Kennedy, renowned historian and biographer of the Kennedy years, Arthur M. Schlesinger, Jr., presents a very poignant memoir of JFK and his legacy. In an extract from his bestseller, *A Thousand Days,* Schlesinger reviews the Kennedy years and the effects of the President's death on the nation and the world. He also recounts the reactions of many people from around the globe — whether the leaders of Cuba and the Soviet Union, or poor tribesmen in Africa.

Twenty-five years after his death, the memory of John Kennedy still evokes a dichotomy of emotions—joy at the memory of an era that reflected his energy and vitality, and sadness because it ended so quickly and so tragically. From the individual recollections of two hundred-fifty Americans, this book presents a unique portrait of one memorable day in American history. *Reflections of JFK's Assassination* forever preserves the feelings of a nation on the day it lost its President.

ALPHABETICAL LISTING OF
CONTRIBUTORS TO THIS BOOK

I

JOHN FITZGERALD KENNEDY: A PROFILE

> "Dad persuaded us to work hard at whatever we did. We soon learned that competition in the family was a kind of dry run for the world outside. At the same time, everything channeled into public service."
>
> "Just as I went into politics because Joe died, if anything happened to me tomorrow, my brother Bobby would run for my seat in the Senate. And if Bobby died, Teddy would take over for him."
>
> — *Senator John Kennedy in 1957*

By James Edward Peters

When John Kennedy took the oath of office on the steps of the United States Capitol on January 20, 1961, he was the youngest man ever elected President. When his body was returned to the Capitol on November 24, 1963 to lie in state, John Kennedy had become the youngest President ever to die in office. In one dark moment, an assassin ended the life which began with so much hope and promise forty-six years earlier.

John Fitzgerald Kennedy was born on May 29, 1917 in Brookline, Massachusetts, a suburb of Boston. He was the second child and the second son of Joseph P. Kennedy and Rose Fitzgerald Kennedy. His parents were both well-educated members of prominent, political Irish-American families. Joseph Kennedy's father, Patrick J. Kennedy, had been a Boston saloonkeeper whose understanding of the value of patronage made him a respected ward leader and state senator; while

James Edward Peters is the author of Arlington National Cemetery: Shrine to America's Heroes.

Rose's father, John F. "Honey Fitz" Fitzgerald (after whom the President was named), served in the U.S. House of Representatives and later as Mayor of Boston.

Joseph Kennedy taught each of his nine children to be competitive in all aspects of their lives, whether it was playing touch football on the lawn of their Hyannis Port home, or playing political football in the arena of public office. Jack — as he was known by his family and friends — learned this lesson well. He and his much-revered older brother, Joe Jr., were in constant competition, physically and intellectually. "Let 'em fight," commented their father. "The important thing is that they fight together." It was that sense of clansmanship that later became a hallmark of the Kennedy family when John Kennedy embarked on his bid for the Presidency.

In 1931, John entered Choate, a prestigious college preparatory school in Wallingford, Connecticut. Following his graduation in 1935, Kennedy enrolled at Princeton, and spent his first summer studying at the London School of Economics. While in England, he contracted jaundice, and when it recurred during the winter term at Princeton, Kennedy was forced to leave school. In the fall of 1936, fully recovered, Jack Kennedy entered Harvard University. While there he majored in government and became a member of the varsity swim team. But it was also at Harvard that Kennedy seriously injured his back playing football, an injury which plagued him the rest of his life.

While Jack was at Harvard, his father was appointed Ambassador to Great Britain by President Franklin Roosevelt in 1937. During his junior year, Jack sought and received permission from school authorities to join his father's staff in London. From this position, he was able to travel throughout Europe, witnessing first-hand the events that would lead to World War II. Jack Kennedy was in Europe when British Prime Minister Neville Chamberlain met with Adolf Hitler in Munich in September 1938, a meeting which many historians believe paved the way for Hitler's advance across Europe. Upon his return to Harvard, Kennedy wrote his senior thesis about Britain's military unpreparedness prior to World War II, entitling it "Appeasement at Munich." Following his graduation with honors in 1940, Kennedy was encouraged by veteran *New York Times* journalist Arthur Krock to publish his thesis. Expanded and retitled *Why England Slept,* the book became a national bestseller for the twenty-three-year-old Kennedy.

After graduation, Jack Kennedy considered the options for his future, but those considerations did not include concern for his financial support. Like each of his eight brothers and sisters, Kennedy had received a million dollar trust fund from his father when he turned twenty-one, and as his father had intended, it gave Jack the freedom to consider his career without financial worry. So Kennedy entered the Stanford University Business School for the 1940 fall term, but withdrew after six months. He then took an extended tour of South America. By this time, Europe was embroiled in war and America seemed certain to be drawn into the conflict. In the spring of 1941, Jack Kennedy attempted to enlist in the United States Army, but was denied admission because of his weak back. Throughout that summer he underwent physical therapy and training, and was finally accepted into the U.S. Navy in September 1941, more than three months before the Japanese attack on Pearl Harbor.

After stints in Washington, D.C. and Charleston, South Carolina, Ensign Kennedy was promoted to Lieutenant (jg) and given command of a motor torpedo patrol boat, the PT-109. By August 1943, Kennedy's boat was assigned to Rendova Island in the Solomon Islands. The Japanese Imperial fleet often dispatched their fast destroyers into this area of the South Pacific to interrupt Allied shipping. It was the mission of the PT boats to intercept and destroy those Japanese vessels.

On August 1, 1943, the PT-109 joined thirteen other PT boats to set up a blockade in the Ferguson passage near the Japanese-held islands of Vella Lavella and Gizo. Shortly after 2:00 A.M. on August 2, the Japanese destroyer *Amagiri* and several other enemy vessels were spotted. In the ensuing battle, the PT boats were scattered as the *Amagiri* engaged several vessels at once. Suddenly—silhouetted by exploding cannon shells and gasoline fires—the PT-109 lay directly ahead of the *Amagiri.* The Japanese commander ordered a collision course, ramming Kennedy's 80-foot wooden craft. The impact splintered the 109, propelling the young Lieutenant and his crew into the firey waters of Ferguson passage. Two crewmen were killed instantly, another was badly burned. Aware that the nearby islands were occupied by the Japanese, Kennedy lead his men to a tiny, unoccupied coral atoll. Clenching the straps of the injured sailor's life jacket between his teeth, Kennedy towed the suffering crewman for more than five hours.

Jack Kennedy spent the next several days swimming through the open channels of the Solomon Islands with a small lantern and a .38 caliber pistol tied around his neck, hoping to signal a passing American boat. As time passed, the situation grew worse. The men were without fresh water, food, and badly-needed medical supplies. Their feet were swollen from coral reef cuts and, as a result of swallowing too much salt water during their swim, they vomited frequently. Kennedy had re-injured his back when the *Amagiri* hit the PT-109, and now suffered extreme fatigue as he swam in dangerous tidal currents seeking help. Luckily, he was spotted struggling in the water by a canoe of friendly natives who took him aboard. Discovering that none of the natives spoke English, Kennedy found a smooth coconut husk and, with a pen knife, scrawled the now famous message: NATIVE KNOWS POSIT HE CAN PILOT 11 ALIVE NEED SMALL BOAT KENNEDY. The natives took the husk to an Australian coast watcher who helped to arrange the rescue of Kennedy and his crew, six days after they were thrown into the sea.

For his heroism, Kennedy was awarded the Navy and Marine Corps Medal and the Purple Heart. Although he had hoped to regain his vitality and remain in the South Pacific, Kennedy had contracted malaria, and his weight fell to less than 125 pounds. He was returned to the United States for treatment of the malaria and his recurring back problems. It was during this period of convalescence that Jack learned that his beloved older brother, Joe, had been killed in the explosion of an Army plane on a secret mission in Europe. His injuries ultimately resulted in his discharge from the Navy in 1945.

Following his military discharge, John Kennedy spent a brief tenure as a reporter for the International News Service, covering the founding of the United Nations, the Potsdam Conference, and the British elections. But after a few months he resigned. "I felt it was too passive," he concluded. "Instead of doing things, you were writing about people who did things." But he was still unsure of just what direction his life should take.

It was well-known among the Kennedy family that Joe Jr. had been chosen by his father for a political career, but those hopes died with Joe during the war. So Joe Sr. was reported to have issued Jack an order. "I told him Joe was dead and it was his responsibility to run for Congress," the older Kennedy was quoted as saying. "He didn't want to. But I told him he had to."

Whatever the motivation, John Kennedy moved into the 11th Congressional District in the Charlestown section of Boston to seek the seat once held by his maternal grandfather. Although shyer and more withdrawn than his older brother had been, Kennedy soon enlisted the help of the man who became one of his closest friends and oldest political associates, Dave Powers. Powers was an affable but savvy Charlestown Democrat, born and bred among the three-deckers that surrounded Bunker Hill, and he soon schooled Kennedy in the facts of political life in Boston. Jack Kennedy was a quick learner. Although he faced eight opponents in that first primary race in 1946, he defeated them handily. After his victory in the general election, Kennedy took his seat in Congress, joining a freshman class which included a young Congressman from California, Richard Nixon.

Kennedy served three terms in the Congress, but was frustrated that his was just a single voice in the 435-member House of Representatives. So in 1952, the 35-year-old Democrat chose to give up his safe House seat to face the three-term incumbent Republican Senator, the venerable Henry Cabot Lodge. Political experts gave Kennedy little chance of beating Lodge, especially when the Republicans nominated Dwight Eisenhower for President. But Kennedy campaigned relentlessly, aided by his large and energetic family. His younger brother, Bobby, managed the campaign, and his mother and sisters hosted teas throughout the state, inviting voters to meet the candidate. It was also during the Senate campaign that Kenneth P. O'Donnell and Lawrence F. O'Brien joined the Kennedy campaign team. Years later, when Kennedy was in the White House, the close-knit team of Powers, O'Donnell and O'Brien would be labeled "The Irish Mafia" by the media. On election night when the votes were tallied, Eisenhower carried Massachusetts, but Kennedy defeated Lodge by more than 70,000 votes.

In January 1953, Jack Kennedy entered the United States Senate. Shortly thereafter, he was invited to dinner at the home of Charles Bartlett, a good friend of Kennedy's and a columnist for the *Saturday Evening Post*. While at dinner, Kennedy was introduced to a young writer and photographer for the *Washington Times-Herald*. Her name was Jacqueline Lee Bouvier. Kennedy later recalled the encounter, "I leaned across the asparagus and asked her for a date."

Jacqueline Bouvier was a graduate of Vassar and had studied at the Sorbonne in Paris. She was fluent in several languages, and shared Jack Kennedy's interest in history and journalism. In 1951, she was awarded *Vogue's* Prix de Paris for an essay she had written about the three men she would most liked to have known—19th century French poet Charles Baudelaire, Irish dramatist and poet Oscar Wilde, and early 20th century Russian promoter of the arts Sergey Diaghilev. Jackie, as she became universally known, was the daughter of New York banker John Bouvier and Mrs. Hugh D. Auchincloss of Georgetown.

Jack Kennedy kept his relationship with Jacqueline very private. Many of his friends and staff members were unaware of the romance until shortly before their engagement was announced in June of 1953. That announcement was delayed, however—to the reported annoyance of Jackie—so as not to pre-empt a politically-favorable article that headlined the June 13 edition of the *Saturday Evening Post*: "Jack Kennedy: The Senate's Gay Young Bachelor."

On September 12, 1953, John Fitzgerald Kennedy (age 36) and Jacqueline Lee Bouvier (age 24) were married in a spectacular wedding in St. Mary's Church in Newport, Rhode Island. The reception was held on the Newport estate of Jackie's stepfather, Hugh Auchincloss. "It was just like a coronation," one guest observed. Following a honeymoon in Acapulco, the couple settled into the home of the late Supreme Court Justice Robert Jackson in McLean, Virginia.

The Kennedys' first year of marriage was not a happy one. Jackie suffered her first miscarriage, and Senator Kennedy was plagued with debilitating back pain, forcing him onto crutches in order to walk. The pain became so intense that he finally agreed to undergo a still-experimental lumbar fusion operation, and to have a steel plate inserted in his spine. The operation took place on October 21, but the steel plate lead to a serious infection, and his condition deteriorated. Twice during the succeeding month, John Kennedy was so close to death that a Catholic priest was called to his bedside to administer the last rites.

Finally, in a second operation, the plate was removed, and Senator Kennedy rallied. But his back remained weak, so he began a regimen of exercises to strengthen his back muscles. It was during this period, while visiting a doctor's office, that Jack found relief sitting in a rocking chair, and decided to acquire one for himself. That rocking chair became a Kennedy trademark in 1955, and it accompanied him to the Oval Office in 1961.

Senator Kennedy spent the first half of 1955 convalescing at his father's home in Palm Beach, Florida. Unable to sleep for more than a couple of hours at a time because of the severe back pain, he spent many hours reading or having Jackie read to him. His interest in political biographies and history seemed insatiable. And his time alone offered him a chance to reflect on the dilemmas of political life. "Politics is a jungle," he later wrote. "...torn between doing the right thing and staying in office; between the local interest and the national interest; between the private good of the politician and the general good." So it was no surprise to his friends and family when he conceived the idea of writing a book about courageous historic figures who defied the popular will to take unpopular, but principled positions. The book was entitled *Profiles In Courage*.

The men Kennedy chose to profile were–like himself–United States Senators: Daniel Webster, Sam Houston, George W. Norris, Lucius Lamar, Thomas Hart Benton, Edmund G. Ross, and Robert Taft. The book became a best-seller, and was later awarded the Pulitzer Prize for biography in 1957.

After several months at his father's home in Florida, John Kennedy returned to the U.S. Senate in May of 1955. His well-publicized book brought national attention to the junior Senator from Massachusetts, and he received an increasing number of invitations to appear across the country. By 1956, he was ready to test the national political waters.

In a bold move, Kennedy allowed his name to be placed in nomination for Vice President at the 1956 Democratic Convention, hoping to be chosen as Adlai Stevenson's running mate. In a close race, he lost the nomination to Senator Estes Kefauver of Tennessee by 38 votes. Many political pundits considered this a fatal blow to Kennedy's future chances for a national office. But the Stevenson/Kefauver ticket was soundly defeated by President Eisenhower in the 1956 election, and Kennedy's own overwhelming re-election to the Senate in 1958 again put Kennedy's name in the forefront of the Democratic Party.

On January 2, 1960, John Kennedy announced his candidacy for the office of President of the United States. He knew then that the road to the White House would not be an easy one to travel. The Republicans seemed certain to nominate Vice President Richard Nixon, who would be a formidable foe in the November election. But before he could face Nixon, Senator Kennedy would have to wrestle the Democratic nomination away from fellow Senators Hubert Humphrey of Minnesota, Lyndon Johnson of Texas, and Missouri's Stuart Symington, and from the undeclared Adlai Stevenson who had been the Democrats' standard-bearer in 1952 and 1956.

As the political jostling began, it became clear that there were few ideological differences between the candidates. What soon became the dominant issue in the campaign was John Kennedy's religion. He was a Catholic, and no Catholic had ever before been elected President. His critics charged that if he were elected, he would be influenced by the Vatican; that his Church, not his country, would claim his first allegiance. The religion issue came to a head during the West Virginia primary where there were only two major candidates on the ballot: Kennedy and Humphrey. Johnson and other anti-Kennedy forces threw their support behind Humphrey, hoping that by defeating Kennedy here, Humphrey could eliminate him from the race. And their greatest chance of defeating Kennedy was by raising the religion issue in this state which was 97% Protestant.

Kennedy decided to confront the issue head-on. As he toured the state, he reminded voters, "Nobody asked me if I was a Catholic when I joined the United States Navy....Nobody asked my brother if he was a Protestant or a Catholic when he climbed into an American bomber to fly his last mission." On May 10, 1960, West Virginians went to the polls to give their endorsement to John Kennedy by a 60% to 40% margin, and religion seemed dead as a campaign issue.

By the time the Democrats convened in Los Angeles in July, John Kennedy had accumulated the greatest number of delegates, but still not enough to secure a first ballot nomination. So the political wrangling intensified. Candidates and would-be candidates scurried from one state caucus to another in search of uncommitted delegates or delegates whose candidates had withdrawn. The city was rife with reports of political deals involving offers for the second spot on the ticket. There were movements to stop the frontrunner. A groundswell of support emerged for Adlai Stevenson, especially among party leaders. Stevenson had not declared his candidacy prior to the convention, but was still enormously popular among party regulars. Lyndon Johnson—the second choice of many delegates—encouraged the stop-Kennedy movement, hoping to benefit from any loss of support for JFK. Finally, the names of Johnson, Kennedy, and Stevenson were placed in nomination.

Then the first ballot roll call began: Alabama...Alaska...Arizona.... The Kennedy forces were well aware that if they failed to win on the first ballot, their support could erode. New Jersey...New Mexico...New York.... As the roll coll continued, it was clear there would be no early victory for the Massachusetts Senator. When the list of states neared the end—Washington, West Virginia, Wisconsin—Kennedy still had not reached the number of votes needed for nomination. The chair finally called, "Wyoming," the last state. The convention hall fell silent; everyone knew that it was going to be close. The chairman of the Wyoming delegation approached the microphone, and as he announced his state's votes, it became clear that the nomination belonged to Kennedy. When the chair made it official, pandemonium reigned, both in the hall among Kennedy's supporters, and in the Senator's suite at the Biltmore Hotel.

The nomination secured, Kennedy's next step was to choose a running mate. He had not made a choice before the convention, though he had indicated that he favored a Midwestern liberal. His personal favorite was Hubert Humphrey, but that was before Humphrey endorsed Stevenson during the convention. Much to the surprise of his brother Bobby, his staff, labor and civil rights leaders, and perhaps most of all the man he chose, Kennedy picked Lyndon Johnson as his running mate.

Amid a storm of protests, Kennedy attempted to explain the choice to his long-time friend Ken O'Donnell. Kennedy confided, "I'm forty-three years old, and I'm the healthiest candidate for President in the United States. You've traveled with me enough to know that. I'm not going to die in office. So the Vice Presidency doesn't mean anything. I'm thinking of the leadership in the Senate....Did it occur to you that if Lyndon becomes the Vice President, I'll have Mike Mansfield as leader in the Senate, somebody I can trust and depend on." Johnson was nominated.

The Republican Party nominated Vice President Richard Nixon as expected, and Nixon chose as his running mate Henry Cabot Lodge, the man John Kennedy had defeated to win his Senate seat in 1952. But neither ticket was taking anything for granted. It promised to be a vigorous campaign fought by two tireless campaigners. Jack Kennedy was 43 years old, and Richard Nixon was 47, making them the two youngest nominees to ever compete for the Presidency.

As the campaign began in earnest, the question of John Kennedy's religion was again raised. In order to quash this issue once and for all—and to allow the campaign to focus on what he considered the real issues—Kennedy decided to present his case before the most critical of juries. On September 12, he accepted an invitation to address, and to answer questions from, members of the Greater Houston Ministerial Association. Against the advice of every person he asked, Kennedy chose this forum to state as clearly and forcefully as he could his views on the separation of church and state:

> "I am not the Catholic candidate for President. I am the Democratic Party's candidate who happens to be Catholic. I do not speak for my church on public matters—and the church does not speak for me....But if I should win this election, I shall devote every effort of mind and spirit to fulfilling the oath of the Presidency—practically identical, I might add, with the oath I have taken for fourteen years in Congress. For, without reservation, I can, and I quote, "solemnly swear that I will faithfully execute the office of President of the United States and will to the best of my ability preserve, protect and defend the Constitution, so help me God."

John Kennedy ranked his speech in Houston among the best he ever delivered. He felt that only his inaugural address, his address at the Berlin Wall, and his foreign policy speech at American University in 1963 were better. The Houston speech silenced religion as a vocal issue in the campaign, although it was shown to have still influenced the decision of many voters.

John Kennedy's 1960 run for the Presidency introduced a campaign tool to the American political scene which is now considered indispensable: the airplane. Kennedy's extensive use of the *Caroline*, (his family's private plane named after his daughter born in 1957) allowed him to crisscross the country, appearing in several states in a single day. It gave him a distinct advantage during the primary elections, and promoted his image as an agressive campaigner. The other contribution to Presidential politics that resulted from the 1960 campaign was the televised debate.

The series of four televised debates between Nixon and Kennedy became the highlight of the 1960 campaign. Kennedy issued the challenge, and Nixon—who held a large lead in the polls—accepted. This was not the first time that these two men had debated, however. It is often forgotten that the first Kennedy-Nixon debate actually occurred in April 1947 in McKeesport, Pennsylvania. On that occasion, while both men were freshman Congressmen, they exchanged sharp comments on the merits of the Taft-Hartley Act.

It is widely agreed that the series of presidential debates between the two candidates, especially the first debate in Chicago, was the single most important factor of the campaign. Much has been said about the way the candidates appeared, even more perhaps than about what they said. To most viewers, Vice President Nixon appeared tired, and his heavy beard gave him a dark and sinister look. His responses also seemed hesitant and unsure. Senator Kennedy, on the other hand, appeared relaxed and healthy, delivering his responses with poise and wit. Kennedy's apparent firm grasp of the issues dispelled the criticism that he was too immature, too inexperienced to stand up the the likes of Soviet Premier Khrushchev.

Nixon was considered ahead in the polls before the debates in September and October. But by the time the last debate ended, the race had narrowed to a dead heat.

Election Day was November 8, and John Kennedy appeared nervous as he accompanied his wife to their polling place near their legal residence on Beacon Hill in Boston. But it was not the election which prompted his nervousness, it was his wife. As he lead Jackie through the throng of cheering supporters outside the poll, he shielded his wife from the jostling crowd. Jackie was more than eight months pregnant, and he wasn't ready to take any chances. After they voted, the couple flew to Cape Cod.

During the next three years, Americans would hear a great deal about the Kennedy Compound at Hyannis Port on Cape Cod. There would be photographs and news reports about the touch football games on the lawn, sailing off the coast, walks along the shore, all connoting the tranquility that President Kennedy sought and cherished there. But on November 8, 1960–Election Day–the Kennedy Compound was anything but tranquil.

Robert Kennedy's house was converted into an election command center. Additional telephone lines had been installed in the large enclosed porch to keep campaign staffers in touch with poll watchers around the country. News service teletype machines were now up and operating, cranking out news from the larger states. And the dining room was equipped with a phalanx of adding machines to tabulate the results as they poured in, ready to be analyzed by pollster Lou Harris. Senator Kennedy walked over from his cottage at about 7:30 that evening to join the masses of people huddled around television screens and telephones. The early returns, all from the East, were good. He returned home to have dinner with Jackie, but when he reappeared at Bobby's house around ten o'clock, the happy faces he had seen earlier had turned sour. Returns from the Midwest were not good. He was doing worse than expected in Illinois and Michigan, and was actually losing in Ohio, Kentucky, Wisconsin, and Tennessee. News west of the Mississippi was even worse.

Later in the evening, after Ohio was lost, Kennedy received an update from his running mate in Texas, who assured him that the Lone Star State was going their way. After LBJ hung up, Kennedy reported that Johnson had quipped, "I see *we* won in Pennsylvania, but what happened to *you* in Ohio?"

At about three in the morning, having claimed 261 of the 270 electoral votes needed for election, Jack Kennedy went to bed. When he woke up the next morning, he had lost California, but had carried Illinois, Michigan, and Minnesota, giving him 303 electoral votes, and the election. But it had been a very narrow victory. Out of more than 68 million votes cast, Kennedy won by a little more than 100,000 votes—or about one vote per precinct. It was the closest popular vote in history. If Nixon had won Illinois (where he lost by only 8,000 votes) and Texas (where it was also close), he would have been elected President.

The National Guard armory in Hyannis had been converted into a press center for Election Day, and it was here that President-elect John Kennedy appeared with his wife on Wednesday morning to declare, "Now my wife and I prepare for a new administration, and a new baby." With that, President-elect Kennedy began the process of forming a government. He had just ten weeks to name a Cabinet and to fill more than 1,200 other positions.

The President-elect divided his time between his father's home in Palm Beach and his own home on N Street in Georgetown. He and Jackie had moved there after Caroline was born. Shortly after the election, Kennedy visited the Vice President-elect at the LBJ Ranch, and he made a call on Richard Nixon at his home in Key Biscayne, Florida.

Kennedy had planned to spend Thanksgiving with Jackie and Caroline in Georgetown, and then to fly back to Palm Beach to continue working on Cabinet appointments. After Thanksgiving dinner, Kennedy left Washington aboard the *Caroline,* followed by a charted DC-6 filled with members of the press. En route, Kennedy received word that Jackie had gone into labor. About to land in Florida, Kennedy decided to return immediately to Washington aboard the much faster DC-6. On board the press plane, Kennedy scrambled into the cockpit to await further reports. At 1:17 A.M., he received word that John Kennedy, Jr. had been born and, although it had been a rough

John Kennedy at the helm of his sailboat, Victura, *off the coast of Cape Cod.*

delivery, mother and son were doing fine.

Kennedy spent a great deal of time in Georgetown after that, staying close to his family and working on his Cabinet. The work progressed smoothly, except for the position of Attorney General. Kennedy had offered it to Connecticut Governor Abraham Ribicoff, but Ribicoff preferred to head the Department of Health, Education, and Welfare. Finally, JFK decided to offer it to his brother Bobby.

Bobby had been Jack's right-hand man since his first Congressional race in 1946. When Jack was in the Senate, Bobby was also on Capitol Hill, serving as legal counsel for two different Senate Committees. So now the President-elect was anxious to have Bobby close at hand in Washington, and he needed an Attorney General in whom he had absolute trust. In the President-elect's view, that meant Bobby. But he knew that the appointment would raise eyebrows. After first objecting for political reasons, Bobby accepted. Then came the question of how and when to make the announcement.

The steps of Kennedy's Georgetown home had become a familiar site on the evening news because it was from here that Kennedy announced many of his Cabinet appointments. When considering how to announce

Bobby's appointment, he suggested, "I'll open the front door of the house some morning about 2:00 A.M., look up and down the street, and if nobody's around, I'll whisper, 'it's Bobby.'" When the President-elect finally made the formal announcement, there was some criticism. He was confident of the appointment, however, and unabashedly brushed aside objections saying, "I can't see that it's wrong to give him a little legal experience before he goes out to practice law."

After Bobby's appointment was announced, President-elect Kennedy was scheduled to fly to Palm Beach for the weekend, deciding at the last moment to take Jackie and the kids along with him. As it turned out, having Jackie and Caroline with him in Florida that weekend may have saved his life.

President and Mrs. Kennedy with their children, John, Jr., and Caroline, after church services on Easter Sunday, 1963. (Cecil Stoughton)

Also in Florida that weekend was a man named Richard Pavlik. Pavlik, a resident of New Hampshire, had developed a deep hatred of John Kennedy, believing that somehow Kennedy had, in Pavlik's words, "bought the Presidency." Pavlik knew that when Kennedy was in Palm Beach, he drove himself to mass on Sunday mornings. On this particular Sunday, Pavlik was parked outside the Kennedy home in an automobile loaded with seven sticks of dynamite. It was Pavlik's intention to ram Kennedy's car as JFK drove to church, setting off an explosion that would kill himself and the President-elect. As Kennedy left the house to get into his car, Jackie and Caroline came to the door with him, and watched as he drove away. Pavlik later confessed that, although he hated Kennedy and wanted to kill him, he could not do it in front of Kennedy's wife and daughter. Seeing Jackie and Caroline standing in the doorway that morning, he decided to postpone his attempt until the following Sunday. During the intervening week, the Secret Service received a tip from Pavlik's hometown that he was in Florida intending to kill the President-elect. A manhunt was ordered, and on Wednesday Secret Service agents took Pavlik into custody. John Kennedy did not learn of the plot until a few days later, after Pavlik had been arrested.

As usual, the Kennedy family gathered at Ambassador Kennedy's house in Palm Beach for Christmas. By that time, JFK had his Cabinet in place, so his attention then turned to the Inauguration. The President-elect spent much of his time working on his inaugural address, while supervising the appointment of the remaining 1,200 executive positions to be filled.

On January 19, President-elect Kennedy met with President Eisenhower in the Oval Office for the last in a series of briefings which had taken place since the election. Throughout the capital, final preparations were being made for the peaceful transition of power, a transition which the United States first pioneered more than 170 years before. At about five o'clock in the afternoon, it began to snow. By morning, the skies had cleared but a thick blanket of snow covered the capital, and the temperature had plummeted.

Shortly before 11:00 A.M. on Friday, January 20, 1961, the Chairmen of the Congressional Inaugural Committee—Speaker Sam Rayburn and Alabama Senator John Sparkman—called on President-elect and Mrs. Kennedy at their home in Georgetown to escort them to the White House where they were to meet the Eisenhowers. Brilliant sunshine reflected off the deep snow which had fallen the night before as the group drove to the Capitol for the oath-taking ceremonies.

On the steps of the United States Capitol, Richard Cardinal Cushing opened the ceremonies with the invocation. Just as he was finishing, a short circuit below the lectern began to smoke. A horrified Secret Service chief considered evacuating the platform, but the smoke cleared before the order was issued. Then the venerable poet Robert Frost rose to recite an original poem which he had written for the occasion, but the bright sun reflecting off the new-fallen snow blinded him, making him unable to read. Instead he recited another poem from memory.

Finally, the new President followed Chief Justice Earl Warren to the podium to take the oath of office. He raised his right hand, while his left hand rested upon the Fitzgerald Family bible, and he swore to uphold the Constitution. It was 12:51 P.M. John Fitzgerald Kennedy was the 35th President of the United States.

President Kennedy then turned to face the cheering crowd who had braved sub-freezing temperatures to hear his inaugural address. But when he spoke, he spoke not just to the tens of thousands of people gathered before him. Rather he directed his words to the hundreds of millions of people who were watching and listening around the world:

> "Let every nation know, whether it wishes us well or ill, that we shall pay any price, bear any burden, meet any hardship, support any friend, oppose any foe to assure the survival and success of liberty....
>
> In the long history of the world, only a few generations have been granted the role of defending freedom in its hour of maximum danger. I do not shrink from this responsibility–I welcome it. I do not believe that any of us would exchange places with any other people or any other generation. The energy, the faith, the devotion which we bring to this endeavor will light our country and all who serve it–and the glow from that fire can truly light the world.
>
> And so, my fellow Americans: ask not what your country can do for you–ask what you can do for your country.
>
> My fellow citizens of the world: ask not what America will do for you, but what together we can do for the freedom of man."

John Kennedy had pointed to the New Frontier, and invited every American to explore it with him:

> "Beyond that frontier are uncharted areas of space and science, unsolved problems of peace and war, unconquered pockets of ignorance and prejudice, and unanswered questions of poverty and surplus. I believe the times demand invention, innovation, imagination, decision. I am asking you to be new pioneers on that New Frontier."

The new President hit the ground running. Although he had taken office on a Friday–and had celebrated his inauguration late into the night–John Kennedy was up and at 'em, bright and early on Saturday morning. And he had made it clear to his staff that he expected them to be there as well, at 8:00 A.M. He spent much of the first day adjusting to his new surroundings–learning just whose office was located where. Former President Harry S Truman made a courtesy call, his first call at the White House since he left office eight years earlier. President Kennedy escorted the former President back to the living quarters to visit with Jackie. Later that day, Mayor Richard J. Daley of Chicago stopped by with his family for a picture with the President.

Like every President, John Kennedy looked for successes in foreign policy, while developing a strong domestic program. Unfortunately, the new President's first venture into foreign affairs was a fiasco, the most serious setback of his Presidency. Shortly after John Kennedy's election in November, President Eisenhower informed him of a plot to overthrow Fidel Castro in Cuba. A strike force made up of 1,400 Cuban nationals—trained and equipped by the CIA—were planning to invade the Cuban mainland, intending to spark a general uprising against Castro. The Joint Chiefs of Staff had unanimously endorsed the plan, and President Eisenhower urged Kennedy to allow the operation to go forward. The new President concurred, and plans were made to implement the operation.

On April 15, the insurgents landed at Bahía de Cochinos—The Bay of Pigs. Ill-trained and inadequately armed, the strike force was outnumbered by Cuban military forces, 143-1. Every insurgent was either captured or killed. The captives who survived were later paraded through a humiliating trial, and then imprisoned. When the extent of the failure became clear, the President immediately accepted "sole responsibility."

Within a couple of weeks, however, public opinion polls indicated that 83% of the American people backed the President's handling of the affair. But the President was more concerned about the reaction in Moscow. He did not want Soviet Premier Nikita Khrushchev to interpret his actions at the Bay of Pigs as a sign of indecision or weakness, especially in light of the summit meeting scheduled for June in Vienna. But Khrushchev let it be known that the summit was still on. President Kennedy was pleased because he was anxious to meet his Soviet counterpart.

The Vienna summit was not the first time Kennedy and Khrushchev had met—Kennedy had been a member of the Senate Foreign Relations Committee when they met with Khrushchev during his 1959 trip to the United States. The Vienna talks were lively, but produced no agreements on the two issues which concerned Kennedy, nuclear testing and the status of Berlin.

Khrushchev flatly stated that in December of that year he was planning to sign a treaty with East Germany which included the unilateral reunification of Berlin. Khrushchev threatened Kennedy that if the United States and the Allied powers interfered with the Soviet's plan to unify Berlin as part of an East German nation, "force would be met with force." Annoyed by Khrushchev's belligerence, Kennedy retorted, "It's going to be a cold winter."

On August 13, 1961 – under the cover of darkness, the East Germans hastily constructed the Berlin Wall, surrounding those sections of the city under the jurisdiction of the United States, Britain, and France, and separating them from the rest of Berlin and East Germany. Although it outwardly appeared to be an act of defiance by Khrushchev, Kennedy saw it as a method of defusing the threats the Soviets had made in Vienna. "Why would Khrushchev put up a wall if he really intended to seize West Berlin?" he wondered rhetorically. "There wouldn't be any need of a wall if he occupied the whole city. This is a way out of his predicament. It's not a very nice solution, but a wall is a hell of a lot better than a war."

But the world saw it differently, and waited for a response from Washington. President Kennedy dispatched a reluctant Vice President Johnson to West Berlin to pledge American support. He also ordered 1,500 American troops to move into West Berlin from Helmstedt, West Germany. In order to get to Berlin, the convoy had to travel along the autobahn through East Germany, raising the prospects of antagonizing Soviet occupation forces. But there was no interference from the Soviets, and Vice President Johnson's welcome of American troops into West Berlin was hailed as an American triumph.

But Kennedy's problems with the Soviets were not over yet. On October 14, 1962, American U-2 reconnaissance planes photographed Soviet offensive missile installations near San Cristobal, Cuba. The sites were re-examined, and the installations were confirmed. Kennedy quietly called a meeting of his National Security Council – his top military and State Department officials – for the 16th, keeping the rest of his schedule intact so as not to cause alarm.

At that first meeting of the group – which would become known as the Ex Comm – it was learned that the missile sites were not yet operational, and would not be for another ten days. This gave the group time to consider the options. Strict secrecy surrounded the discussions. The nation and the world would not know of the American reaction until the President went before the public on the following Monday evening. Kennedy kept up his normal schedule, including campaign appearances for the off-year Congressional elections, and, ironically, a previously scheduled meeting on Thursday with Andrei Gromyko, the Soviet Foreign Minister.

The evidence of a Soviet nuclear build-up in Cuba mounted. It was determined that the missiles were medium- and intermediate-range, capable of striking Washington, D.C., New York, or Chicago, and that they carried warheads four times as powerful as the bombs dropped on Hiroshima. A single volley could have killed 80 million Americans. The Ex Comm group met on a daily basis to evaluate new evidence and options.

On Thursday, now four days since the first photographs were taken over Cuba, President Kennedy met with Foreign Minister Gromyko in the Oval Office. Ostensibly, the meeting was requested by Gromyko to discuss Berlin, but eventually the topic turned to Cuba. Kennedy was not yet ready to tip his hand to the Soviets, wanting them to believe that the U.S. was still ignorant about the existence of their bases on Cuban soil. Gromyko assured the President that all the Soviets wanted was peaceful co-existence between the Cubans and the Americans. The President warned that no offensive weapons would be tolerated in Cuba, and Gromyko assured Kennedy that the thought had not even entered Premier Khrushchev's mind.

On Monday evening, October 22, President Kennedy addressed the American people from the Oval Office. In a solemn voice, Kennedy informed the American public that unmistakable evidence established that Soviet missiles were in Cuba with no other purpose than to provide a nuclear strike capability against the United States. "We have no wish to war with the Soviet Union," the President assured his listeners, "for we are a peaceful people who desire to live in peace with all other peoples....The cost of freedom is always high, but Americans have always paid it. And one path we shall never choose, and that is the path of surrender or submission." He then announced a "quarantine" of Cuba. Any ship heading toward Cuba carrying weapons—but not necessities of life—would be stopped and turned back. Then the waiting began.

The quarantine was to take effect on Wednesday morning at 10:00. At that hour, it was reported that two Soviet vessels were heading toward the blockade accompanied by a Soviet nuclear submarine. The President was all too aware of the possible consequences. A small skirmish at the blockade could escalate into a full-fledged nuclear war. American troops were on alert throughout the world, ready to respond to orders from the Pentagon. Kennedy had even brought his wife and children back to the White House from their country estate in Virginia. Plans were made to evacuate the White House upon the President's order in the event of a nuclear attack on Washington.

As Ex Comm was gathered in the Cabinet Room awaiting word from the blockade line, Secretary of State Dean Rusk observed, "We're eyeball to eyeball." Then the first reports from the scene arrived; the Soviet ships were stopping. Khrushchev had blinked.

The crisis was not over yet, however. Indirect, secret negotiations continued between Kennedy and Khrushchev. The President received a private letter from Khrushchev which agreed to the removal of the Soviet missile installations in exchange for a promise that the United

States would not invade Cuba. This was certainly acceptable to the United States. But before Kennedy could respond, the Soviets issued another letter demanding removal of U.S. Jupiter missiles from Turkey. The President was upset—not because of Khrushchev's new demand—but because Kennedy himself had previously ordered the removal of the Jupiters from Turkey at least two months earlier. Now those Turkish missiles could be the stumbling block to a resolution in Cuba. Kennedy decided to risk a response to the first letter—agreeing to a promise of non-agression against Cuba in exchange for removal of the Soviet missiles—and ignoring the second letter. The ploy worked. The Soviet missiles were withdrawn, and the U.S. promised no intervention into Cuba. Several months later, the U.S. unilaterally removed the Jupiter missiles from Turkish soil.

As successful as the Cuban Missile Crisis was for John Kennedy, he did not consider it his most important foreign policy victory. That came the following year with the signing of the first nuclear atmospheric test ban treaty between the United States and Britain and the Soviet Union. Announcing the agreeement, Kennedy declared:

> "Yesterday, a shaft of light cut into the darkness. Negotiations were concluded in Moscow on a treaty to ban all nuclear tests in the atmosphere, in outer space and under water....According to the ancient Chinese proverb, a journey of a thousand miles must begin with a single step....Let us take that first step. Let us, if we can, step back from the shadows of war and seek out the way of peace. And if that journey is a thousand miles or even more, let history record that we, in this land, at this time, took the first step."

On October 7, 1963, Kennedy executed the agreement in the Treaty Room on the third floor of the White House.

Foreign policy was always of great interest to John Kennedy, and throughout his career he considered his best foreign policy speech to have been the address he made at the American University commencement exercises in June, 1963. Kennedy was anxious to make a bold statement on world peace at that time, and he chose that commencement as the forum. During the address, he decried the amount of resources the two super powers were using to enlarge their nuclear arsenals instead of combating ignorance, poverty, and disease. Kennedy called for "not merely a peace for Americans, but a peace for all men; not merely a peace in our time, but peace for all time." He concluded:

> "If we cannot end now our differences, at least we can help make the world safe for diversity. For, in the final analysis, our most basic common link is that we all inhabit this small planet. We all breathe the same air. We all cherish our childen's future. And we

are all mortal."

Many observers feel that this speech paved the way for a thaw in U.S.-Soviet relations. Khrushchev said that it was the best speech delivered by an American President since Franklin Roosevelt, and he allowed it to be reprinted in the Soviet press. Within thirty days, both parties had concluded the test ban treaty.

John Kennedy enjoyed face-to-face discussions with foreign leaders as a means of avoiding breakdowns in communication. The President traveled a great deal during his brief thirty-four months in office. In this hemisphere, he visited Canada, Venezuela, Colombia, Mexico and Costa Rica. On his way to Austria to meet with Nikita Khrushchev earlier in June 1961, he and Jacqueline made a triumphant visit to Paris to meet with President Charles De Gaulle. Following the enthusiastic reception that Mrs. Kennedy received from the French people, Kennedy later quipped, "I'm the man who accompanied Jackie Kennedy to Paris.

Kennedy also made a solo visit to Europe in June, 1963. Jackie was pregnant with their third child, so she chose not to accompany her husband. Kennedy's first stop was West Germany. In Cologne, a crowd of four hundred thousand people turned out to welcome him. Two days later, he made a forty-mile tour of West Berlin where an estimated 1.5 million Berliners hung from balconies, crowded rooftops, and lined the streets to see the American President. The reception left Kennedy ecstatic as he prepared to visit the Berlin Wall, but when he climbed the steps to look at the Wall—and to look beyond it into East Berlin—he became angry and shaken. Kennedy then faced the hundreds of thousands of Berliners packed into Rudolpf Wilde Platz to hear the American President. Still angered by the sight of the Wall, John Kennedy addressed the excited throng in a defiant voice—

> "There are many people in the world who really don't under-
> stand, or say they don't, what is the great issue between the free
> world and the communist world.
> Let them come to Berlin.
> There are some who say that communism is the wave of the fu-
> ture.
> Let them come to Berlin!
> And there are some who say in Europe and elsewhere we can
> work with communists...
> *Lass sie nach Berlin kommen!* Let—them—come—to—Berlin!"

The crowd roared its approval, encouraging Kennedy to tell them more. He shouted back to them—

> "All free men, wherever they may live, are citizens of Berlin,

and, therefore, as a free man, I take pride in the words *'Ich—bin—ein—Berliner!'*

The sea of spectators erupted into a chorus of "Ken-ah-dee, Ken-ah-dee!" He had won the hearts of the German people, and had scored a foreign policy victory. As he left Germany later that day, Kennedy understated, "We'll never have another day like this one."

When President Kennedy left Germany, he made an emotional visit to the homeland of his ancestors, Ireland. It was a visit that he would recall with an air of nostalgia when he returned to the United States, and one which his close friends considered to be a personal highlight of his life. From Ireland, he flew for a short visit to England where he met with Prime Minister Harold Macmillan, and visited the grave of his sister Kathleen, who had died in a plane crash in France in 1948. It was the first and only time he ever visited the grave site.

The final leg of his trip to Europe took him to Italy where he met Italian officials, and received an audience with newly-installed Pope Paul VI—a visit which seemed anticlimactic considering what an issue the Pope's influence had become in the 1960 campaign. Then John Kennedy returned home.

On August 7, while Jackie and the children were in Hyannis Port, and the President was at the White House, word was received that Jackie was undergoing emergency surgery in Massachusetts. She had gone into labor, five weeks premature. By the time the President reached her side, she had delivered a four-pound, ten-ounce baby boy. He had already been baptized, Patrick Bouvier Kennedy, but both Jackie and the baby were doing well. The baby later developed breathing problems and was transferred to Children's Hospital in Boston. His condition worsened, and he was moved again, this time to the Harvard medical school. President Kennedy stayed with his son in the hospital that night, but at two o'clock in the morning, little Patrick grew worse. Two hours later, he died. When the President heard the news, he sat on his bed and wept. The baby was buried in Brookline, Massachusetts, and later reinterred next to his father in Arlington National Cemetery.

Following his successful trip to Europe earlier in the summer, one of the problems which greeted the President upon his return to the United States was in Vietnam. The United States had supported its leader Ngo Dinh Diem, but Kennedy was having second thoughts about that support. Diem and his brother were considered ruthless in dealing with their opposition. So Kennedy requested Senate Majority Leader Mike Mansfield to undertake a fact-finding mission to Saigon. When Mansfield returned, he unequivocally advocated withdrawing completely from Vietnam. The President balked, unhappy that

Mansfield disagreed so completely with his policy. Several months later, however, Kennedy informed Senator Mansfield that he would in fact withdraw all American advisors in 1965. He felt that politically he could not do it until after the 1964 election. On October 2, 1963 Kennedy instructed Secretary of Defense Robert MacNamara to make the planned withdrawal administration policy, and to withdraw one thousand of the 16,000 American military personnel currently in Vietnam before the end of the year. That was Kennedy's policy on November 1, 1963 when Diem was assassinated in a coup by his military generals. That policy was still in effect three weeks later when Kennedy was assassinated in Dallas.

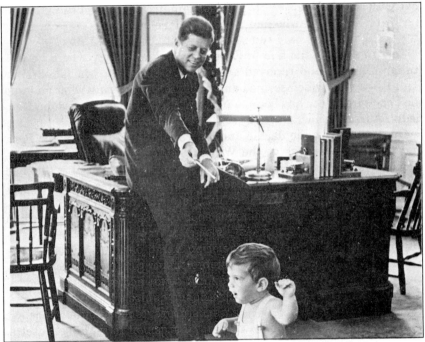

John F. Kennedy, Sr., playing with John F. Kennedy, Jr., in the Oval Office.

By the fall of 1963, John Kennedy had been less successful with his domestic programs than he had hoped. He had increased aid to higher education; established a limited program of urban renewal; created the Peace Corps; and had passed legislation increasing the minimum wage. He had challenged the country to expand the space program, and to put a man on the moon by the end of the decade. But Congress had rejected his ideas about creating a Department of Urban Affairs, medical care for the elderly, and a sweeping civil rights reform program.

Kennedy had always supported the Civil Rights movement. He endorsed Dr. Martin Luther King, Jr.'s march on Washington in 1963. He sent U.S. marshals and National Guardsmen to the University of Mississippi when Governor Ross Barnett threatened to block the court-ordered admission of its first black student, James Meredith. The President hoped to enact legislation giving equal access to minorities in housing, voting, education, and employment. But the President realized that such controversial legislation would only pass the Congress if he was re-elected by a large majority in 1964, elected with a mandate from the American people for such change.

So it was with an eye on that mandate that on November 13 John Kennedy held the first major meeting to plan his re-election campaign. Among the items discussed were the upcoming trips to Florida and to Texas—two states which Kennedy knew he would have to carry in order to secure his much-desired mandate. The President was looking forward to the Texas trip because Jackie had agreed to accomany him. It was to be her first public appearance since Patrick had died in August.

On November 21, the Kennedys flew to San Antonio, and then on to Houston to attend a rally for Congressman Al Thomas, one of Kennedy's favorite Congressmen. Then, shortly after midnight on the 22nd, they arrived in Fort Worth. Following a morning breakfast meeting in Fort Worth, the President and Mrs. Kennedy flew to Dallas. In each of their stops, the crowds greeted the President and First Lady with great enthusiasm, but nowhere was their welcome more enthusiastic than in Dallas. From the airport into the center of the city, the crowds got larger and friendlier.

Traveling in the limousine with the Kennedys were Texas Governor John Connally and his wife, Nellie. Just as the Presidential limousine entered Dealey Plaza, Mrs. Connally turned to the President and said, "You can't say that Dallas doesn't love and respect you, Mr. President." "You sure can't," he replied. Then there were three shots, and in a matter of seconds, John Fitzgerald Kennedy, 35th President of the United States, was dead. He died November 22, 1963 at 12:30 P.M. CST.

President Kennedy's body was returned to the White House shortly after 4:00 A.M. the following morning, and placed in the East Room. On Sunday, the casket bearing the fallen President was taken to the United States Capitol to lie in state in the Rotunda. Memorial services were held there, and throughout the day and night, more than one quarter of a million people passsed through the Rotunda to pay their respects. At times the line outside the Capitol reached for more than two miles. On Monday morning, Mrs. Kennedy led the funeral procession to Washington's St. Matthew's Cathedral where Richard Cardinal Cushing, the long-time Kennedy family friend who had married the Kennedys ten years earlier, said the Requiem mass. The funeral cortege then marched to Arlington, where the Kennedy family was joined by President and Mrs. Johnson, former Presidents Truman and Eisenhower, and members of the Cabinet, the Congress, and the Supreme Court.

Also standing on that hillside in Arlington were leaders from every corner of the globe; they had come to grieve with the American people, and–whether friend or foe–to pay their respects to John Kennedy: President DeGaulle of France, Emperor Selassie of Ethiopia, King Baudouin of Belgium, Prince Philip of England, Queen Frederika of Greece, President Park of South Korea, President Macapagal of The Philippines, Chancellor Erhard of West Germany, Prime Minister Ikeda of Japan, Deputy Premier Mikoyan of the Soviet Union, and many, many more. Then, at 3:34 P.M., following brief graveside services, forty-six-year-old John Fitzgerald Kennedy was buried at Arlington National Cemetery. "So now he is a legend," observed his young widow, Jacqueline, "when he would have preferred to be a man."

The gravesite of John Kennedy is now the most visited site–not just at Arlington Cemetery–but in Washington, D.C. Each year, more than four million people from every corner of the globe come to pay their respects at the grave, marked by a marble tablet which simply proclaims:

John Fitzgerald Kennedy
1917–1963

Above his grave stands the Eternal Flame which was lit by Mrs. Kennedy during the President's burial service. His two infant children–Patrick Bouvier Kennedy, and the unnamed baby girl who predeceased the President in 1954–were reinterred on either side of him on December 4, 1963. When the permanent gravesite was completed, the bodies of President Kennedy and his two children were removed to their final resting places on the evening of March 14, 1967, and were blessed by Cardinal Cushing the following morning. The grave of Robert Kennedy, who was assassinated in 1968, is located a short distance away.

II

THE TRIP TO DALLAS: EYEWITNESSES RECOUNT THE TRAGEDY

"This trip is turning out to be terrific. Here we are in Dallas, and it looks like everything in Texas is going to be fine for us."
—President Kennedy as he landed in Dallas, November 22, 1963

President Kennedy traveled to Texas in November 1963 to get a head start on his 1964 re-election campaign. He had carried Texas in 1960, but by a narrow margin. Now he hoped that several joint appearances with Vice President Lyndon Johnson would strengthen his standing in the state. The President also felt his visit would help to heal the split in the Democratic Party between Governor John Connally and long-time Senator Ralph Yarborough.

Many of President Kennedy's policies were unpopular among Texans, prompting those traveling with him to keep a wary eye on the public's reception. Just one month earlier on a visit to Dallas, U.N. Ambassador Adlai Stevenson had been spat upon and struck with picket signs. So President Kennedy knew full well that he was entering potentially unfriendly territory. Ironically, until he was shot, the biggest news story that day had been how enthusiastically Texans had welcomed the Kennedys.

The initial reports from Dallas indicated that the President was seriously injured, but alive. Across the country Americans held their breath as they awaited details. But when the worst fears were confirmed, the world clamored to know how it had happened and why.

Traveling with the President were journalists Robert MacNeil and Douglas Kiker; one of Kennedy's closest friends and advisors, Larry O'Brien; Jack Valenti, an LBJ confidant; and Congressman Jim Wright, now Speaker of the House of Representatives. These five distinguished Americans recount the events as they witnessed them firsthand that dark day in November. Never before presented together, their combined accounts offer an informed and comprehensive look at the events in Dallas.

25

Robert MacNeil

Robert MacNeil, co-anchor of the "MacNeil/Lehrer Newshour," was covering President Kennedy's trip to Dallas for NBC News. He is a recipient of the Peabody Award for excellence in broadcast journalism.
[32]

We all wear a protective covering, like a membrane, around our subjective lives. Few outside events ever penetrate it; but the killing of John F. Kennedy was one that did and did so universally. I have never run into anyone, in any country, who does not remember precisely where he was when he heard the news.

It happened that I was in Dallas, traveling with Kennedy....It was my first big presidential trip....On November 22, obviously, we did not know what would happen. I describe it now, as nearly as I can, as it seemed then, before we knew....

[In Fort Worth], it was chilly, dark and drizzling at 6 A.M. I checked out of my room,...and went to the press room....We drank our coffee beside our typewriters and studied advance copies of the speech JFK was to deliver at the lunch in Dallas. It was a spirited attack on his conservative critics....

It was significant that Kennedy had chosen to attack the spirit that had made Dallas seem such a nest of extremists. Right-wing demonstrators had assaulted fellow Texan Lyndon Johnson during the 1960 campaign. Just a few weeks before the Kennedy visit, United Nations Ambassador Adlai Stevenson had been spat upon and struck with posters. Dallas city officials were determined there would be no repetition of such incidents. Dallas police had mounted the biggest security operation in the city's history. That was the atmosphere, we all knew, that awaited Kennedy, and in which he would deliver [the] provocative remarks....

At 8:45 JFK came out looking very rested and tanned, his hair still damp from the shower. With him were Governor John Connally, Vice President Lyndon Johnson, Senator Ralph Yarborough, and the local congressman, Jim Wright. When they all lined up, flanking Kennedy,

Reprinted with permission from The Right Place at the Right Time, *by Robert MacNeil, Little, Brown & Company, Boston, Massachussetts, 1982.*

they looked a little like guilty schoolboys made to stand together after being caught fighting, which is what they had been doing. The feuding between the liberal Yarborough and the conservative Connally–and the efforts to cover it up–had been preoccupations of the trip. So far Connally had managed to prevent Yarborough from ever riding in the limousine with the president.

There was just a taste of rain when Kennedy spoke [to a crowd in a parking lot across from the hotel]. He said, "You'll have to excuse my wife for not being here. She's still organizing herself–but that's because she looks better than we do." The wide grin and sparkle in his eye at this remark, his way of beginning to laugh at his own joke before he quite finished delivering it, triggered a warm ovation from the crowd....

There was a large crowd in the hotel lobby, held back by a rope, leaving a path to the elevator....Merriman Smith of the UPI found an opening under the rope through the crowd on the stairs and we got into the Chamber of Commerce breakfast....

...There was only one seat vacant at the head table and the entire room began twisting and muttering, "Where's Jackie?" Then Bob Kahn of the USIS pointed to the kitchen door. I went over and saw Jackie wearing a broad mischievous smile waiting outside with the Secret Servicemen....

The preliminary speeches finally ended and Jackie was announced. The band struck up, the cameras whirred and followed her through the crowd until she emerged in the lights at the end of the head table, resplendent in a suit the color of strawberry ice cream, with a pill box hat and a dark blouse. She caused a sensation. She was cheered all the way to her seat. And in the back of the room the reporters laughed and wondered how they could describe so blatant a bit of staging without going too far. Kennedy's Air Force aide, Godfrey McHugh, was standing beside me with a big smile. "What kind of an entrance do you call that?" I asked. "Tactical," he replied.

...JFK began his speech, "Two years ago, I introduced myself in Paris by saying that I was the man who had accompanied Mrs. Kennedy to Paris. I am getting somewhat the same sensation" (he began to laugh himself and the crowd laughed too) "as I travel around Texas. Nobody wonders what Lyndon and I wear!" That brought the roof down. It was a full minute before the crowd was composed enough for Kennedy to go on with the main point of his speech....

By the time we got outside and into the press bus, there was bright sunshine, a sparkling day getting quite warm....[We] ran straight up to the press plane...for the takeoff [to Dallas]....Air Force One landed and taxied in with the usual ear-splitting whine.

I don't know whether hindsight makes me remember the next moments extra vividly, or whether—as I think was true—the image of the Kennedys framed in the doorway of the plane was thrust into my consciousness with more than usual force. The sunshine hit Mrs. Kennedy's pink suit, it was like a blow between the eyes. As they descended the ramp, they seemed enveloped in an aura of extra light. At the foot of the stairs, someone gave Jackie a huge bunch of deep red roses and the effect of those, almost blood red against the pink suit was electrifying....Eventually they both came over to the wire fence which bulged with the enthusiastic crowd pressing on it....

Finally they settled themselves in the Lincoln convertible, JFK in the right rear seat, Mrs. Kennedy beside him; Governor and Mrs. Connally on the jump seat in front of them. We ran for the press buses....I was sitting at the right front on the side-facing bench seat, able to get a clear view out of the front window....Although we were higher up in the bus, there were two cars of photographers and cameramen ahead of us and they were sitting up on the back of their seats. We could just see the presidential limousine, which was seven cars ahead.

The crowds were sparse on the outskirts of Dallas and only one or two deep in the suburbs. We were all watching for some kind of demonstration but didn't know quite what to expect. The route was thick with policemen. But indications of opposition were pretty innocuous, a few Goldwater signs, perhaps half a dozen all the way in....But the crowds were very friendly....

Just as we turned the corner on Houston Street, I looked at my watch. I know it was roughly five minutes fast and it said something like 12:36. I began to go over my personal schedule; to figure when to write a one-minute radio spot based on the text JFK would deliver at 2 P.M., in time to phone it to NBC in New York for the News on the Hour. I had just decided, "Well, I won't worry about it till we get there," when we heard what sounded like a shot. The bus was still on Houston Street.

I said, "Was that a shot?"

Several people said, "No, no," and others said, "I don't know."

That reaction took a few seconds, then there were two more explosions, very distinct to me. I jumped up and said, "There *were* shots! They were shots! Stop the bus! Stop the bus!"

The driver opened the door and I jumped out, just as the bus was turning the corner of Elm Street. I couldn't see the president's car but I really started to believe there was shooting because on the grass on both sides of the roadway people were throwing themselves down and covering their children with their bodies. The air was filled with screaming, a high unison soprano wail. The sun was intensely bright.

I saw several people running up the grassy hill beside the road. I thought they were chasing whoever had done the shooting and I ran after them. It did not enter my head that Kennedy had been hit. I was thinking, It must have been some crazy right-wing nut trying to make a demonstration by firing a gun off. He couldn't be trying to hit Kennedy....I thought I had better look for a telephone.

I ran to the right and into the first building I came to that looked as though it might have a phone. It was the Texas Book Depository. As I ran up the steps and through the door, a young man in shirt sleeves was coming out. In great agitation I asked him where there was a phone. He pointed inside to an open space where another young man was talking on a phone situated near a pillar and said, "Better ask him." I ran inside and asked the second man, who pointed to an office at one side. I found a telephone on the desk. Two of the four Lucite call buttons were lit up. I pushed another, got long distance, and was through to NBC Radio news in about ten seconds....I recorded a bulletin ad lib of all I could safely say at that point:

"Shots were fired as President Kennedy's motorcade passed through downtown Dallas. People screamed and lay down on the grass as three shots rang out. Police chased an unknown gunman up a grassy hill. It is *not* known if the shots were directed at the president. This is Robert MacNeil, NBC News in Dallas."

...I still did not realize the president had been hit. Just then a woman ran up crying hysterically. Seeing my White House press badge, she asked dementedly, "Was he hit? Was he hit?" I said, "No, I'm sure he wasn't." And then it began to dawn on me that what I thought was so impossible could have happened. I rushed over to a policeman who was listening intently to his motorcycle radio, "Was he hit?"

"Yeah. Hit in the head. They're taking him to Parkland Hospital."

That put me in a frenzy. The president had been hit and I was now separated from the story! I had to get to the hospital....I ran across Dealey Plaza to Main Street and dashed in front of the first car that came along. He stopped and I opened the door.

"This is a terrible emergency. The president's been shot. I'll give you five dollars to take me to Parkland Hospital."

He was about thirty, not very bright. With a smile, he said, "Okay,"...

The traffic was infuriatingly jammed up. I kept urging the young man on, telling him to go any speed, take any risks, go through red lights. I would pay any fines. Besides, what could the police care right now? In fact, police cars were still racing by us going the other way....Eventually–it seemed like half an hour but was only a few minutes–we got to the hospital....The bus I had left was just arriving. So I was still competitive. There was a cluster of reporters around

Senator Yarborough, who said the president was "gravely wounded." I looked into the limousine. The roses from Mrs. Kennedy's bouquet were scattered in the bloody back seat. In the corridor inside the emergency section, I got more details from Bob Clark of ABC, who had been in the pool car. He had seen the president carried in on a stretcher, bleeding and apparently unconscious....The corridor was jammed with reporters, Secret Servicemen, and White House staffers, and the hospital personnel were trying to clear it....I opened the door of a small waiting room. Behind the door were three pay phones no one had noticed. I grabbed the one nearest the door and never gave it up for the rest of the afternoon....

I got a hospital intern to hold the phone open for me periodically while I went down the corridor to talk to the FBI, Secret Servicemen, or White House staffers who stood around with ghastly, expressionless faces. Then I would go back to the phone....

I left the phone when Lady Bird Johnson came down the corridor looking very unsteady. She would only say: "Lyndon is all right." She wouldn't comment on Kennedy.

A priest, Father Huber, came out and said that he had delivered the last rites to the president. Bob Pierrepoint of CBS and I talked together. We both understood him to say, under our repeated questions, that the president was not dead when he administered the rites....

Another dash from the phone when Lyndon Johnson and a circle of worried Secret Servicemen came barging through the swinging doors. The FBI had cleared the area but had missed Pierrepoint and me behind the doors of the waiting room. I stepped in front of the vice-president to ask, "Is the president dead?" LBJ stared at me, his face white with shock, and said nothing, practically bowling me over as he walked out. He entered his limousine and was driven off at great speed....

We followed Mac Kilduff, [the assistant White House press secretary], ...[to] a nurses' classroom where a press room had been set up. It was full. Kilduff stood behind a wooden desk on a small platform. The cameras were switched on. His face was very white and he kept twisting it to avoid crying, but his cheeks were shining with tears. His hands were shaking and he tried to steady them by pressing down firmly with his fingers on the desk. With great difficulty in controlling his voice, Kilduff said: "President John F. Kennedy—"

Someone said, "Wait, what time is it?"

Someone else: "One thirty."

"That'll be it then." Again reporters wanting a consensus.

Then Kilduff: "President John F. Kennedy died at approximately one o'clock Central Standard Time of a gunshot wound in the brain."

Bob Pierrepoint broke for the door and I followed. We raced all the way back around the outside of the building to the emergency section. I was grasping for breath as I grabbed the phone receiver and did the announcement that Kennedy was officially dead.

Then the coffin came out on an undertaker's cart. Jackie walking with one hand on it, possessively, her pink suit still spattered with the darker spots of her husband's blood.

There was a great quiet when they drove off. We heard that Lyndon Johnson had been sworn in and that Air Force One had taken off for Washington. I waited for further instructions from New York, about whether to stay in Dallas or go to Fort Worth to the NBC affiliate to start preparing a report.

It was then that I heard on television that a young man called Oswald, arrested for the shooting, worked at the Texas Book Depository and had left by the front door immediately afterwards. Isn't that strange, I told myself. He must have been leaving just about the time I was running in. But I had no memory of a face. My attention had been focused solely on finding a telephone, and the Book Depository had no other significance for me at that point. When Lee Harvey Oswald's picture appeared shortly afterwards, there was no leap of instant recognition....

It was not until Monday, three days after the shooting, that my private emotions caught up with the professional drive that preoccupied me. From the moment the shots were fired and I got out of the press bus, I was thinking, What a story, what an incredible story. How do I cover this? Where should I be?—as though I were a reporting machine with no emotions....It was when I heard the lament played by the bagpipes of the Black Watch Regiment, marching in the funeral procession, that I really understood, with my feelings, what had happened. I sat there in the sunshine with the tears running out of my eyes; aware of how much the salt in them burned because crying was such an unaccustomed thing to do.

Two weeks earlier I had watched those same pipers playing on the South Lawn of the White House. It was a glorious autumn day, with President and Mrs. Kennedy, watching from the balcony, with Caroline and John John.

My own two children, a girl and a boy, were the same ages....

It was about a year and a half later that I got a call in New York from William Manchester, who was writing *The Death of a President.* He said he had gone carefully over the ground to find out who had been in the Book Depository before and right after the shooting. He had seen a statement I had made to the FBI. He had traced my call through the telephone company to 12:34, four minutes after the shooting, and he was convinced that I had spoken to Lee Harvey Oswald. Could I tell him any more about it? I couldn't; it was possible, but I had no way of confirming that either of the young men I had spoken with was Oswald.

Then Manchester asked if I knew about the statement Oswald had made to the Secret Service. Oswald had told them that as he left the Book Depository, a young Secret Serviceman with a blond crewcut had rushed up the steps and asked him for a phone. Since no Secret Serviceman had entered the building, Manchester concluded that Oswald had mistaken me for one. I could only say that it was possible. I am blond. My hair was very short then and I was wearing a White House press badge he might have mistaken for Secret Service ID. But I had no way of proving it.

"Well," Manchester said, "I'm ninety-five percent convinced that it was you and I'm going to do some checking."

Evidently he overcame his five percent of doubt because he states flatly in *The Death of a President* that at 12:33 P.M. Oswald "leaves Depository by front entrance, pausing to tell NBC's Robert MacNeil he can find a phone inside: thinks MacNeil is a Secret Service man."

It is titillating but it doesn't matter much.

Lawrence F. O'Brien

Larry O'Brien was JFK's Congressional Liaison at the time of the assassination. He subsequently held positions as U.S. Postmaster General and as Commissioner of the National Basketball Association.
[46]

By November 1963 it seemed possible that Senator Barry Goldwater might be the Republican nominee for President the following year. We viewed Goldwater as an ultra-conservative, out of touch with the American political mainstream and thus the easiest man for Kennedy to defeat. President Kennedy's trip to Dallas in November was a bit of early-bird campaigning in a key state, and it was also part of his continuing effort to increase his personal influence with powerful members of Congress.

...Jackie, who wasn't always enthusiastic about political journeys and who had suffered a miscarriage only three months before, decided to join her husband on the Texas trip. Kennedy was delighted. When we left Washington on the morning of the twenty-first, he was concerned about the weather in Texas, afraid it might not be right for Jackie's wardrobe, and he kept asking General Godfrey McHugh, one of his military aides, to check it.

The weather, the general reported, was variable, perhaps a little warm.

"Damn it, Mac, make up your mind," Kennedy protested. He struck me as being excited as a little boy to have Jackie accompanying him on this trip.

We flew first to San Antonio,...and then to Fort Worth, arriving around midnight. By the end of that first day, we realized we had a problem on our hands. A bitter feud existed between Vice President Johnson and Texas Senator Ralph Yarborough. Johnson, as Vice President, had continued to involve himself in matters of Texas patronage, and Yarborough, as the state's senior senator and an old foe of Johnson's in Texas politics, bitterly resented what he regarded as a challenge to

Reprinted with permission from No Final Victories: A Life in Politics from John F. Kennedy to Watergate *by Lawrence F. O'Brien, Doubleday and Company, Garden City, New York, 1974.*

his prerogatives. Consequently, Yarborough refused to ride in the same car with Johnson. That quickly became a big news story in Texas, so big it threatened to overshadow the visit of the President. On Friday morning, at the Hotel Texas in Fort Worth, Kennedy told me he wanted me to end the Johnson-Yarborough sideshow.

"I don't care if you have to throw Yarborough into the car with Lyndon," he said. "Get him in there."

As we talked in his hotel suite, Kennedy went to a window and looked down at the speaker's platform that had been erected for his appearance. He stared at it for a moment and shook his head.

"Just look at that platform," he said. "With all these buildings around it, Secret Service couldn't stop someone who really wanted to get you."

I later went downstairs, where the motorcade was waiting, and found Senator Yarborough on the sidewalk. The newspapermen were already on the press bus, but I could see them watching us out the windows.

"Damn it, Ralph," I told the senator. "Look at those reporters watching to see what you do. It's not fair to the President. Why should he suffer because you and Lyndon have a problem? If you really want to help him, you'll get in the car with Lyndon before this thing gets worse."

Ralph protested he had not intended to hurt the President. He said, "He's having a great trip, the crowds are terrific, everyone's excited. I'm proud to be with him here." He then took another long look at the press bus, turned back to me and quickly agreed to join the Vice President in the car.

I immediately signaled the Secret Service agent standing by the Vice President's car a few feet away and told him Yarborough would be riding with the Vice President and Mrs. Johnson.

"Keep close to the senator and be sure he gets into that car. This is a must." I added.

Then I saw Johnson come out of the hotel.

"Yarborough 's going to ride with you," I told him.

"He is?"

"Right."

"Fine," Johnson said, and moments later the two of them drove off together in the open car, all smiles....

[In Dallas] Kennedy's car was four or five cars ahead of us and we could see him waving to the crowds....On the outskirts of Dallas, the crowds were large, but not enthusiastic. My impression was that they'd come out of curiosity and perhaps to glimpse Jackie....

The mood changed, however, as we entered downtown Dallas. Suddenly there were cheering crowds pressing in on the motorcade and throwing confetti. The scene reminded me of New York City's Broadway....We were rounding a corner...when we heard a shot.

"What was that?" I immediately asked our driver.

"I don't know," he said. "They must be giving him a twenty-one gun salute."

As he spoke we heard additional shots. We had no idea what had happened. The motorcade began to move faster and there was confusion all around us....

[We] moved at a high speed, trying to keep up with the cars ahead. We lost them, so we went to the scheduled destination, the Trade Mart, where Kennedy was to go next. When we got there, other cars from the motorcade were waiting, but not the President's car and I realized something terrible must have happened. Then someone called to us, "He's been shot, he's draped over the back seat!"

We raced to the nearest hospital, where we found the rest of the motorcade, police cars, and great confusion. The police stopped me at the door, but Congressman Al Thomas intervened.

"This is Mr. O'Brien, the assistant to the President," he said, and the policeman stepped aside.

I ran through a maze of corridors until I reached an anteroom where Jackie and Nellie Connally, Governor John Connally's wife, were sitting together. Jackie's pink suit was spattered with blood and she was sitting like stone. As I entered someone said, "John Connally is being moved upstairs to surgery." My immediate thought was he was the one who was seriously wounded. Then Ken [O'Donnell] whispered to me there was little or no chance that the President would live. I turned to Jackie to try to comfort her, but I could not speak.

The next hour was a nightmare. Everything was unreal. I was functioning entirely on reflex action. What is happening? I thought. What will happen next? Events seemed fragmented then and they still seem fragmented in retrospect.

It was chaotic, doctors, nurses running in and out. Medical equipment being wheeled into the room. At one point Jackie and I stepped into the adjoining room where the President's body lay. All I recall is I thought he looked as he always had.

Mac Kildruff, the acting press secretary, kept checking with us. He was distraught. What could he tell the press, he asked? What could he report to the Vice President, who was in another part of the building?

At one point Mac said, "He's dead, isn't he?" near tears. "I've got to tell the press."

"You can't say anything," Ken told him, and the confirmation of the President's death was kept from the world for perhaps half an hour, simply because Ken and I could not bring ourselves to accept it.

Someone sent for a priest and a casket. The casket arrived, and three priests, and a man who said he was the coroner. He ordered that the body could not be removed from the hospital until there had been an autopsy. Jackie had already said, "I won't leave here without Jack." It became an intolerable situation. We argued bitterly with the first official, then with a second official who called himself a judge. Their attitude was that this was no more than another homicide and local rules must be observed.

Finally, we demanded that they get out of our way, that we were taking the President out of there. Ken, Dave Powers, General McHugh, and I proceeded to push the casket down the corridor, with Jackie following behind us. The Dallas officials continued to protest, but we pushed past them. Near the exit we encountered one of the priests, who blocked our path and insisted that he say more prayers over the body. I shoved him aside. We knew that Jackie couldn't stand any more delays and we were fearful the Dallas officials might use additional force to stop us. We finally got the casket into a hearse that was standing by and we piled into a car and sped to the airport behind the hearse.

Secret Service agents managed to get the five-hundred pound casket up the stairs and into Air Force One, but the stairs were too narrow and they scratched the casket and broke one of the handles.

Ken, Dave, and I assisted the agents in placing the casket on the floor of the compartment and securing it. As Jackie and the three of us moved to seats opposite the casket, Vice President and Mrs. Johnson appeared. Lady Bird put her arms around Jackie, whispered her condolences, and the Vice President murmured something to her. The Johnsons then withdrew....

Shortly afterward, Judge Sarah Hughes arrived. She was handed a typed sheet of paper with the wording of the oath. Johnson asked me if I thought Mrs. Kennedy would join him, and I said that I would ask her....Soon Jackie appeared and slowly walked over to join the Johnsons. The group on the plane gathered around....The oath was quickly administered. Jackie, Ken, Dave, and I took our places opposite the casket at the rear of the plane, and we were soon airborne....

For most of the flight back to Washington...we were alone with Jackie. She spoke at length of what we three had meant to the President. I think that his reaction to his trip to Ireland that summer, his rekindled interest in his Irish heritage, had made her more understanding of the bond that united us.

"You were with him in the beginning and you're with him now," she would say. "That's as it should be." I had never been close to Jackie, but tragedy had made us all part of the same family.

On arrival at Andrews Air Force Base, Bob Kennedy immediately boarded the plane. A ramp was placed at the rear door and an honor guard stepped forward to remove the body. We asked them to stand aside and, with Bob, the three of us moved the casket onto the ramp and it was lowered and placed in the hearse. Bob and Jackie rode in the hearse followed in a car by Ken, Dave, and me, to Bethesda Naval Hospital in Maryland where an autopsy was to be performed....

We brought the dead President's body to the White House at 4 a.m. and we placed it in the East Room. Jackie asked Ken and me to spend the remainder of the night in the White House. Ken and I went to a bedroom, but we could not sleep, so we talked for hours.

A Mass would be said at 10:00 A.M., to be attended by the family and close friends....

Minnesota Senator Hubert Humphrey confers with JFK in the Oval Office while Larry O'Brien (at right), Kennedy's Congressional Liaison, waits to speak with the President. Also pictured, from left, Speaker of the House John McCormack (behind Humphrey), House majority Leader Carl Albert, Senate Majority Leader Mike Mansfield, and Press Secretary Pierre Salinger (behind O'Brien). (John F. Kennedy Library).

All that weekend, in my White House office, friends came and went, and there were many tears and reminiscences. Hubert Humphrey, our rival in 1960, came to my office on Saturday morning, just after Mass in the White House, and broke into tears....

Monday morning, November 25, Dave and Ken and I were in the upstairs living room of the White House, waiting to join the funeral cortege, which was then on its way from Capitol Hill. We were watching the cortege on television and little John-John Kennedy came into the room and, suddenly, we saw him saluting the televised picture of the cortege.

One of the butlers came in and asked if he could get us anything.

"Let's have a bottle of champagne," Dave said.

The butler brought the champagne and glasses and we toasted Jack Kennedy.

"To the President."

"To the President."

"Good-by, Jack, good-by."

Jack Valenti

Jack Valenti, Special Assistant to President Johnson from 1963–66, was in Dallas with LBJ on November 22, 1963. He became President of the Motion Picture Association of America in 1966 and is the author of A Very Human President *and* The Bitter Taste of Glory.
[42]

MOTION PICTURE ASSOCIATION
OF AMERICA, INC.

JACK VALENTI
PRESIDENT
AND
CHIEF EXECUTIVE OFFICER

I was in Dallas, in the motorcade some seven cars back of the President and Governor Connally, and their wives.

As we entered Dealey Plaza, the motorcade became an Indianapolis Speedway. We saw the disciplined crowd fragment, jostling and milling about. Something was out of kilter but at that moment we had no imagining of a bizarre tormenting of assumed decencies, the unreeling of a senseless act of mindless malice. I was with Liz Carpenter, staff director for Mrs. Johnson, Pamela Tunure, Mrs. Kennedy's secretary and Evelyn Lincoln, the President's secretary. With unspoken terror we sped onto the Dallas Trade Center where the President was scheduled to speak. The Center was filled, but no President. From a Secret Service agent we learned the President and the Governor had been shot.

I commandeered a Dallas County deputy sheriff and he drove us wildly to Parkland Hospital.

After getting Mrs. Lincoln to the Administrator's office, I wandered about the basement of the hospital. Hysteria and gloom hung like Spanish moss from every inch of that unhappy area. I paused monentarily before the stainless steel door of the emergency operating room where lay the body of the 35th President, all life drained from him but that was not yet known.

Suddenly, someone touched me on the arm. It was the late Cliff Carter, chief political agent of the Vice President. He said: "The Vice President wants to see you right now." He paused confusedly. "The President is dead, you know."

I wept unrestrainedly. Cliff held my arm and said, "Compose yourself, Jack. The Vice President is waiting."

I was aboard Air Force One when it flew through the skies from Dallas to Washington. In the aft portion of the plane rested the body of John Kennedy forever enclosed in a flag draped coffin. I was witness to the swearing in of the new President, his wife and Mrs. Kennedy by his side as he took the oath which resides in the Constitution. I learned then from personal anguish/experience that while the light in the White House may flicker, the light in the White House never goes out. The country goes on. That's what the country is all about.

Sincerely,

Douglas Kiker

NBC newscaster Douglas Kiker was covering President Kennedy's trip to Dallas on November 22, 1963 as White House Correspondent for the New York Herald Tribune.
[33]

As White House correspondent for the New York Herald Tribune, brand-new, my first out-of-town trip with the President, I was in the motorcade, in the press bus, about twenty cars back, when President Kennedy was killed, so far in the rear we did not see or hear a thing. In fact, the press bus proceeded on to the Trade Mart, one stop off the freeway this side of the hospital. We learned about the shooting when Marianne Means, the Hearst newspapers correspondent, called her Washington office to check in. The teletype operator had been reading the wires, which were going crazy. You must understand, the two wire service pool reporters, Jack Bell and Merriman Smith, were in the secret service car directly behind the President's limousine, and had a car phone, so they were filing flash dispatches.

When we arrived on the press bus at Parkland Hospital, the President's car was pulled up before the emergency entrance, all four doors open, several of Mrs. Kennedy's roses on the ground. Also there, directly behind it, was the Vice President's car. After a few minutes, Sen. Ralph Yarborough came out and intimated, but did not tell us, that the President was dead. Shortly thereafter a priest, little guy, came out and, in answer to a question from Hugh Sidey of Time said, "He's dead, all right."

It was, obviously, the most important news story I would ever write. I kept minute-by-minute notes. Tom Wicker of the NY Times and I wrote our stories in the Braniff VIP lounge at Hobby airport. I remember thinking that, if the poor man hadn't been killed, my lead that day would have said what a warm welcome Jack Kennedy got in Dallas: no ugly signs, no jeers, a big, friendly crowd. It was a flag day in my life, one I will never forget.

Douglas Kiker

Jim Wright

Texan Jim Wright began his first term in the U.S. House of Representatives in 1955. In 1987, he became Speaker of the House. He was a member of the Kennedy entourage on November 22, 1963.
[40]

JIM WRIGHT

Congress of the United States

On Friday morning, November 22, none could feel but that the Nation and this man who so perfectly symbolized it were in their finest hour.

41

On that morning, I had the privilege of walking with him through a clamorous hotel lobby and across the street to a waiting crowd, tumultuous with the joy of seeing their President. In that inimitable way in which he gave himself, we walked past the speaker's stand and directly to the people. It was his joy to go among them, to shake their hands, to feel the press of their hopes and aspirations....

The President was relaxed, in the high spirits of his characteristic good humor, vibrant and outgoing at his very best, a President sharing himself with his people.

As he talked, another crowd awaited at a breakfast. But he could not bring himself to leave, so hungry were the people assembled in a drizzling rain to hear him and to clasp to themselves forever the imprint of his personality....

On the way from Fort Worth to Dallas, he spoke to me with enthusiastic and obviously sincere appreciation of the unfeigned friendliness of the people, the demonstrative and contagious warmth of the reception they had given him. "They liked you, Mr. President," I told him. "I liked them," he grinned....

I was in the motorcade, several cars behind President Kennedy, when those terrible shots rang out. There were a few seconds of anxious confusion before I learned the magnitude of the tragedy that had befallen the nation. I was stunned and shocked beyond words.

Sincerely,

Jim Wright

III

OFFICIAL WASHINGTON REACTS
TO THE NEWS FROM DALLAS

"With a good conscience our only sure reward, with history the final judge of our deeds, let us go forth to lead the land we love, asking His blessing and His help, but knowing that here on earth God's work must truly be our own."
– *President Kennedy's Inaugural Address, 1961*

The news of John Kennedy's death swept across Washington D. C. like a brushfire, leaving in its wake a city shaken and stunned. Here the effect of the President's death seemed harsher somehow. In the midst of their grief, officials were forced to continue the business of governing while they buried their President.

The eyes of the world followed John Kennedy home from Dallas that Friday evening, quickly focusing on the events in Washington. Political leaders from around the nation and the world watched, waiting to see how the American government would react to his death; many wondering whether there could be a peaceful transition of power following the mysterious assassination of the President.

These are the reflections of more than two dozen people who were in Washington that day, or who--though away from the nation's capital--shared with John Kennedy the solemn responsibility of governing the nation. They paint a compelling picture of events in the capital as they recall the effect of the President's death on the institutions of government, including the orderly tranfer of authority to Vice President Johnson.

Also recounted are the reactions on the floor of the Senate where Edward Kennedy was presiding. Senator Barry Goldwater, on a trip to the Midwest, hurried back to Washington while reflecting on the loss of a friend, and considering the effect on his own presidential campaign. Congressmen, Cabinet members, and a Supreme Court Justice recall their reactions to the news, sharing their personal feelings and their concerns for the country. And former Senator Charles Mathais recounts the memorial services for the President in the Rotunda of the Capitol and burial services at Arlington National Cemetery.

Barry Goldwater

Barry Goldwater was U.S. Senator from Arizona for over thirty years and the 1964 Republican Presidential Nominee. His books include The Conscience of a Conservative, *and* With No Apologies.
[54]

BARRY GOLDWATER
ARIZONA

𝔘𝔫𝔦𝔱𝔢𝔡 𝔖𝔱𝔞𝔱𝔢𝔰 𝔖𝔢𝔫𝔞𝔱𝔢

... I was enroute to Muncie, Indiana, accompanying the body of my deceased mother-in-law for burial in that city, which is the home city of her family. I learned of the assassination of Jack Kennedy as I left the airline and went to Butler Aviation to fly to Muncie in a chartered aircraft.

I could not believe it and that reaction stayed with me all the way to Muncie, where I verified it by a telephone call to my Washington office. One of the cruelest things happened to me that day when Walter Cronkite, talking over CBS, made the statement that I was enroute to a paid speaking engagement and was not available for comment. He later withdrew that statement.

On that date, frankly, I did not have any real reaction as to what impact Kennedy's death might have on the nation. As time went by, though, I realized that his would be a deeply felt loss because he was a young man and, in my mind, had a very, very promising future as a President, even though we didn't agree a lot on political issues.

I knew him as a close friend and I had really looked forward to running against him in the election that was to be held. The news of his passing caused me to withdraw my name because, to be perfectly honest with you, I had no stomach for running against Lyndon Johnson.

44

Jack and I had talked about a campaign. We had discussed the possibility of traveling around the country either together or in separate aircraft, but stumping the country like politicians should do. Standing up to state our points, our issues, and then debating each other. That would have been impossible with Lyndon Johnson and it was. However, I later, rather reluctantly, gave in to the demands, mostly of the young people, that I run, but I sorely missed Jack Kennedy in that campaign and I still think he could have been one of our greatest Presidents.

Sincerely,

Barry Goldwater

Although political rivals, John Kennedy and Barry Goldwater were good friends. Goldwater, seen here at a Rose Garden press conference, considered withdrawing from the 1964 Presidential campaign because he "had no stomach for running against Lyndon Johnson." (John F. Kennedy Library)

Daniel K. Inouye

After five years in the Hawaii state legislature, Daniel Inouye spent two terms in the U.S. House of Representatives prior to his election to the U.S. Senate in 1962. [39]

DANIEL K. INOUYE
HAWAII

United States Senate

I was in an area of the Senate chambers known as the Senators' Private Lobby, reading the Associated Press newswire teletype, when suddenly the news bulletins from Dallas, Texas, appeared.

I was, of course, stunned and shaken at this news. Then I realized that the temporary presiding officer of the Senate at that moment was Senator Ted Kennedy. I immediately dispatched a Senate page to the president's rostrum on the Senate floor, adjacent to the Private Lobby. I instructed the young page to tell Senator Kennedy to leave the rostrum for a matter of utmost emergency. It was then that Senator Kennedy learned of his brother's shooting.

It was difficult, on that date, in an atmosphere of such shock, to foretell the impact of this event on the nation. There were rumors about conspiracies to kill not only the President, but also the Vice President; speculation about whether this was an act of a madman, or an orchestrated effort possibly leading to war; and other such thoughts running through the Nation's Capital on that day.

Aloha,

DANIEL K. INOUYE
United States Senator

46

Nominees John Kennedy and Lyndon Johnson greet Hawaii Senator Daniel K. Inouye during the 1960 Democratic National Convention in Los Angeles.

"...it is the fate of this generation—of you in the Congress and me as President—to live with a struggle we did not start, in a world we did not make. But the pressures of life are not always distributed by choice. And while no nation ever faced such a challenge, no nation has ever been so ready to seize the burden and the glory of freedom."

—State of the Union Address, 1962

Sam A. Donaldson

After ten years as Capitol Hill Correspondent for ABC News, Sam Donaldson became the White House Correspondent in 1977. He is the author of the book, Hold On, Mr. President.
[29]

ABC News

Sam Donaldson

When President Kennedy was shot I was sitting in the press gallery overlooking the U.S. Senate. Senator Edward Kennedy was presiding. I watched a senate aide burst through the door to the cloakroom and, going from desk to desk, inform the few members who were on the floor. Kennedy stiffened, gathered up his papers and hurried out.

I reacted to the news, which was the most schocking I had ever heard, with personal anguish. It was as if a loved one of my own had been killed. At that moment I gave no thought to the impact on the nation of Kennedy's death. I went about my job for the rest of the day without much thought of the future course of events.

Yours truly,

Sam A. Donaldson

George McGovern

South Dakotan George McGovern served in the U.S. House of Representatives from 1957–61 and in the U.S. Senate from 1963–81. He was the Democratic Presidential Nominee in 1972.
[41]

GEORGE MCGOVERN

     ... I was in the United States Senate chamber when I first heard the news of President Kennedy's shooting. I was totally stunned and shocked by this announcement. President Kennedy seemed so young and vital and important to me at the time that it was difficult for me to envision the nation without him. I remember Senator Mansfield adjourning the Senate when the news broke. I then hurried back to my office in the Senate only to learn by means of a small television set in our office that he had died. At that time I felt the nation had experienced a severe and demoralizing setback that we would not recover from for a long time to come.

All the best,

George McGovern

49

President Kennedy introduced his new Food for Peace Director, George McGovern, at a White House ceremony, January 24, 1961. McGovern was on the floor of the Senate when the first reports from Dallas swept across Capitol Hill. (John F. Kennedy Library)

"A newly expanded Food for Peace Program is feeding the hungry of many lands..., providing lunches for children in school, wages for economic development, relief for the victims of flood and famine, and a better diet for millions whose daily bread is their chief concern."

—State of the Union Address, 1962

Claiborne Pell

Claiborne Pell was elected U.S. Senator from Rhode Island in 1960. His books include Megalopolis Unbound *and* Power and Policy.
[45]

CLAIBORNE PELL
RHODE ISLAND

United States Senate

I was in the Senate Chamber when I first heard about the shooting of President Kennedy.

I reacted with immense and very personal grief, shutting myself in my office for a considerable period of time. Next to my father's, his death made me sadder than any other I had then experienced.

On that date, November 22, (which incidentally is my birthday) I know that I felt President Kennedy's death would have a tremendously negative slowing down effect upon our nation. And ever since then I have prayed that the ideas of John F. Kennedy for our country, earth and universe come to be.

Ever sincerely,

Claiborne Pell

Abraham Ribicoff

In addition to serving as Governor of Connecticut and as U.S. Secretary of Health, Education and Welfare, Abraham Ribicoff represented Connecticut in both the U.S. House of Representatives and the U.S. Senate. [53]

... I was on the floor of the Senate on November 22, 1963 when the news that President Kennedy was shot came over the wire. I, together with my fellow Senators, was in silent shock and disbelief. It just seemed impossible that the President, who was a longtime friend, was a victim of such a tragedy. I felt that his death would remove the inspiration and confidence that he had instilled in our people, especially the young, during his years in office.

Sincerely,

Abraham Ribicoff

"...our nation is commissioned by history to be either an observer of freedom's failure or the cause of its success."
—*State of the Union Address, 1962*

The late "Scoop" Jackson served six terms in the U.S. House of Representatives before his election to the Senate from Washington state in 1953, where he was serving when he died in September, 1983.
[51]

HENRY M. JACKSON
WASHINGTON

United States Senate
WASHINGTON, D.C.

... I was in the Senate restaurant having lunch when I received the news of the assassination.

I reacted with total disbelief, a sense of numbness, if you please, a feeling that it could not have happened. The first news indicated, of course, that he had been shot, had been rushed to the hospital. The implication was that he was still alive. Then came the final news of his death.

... I felt there would be an enormous impact on the country with his death. However, what did surprise me was that his death had an impact long after the event. President Kennedy had been having considerable trouble in getting his domestic legislative program approved by the Congress. It is interesting to note that the bulk of his program that had not been approved was passed in the Congress in a relatively short period of time in December of 1963 and the beginning of 1964. The fact that President Kennedy wanted a given piece of legislation made it possible for his successor, President Johnson, to carry his program forward to completion in a relatively short period of time. The presence of the martyred President carried through the election of 1964 giving President Johnson a landslide as well as an increase in the number of seats in the House and Senate for the Democrats.

Sincerely yours,

Henry M. Jackson

Henry M. Jackson, U.S.S.

President Kennedy with the late Senator Henry "Scoop" Jackson of Washington shortly after Kennedy's inauguration. Jackson believed that President Kennedy's death made it possible for LBJ to enact much of the Kennedy legislative program. (John F. Kennedy Library)

"We have no wish to war with the Soviet Union, for we are a peaceful people who desire to live in peace with all other peoples....The cost of freedom is always high, but Americans have always paid it. And one path we shall never choose, and that is the path of surrender or submission."
—*During the Cuban Missile Crisis, October 1962*

Margaret Chase Smith

Margaret Chase Smith, U.S. Senator from Maine from 1948–72, served longer than any other woman in the U.S. Congress.
[65]

THE NORTHWOOD INSTITUTE
MARGARET CHASE SMITH LIBRARY CENTER

... I was in my office, Senate Office Building, the time of the Dallas incident. With me were two NBC men and their camera making a film. After 15 minutes of discussion, the door from the next office quietly opened and my executive assistant, William C. Lewis, Jr., quietly said, "The President has been shot".

The two men left almost before he closed the door, and I continued to sit, shocked at such news. Before the day was over, I cancelled all commitments for the following six weeks out of respect for President Kennedy. Among these were a television program for Jack Paar, a luncheon with the National Press Women in Washington, and others of similar importance.

Sincerely,

Margaret Chase Smith

P.S. What a tragedy—a young man to be shot from afar without regard to person, position, people and nation.

U.S. Senators Edmund Muskie and Margaret Chase Smith, both from Maine, are shown at a White House press conference in 1962. Muskie was in Maine and Smith was in Washington when they heard the news of Kennedy's death.

Edmund S. Muskie

Ed Muskie has served as Governor of Maine, U.S. Senator, and U.S. Secretary of State. In 1968, he was the Democratic Nominee for Vice President.
[49]

On that unforgettable day, I was having lunch with a number of supporters who were organizing my campaign for reelection to the U.S. Senate. The place was the Eastland Hotel in Portland, Maine.

The American Legion was holding an event in the same hotel. As we were about to start our discussions, a friend from the Legion rushed in to tell me that the President had been shot.

We promptly adjourned the meeting and I took the hotel elevator to the studios of WCSH-TV to listen to the news as it unfolded in Dallas. And so we followed the drive to the hospital, the agonizing suspense as the doctors labored to save the President's life, and the sad news of his death and the subsequent events.

I was asked to speak to the people of Maine and re-sponded as best I could to the unbelievable tragedy. I was summoned back to Washington. There was the inevitable speculation, which continues to this day, as to the identity of the perpetrators. What were their motives? Was the Soviet Union or Cuba involved? If so, why and what else might they try?

I was sure the country would respond with steadi-ness and strength, and rally around President Johnson. His theme, "Let Us Continue", struck just the right note.

The weekend that followed was a somber and sad time. I had lost a good friend as well as an inspiring leader.

I have not forgotten that experience.

With best wishes, I am

Sincerely,

Edmund S. Muskie

Robert A. Taft, Jr.

Robert Taft represented the state of Ohio in the U.S. House of Representatives from 1963–65 and from 1967–71, and in the U.S. Senate from 1971–76.
[46]

ROBERT TAFT, JR.

At the time I heard of it I was addressing a section of the American Bar Association at its meeting in Chicago. Of course, I cut off the speech and expressed concern and grief to the audience. My reaction was one of shock and realization that the course of the Congress in which I served would be radically changed.

> "I know my Republican friends were glad to see my wife feeding an elephant in India. She gave him sugar and nuts. But of course the elephant wasn't satisfied."
> —*Before the Gridiron Club, 1962*

Edward J. Gurney

Edward Gurney represented the state of Florida for six years in the U.S. House of Representatives and for six years in the U.S. Senate.
[49]

EDWARD J. GURNEY
FLORIDA

The first news of the assassination of President Kennedy came to me at a luncheon in the officers' club at Patrick Air Force Base in Florida. I was with a group of Congressmen, Members of the House Science and Astronautics Committee, on an inspection visit to space installations.

All of us at the table had the same reaction—total disbelief. Frankly, I thought it was some sort of sick joke.

Perhaps, the best way to point up the severity of this tragic event, to me as well as the other Congressmen, is to relate what followed.

We held a meeting and a discussion. We decided to cancel our inspection visit and return to Washington. The flight back reminded me of being part of a funeral. There was very little talk, each of us concentrating on our own thoughts.

I did have one general feeling. I thought that the change in leadership at the helm of our nation would have a profound effect. It did. It would take volumes to explain that conclusion. I do not believe that any other single event in the history of the United States has brought about greater change in the course of our nation.

Sincerely
Edward Gurney

Gale McGee

Gale McGee has held positions as Delegate to the United Nations General Assembly, as Permanent Representative and Ambassador to the Organization of American States, and as U.S. Senator from Wyoming.
[48]

My wife, Loraine; secretary, Liz Strannigan; and I were enroute by automobile from Casper, Wyoming to Sheridan, Wyoming for an evening Democratic rally and picture-showing of a campaign film in preparation for my own upcoming campaign for re-election to the United States Senate.

We stopped for gas in a tiny, Wyoming town called Kaycee. It was 11:50 a.m., and the news bulletin had just come on the air—the first time we'd had the radio on all morning. We had been enjoying the quiet and wide open Wyoming spaces.

The miles were endless as we waited to hear the news from the hospital in Dallas. The silence was heavy when the final words were received....

Our reaction was total shock—disbelief—a sense of panic to get to a larger community where additional news bulletins might be available.

Our immediate reaction was to make arrangements to get back to Washington, D.C. Air flights were infrequent and unavailable from Sheridan at that time of day. We had to charter a private plane to get Loraine and me back to Denver's Stapleton International Airport in order to get a connection on to Washington....

We couldn't know exactly what this loss of the president portended on an international level, but we knew we had to get back to be ready for any action our Congress would be taking and to assist as best we could. Again, the flight from Denver to Washington was eerily silent.

Sincerely yours,

GALE McGEE

President John Kennedy with Wyoming Senator Gale McGee at the University of Wyoming in 1963.

"But we cannot be satisfied to rest here. This is the side of the hill, not the top. The mere absence of war is not peace. The mere absence of recession is not growth. We have made a beginning, but we have only begun. Now the time has come to make the most of our gains, to translate the renewal of our national strength into the achievement of our national purpose."

—State of the Union Address, 1963

Strom Thurmond

Before his election to the U.S. Senate in 1955, Strom Thurmond served one term as Governor of South Carolina. In 1948 he was the Presidential Nominee of the States Rights Party.
[60]

STROM THURMOND
SOUTH CAROLINA

𝔘nited 𝔖tates 𝔖enate

That tragic day, of course is indelibly etched in all our memories.

...I was attending the dedication of a public water system in Beaufort, S.C., when my staff called to notify me of the tragic news. My reaction, which was similar to the reactions of most people, was profound shock and sadness. President Kennedy had achieved much in a short time, which made this serious course of events all the more difficult to accept and understand. In some countries, an event of this horrible magnitude would have sent the nation into an irrecoverable tailspin. But I knew our country and our people would somehow overcome the assassination and continue to move forward.

Sincerely,

Strom Thurmond

Strom Thurmond

Charles Mathias

Charles Mathias represented Maryland in the U.S. House of Representatives from 1961–69, and in the Senate from 1969–87.
[41]

CHARLES McC. MATHIAS, JR.
MARYLAND

United States Senate

The murder of John Fitzgerald Kennedy was more than the trespass of one man against another. It was more than a crime against a wife and children. It was more even than a blow against all humanity. It was an act which struck at the Constitution of the United States itself....

When I first heard the news of President Kennedy's assassination, I was attending the President's Appalachian Regional Conference in Hagerstown (Maryland). The speaker on that occasion was to have been Under Secretary of Commerce, Franklin D. Roosevelt, Jr. As soon as I had been advised that President Kennedy had been wounded I told Secretary Roosevelt the sad news. We made an announcement to the group gathered there for lunch and we both immediately felt that we should get to a place where we could follow events and be of service in any way possible.

It was all too soon that the announcement was made–the President had died. This unbelievable fact, even more unbelievable because of the vitality and youth of the President, was hard for the country to absorb as a reality. On the following day, Mrs. Mathias and I joined our colleagues at the White House to pay respects. We were met at the door by one of President Kennedy's naval aides and with slow ceremony escorted through the state rooms of the White House into the East

Room where the coffin lay in state....

The next act in the sad drama occurred on the following day when the President's body was moved from the White House to the Capitol. On Sunday the entire Congress gathered solemnly in the rotunda under the great dome. There, in muted light, surrounded by the pictures of the great events which represent more than three centuries of American history, we waited together for the unfolding of yet another chapter in the history of America. As we waited we could hear through the stone walls of the Capitol the drums and music of the funeral cortege approaching Capitol Hill. When the great bronze doors opened, the casket was brought in to rest upon the Lincoln catafalque. No human heart within the great hall could be untouched and unmoved when Mrs. Kennedy, following the coffin of her husband and clasping the hands of her children came forward to bid farewell with dignity, with grace, and with beauty.

On the following day the Congress gathered again in the rotunda accompanied by members of the Cabinet, former Presidents, and many of those who had taken great parts in the life of this Nation. We gathered in complete quiet. The eloquent men, the great orators of the Congress, all stood silent with heads bowed and centered in attention and emotion on the casket carrying the body of the 35th President of the United States. As the pallbearers bore the casket from the rotunda every soul in that assemblage was wrenched by the human suffering of Mrs. Kennedy and of her children—that suffering which she subdued because the wife of a President is not even allowed the privilege of her grief, but must uphold the traditions of the office to which her husband had been called.

In the afternoon, Congress went to Arlington National Cemetery to bid farewell to John F. Kennedy. I was struck by that fact that the Members of Congress gathered on the grass under an ancient oak tree, gnarled, almost leafless—standing on the hill below the home of George Washington Parke Custis in that sunny afternoon as if they were gathering in a country churchyard. There was a simplicity about the fact that these Senators and Representatives—Members of the greatest legislative body in the world—stood there, bareheaded for the most part, waiting for the body of the Chief Magistrate of this Republic to be borne to its final resting place....

From the hillside we saw the funeral cortege coming across Memorial Bridge. And what a procession—representing the peoples of the world—President de Gaulle, Prince Philip, Prime Minister Home, King Baudouin, Emperor Haile Selassie, all these come to salute a great man and a great nation. The day seemed in tune with the event.

As we stood by the grave at Arlington the sun moved over our heads and touched the tops of the trees. The shadow lengthened and it was, indeed, a time for farewell.

How rightly typical of a Republic—what a scene to emphasize the dignity of man—there, not separated by position, rank or favor, the leaders of the nations gathered as one family to pay a last tribute. It was a moving testimonial to the office of the Presidency, to its 35th occupant and to the Nation over which he presided.

Sincerely,

Charles McC. Mathias, Jr.
United States Senator

> "Members of the Congress, the Constitution makes us not rivals for power but partners for progress. We are all trustees for the American people, custodians of the American heritage. It is my task to report the state of the Union; to improve it is the task of us all."
>
> —*State of the Union Address, 1962*

Spark M. Matsunaga

Following seven terms in the U.S. House of Representatives, Spark M. Matsunaga was elected U.S. Senator from Hawaii in 1976.
[47]

SPARK M. MATSUNAGA
HAWAII

United States Senate

      ... I was in the office of "Fishbait" Miller, Doorkeeper of the U.S. House of Representatives. He had his radio tuned to soft music which was suddenly interrupted with the announcement that President Kennedy had been shot. With Doorkeeper Miller, I fell to my knees and prayed, "Please God, don't let him die. He's much too needed."

      My impression of the impact of President Kennedy's death was that this dastardly act would be used by our detractors as irrefutable evidence that ours is a Nation of violence.

      Aloha and best wishes.

Sincerely,

Spark Matsunaga
U. S. Senator

Lindy Boggs

*Following the death of her husband, Hale, in 1973,
Lindy Boggs succeeded him as a Member of the U.S.
House of Representatives from Louisiana. She was
also Chairperson of both the Kennedy and Johnson
Inaugural Balls.*
[47]

LINDY (MRS. HALE) BOGGS, M.C.
2D DISTRICT, LOUISIANA

Congress of the United States
House of Representatives

When I first heard the news of President Kennedy's shooting, I was
in my husband's Majority Whip office in the U.S. Capitol Building.

My first reaction was to turn on a television set. Then, I sank to
knees to pray that my dear friend had not been killed. Next, because
my husband and the Majority Leader and the Speaker were not in the
Capitol building, I called the Sergeant-At-Arms office to make certain
that our staff members would answer inquiries correctly.

The negative impact that President Kennedy's death would have upon
the nation centered around the loss of his special qualities of
vision and charisma, and the violent manner in which it occurred.
However, I knew Lyndon Johnson well and was confident that his
leadership would take our nation forward without a hesitant step
under our remarkably enduring constitutional system.

                    Sincerely,

                    Lindy (Mrs. Hale) Boggs, M.C.

Gerald R. Ford

Gerald Ford represented Michigan in the U.S. House of Representatives from 1949–73. He was also a member of the Warren Commission, which conducted a government investigation into President Kennedy's assassination. The first person ever appointed Vice President, Gerald Ford became President of the United States upon Richard Nixon's resignation on August 9, 1974.
[50]

GERALD R. FORD

My wife, Betty, and I were driving in Washington, D.C., for an interview with an educational counselor for one of our children when we heard about the shooting of President Kennedy.

... We were terribly shocked because we had become reasonably good friends of President Kennedy during our first term in the House of Representatives. JFK came to the House of Representatives in January 1947 and I was sworn in two years later in January 1949. In 1949 and 1950 our staff offices were across the corridor from each other. As a result, JFK and I got well acquainted.

I was especially saddened because a person I admired had met a tragic death and I was angry because this crime could occur in the United States.

On the date of the assassination there was no way I could accurately assess the impact of his assassination. I knew, of course, Vice President Johnson was an able dedicated and effective leader, but had no specific

knowledge as to what his policies might be. Subjectively,
I did thank our forefathers for providing a Constitution
that gave our nation the capability to handle the transfer of authority in such a tragic circumstance.

Sincerely,

Gerald R. Ford

*Then-Congressman Gerald R. Ford (right) joins President Kennedy, Ohio Congressman
Michael J. Kirwan (next to JFK) and other Congresssional leaders at a White House reception. Ford later served on the Warren Commission. (John F. Kennedy Library)*

Robert H. Michel

Illinois Congressman Robert Michel began his first term with the U.S. House of Representatives in 1957, and has served both as House Minority Whip and as House Minority Leader.
[40]

ROBERT H. MICHEL
18TH DISTRICT, ILLINOIS

Office of the Republican Leader
United States House of Representatives

The stunning news came to me as I had started my drive back to Illinois on that fateful Friday, November 22. I was between Hagerstown, Maryland and Hancock, Maryland when the confirmed report came over the radio that the last rites had been administered and that the President had died. I pulled off the side of the road to control my shock and emotion and sought out the first telephone that I might phone my wife. Neither of us could talk very intelligently, but we did decide that I should turn back and return to Washington.

I shall never forget that drive back to Washington along Route 24 which I had driven so many times. Cars were pulling off to the side of the road in numbers and those still on the road were just poking along. It was quite obvious that drivers were listening intently to their radios for every fragment of news.

As I turned onto Embassy Row, down Massachusetts Avenue, I never before have noticed so many flags representing foreign countries and all were drawn to half mast. I guess there never has been so tragic an event that has touched so many capitals around the wrold and certainly attests to the stature this relatively young man achieved in so short a time.

Sincerely yours,

Robert H. Michel
Republican Leader

Arch A. Moore, Jr.

Arch Moore, a former Member of the U.S. House of Representatives, began his third term as Governor of West Virginia in 1985.
[40]

STATE OF WEST VIRGINIA
OFFICE OF THE GOVERNOR

ARCH A. MOORE, JR.
GOVERNOR

    At the time of the President's assassination, I was in Washington, serving as a United States Congressman. I had seen the President only a short time before he left for Texas, and when I learned of the tragedy in Dallas, my first reaction was disbelief. I could not accept for the moment that this man who so recently had appeared smiling and ebullient, with a warm and encouraging word for those around him, would never again walk among us. I was struck, too, by the sad realization that no matter how carefully we try to protect our President, he will always be vulnerable to those who are determined to harm him.

    On November 22, 1963, I think our nation was stunned beyond knowing--or even thinking--what the impact of the President's death would have on us. Rather, I believe our immediate thoughts and prayers were for his wife and two small children.

    In a time of grief and confusion, and God grant that it never happen again, we are fortunate that we can find our way through our Constitution. Designed to be our guide, the Constitution of the United States provides for an orderly transition of government, and it did not fail us in one of the darkest hours in our country's history.

Sincerely,

Arch A. Moore, Jr.
Governor

71

Morris K. Udall

Arizonan Mo Udall was first elected to the U.S. House of Representatives in 1960. He is the author of Arizona Law of Evidence *and* Education of a Congressman.
[41]

Congress of the United States

A second term Congressman, I was having a Friday lunch (with my key staffers) at a restaurant near the Capitol. A waiter informed us that he had heard the tragic news on the radio. We were all shocked and went back to my office to watch the developing story on television.

I felt a range of emotions: Disbelief that this could happen in America; anger at what I assumed (erroneously) was right wing violence and extremism; fear of foreign involvement in the shooting; sadness for Mrs. Kennedy and the two children; and deep sorrow that the Country had to accept the loss of such a remarkable leader.

I feared that the tragedy would deepen division in the Country that President Kennedy had tried to heal. And it seemed likely that the Civil Rights movement might be strengthened by this tragedy.

Sincerely,

Morris K. Udall
U.S. House of Representatives

72

George E. Reedy

George Reedy was LBJ's Legislative Assistant at the time of JFK's assassination. He later served as White House Press Secretary and wrote such books as Who Will Do Our Fighting for Us? *and* The Twilight of the Presidency.

[46]

George E. Reedy
Nieman Professor of Journalism

MU Marquette University

I was in my office on the West front of the Capitol transacting routine business when I received a call from a secretary in the Vice President's office. She said that someone had stuck his head in the door to tell her that President Kennedy had been shot. I walked to my wire service tickers in the outer hall to read the news. Johnson had no major staff members with him as both he and I had deep reservations about the wisdom of the Kennedy trip and he was deliberately reducing his presence to the minimum. (Let me hasten to add that the reservations had nothing to do with the assassination but with a fear that he would worsen a complicated division in Texas politics which should be handled only by experts. We were right but, of course, no one noticed it in the wake of the assassination.)

My immediate reaction was one of mild shock. I called Walter Jenkins and alerted the other members of the Johnson Staff and then waited anxiously for further word. Later in the day, I was called down to the White House to participate in the planning of the return of President Johnson and the martyred President to Washington. I came to the immediate conclusion that it was a "crackpot" killing simply because nothing else happened. A serious "plot" it seemed to me would have used the assassination as a signal for further action. I saw the major problem as moving to reassure the American people that the country would not go down the drain just because a President had been killed.

I was afraid that there might be an outbreak of panic based upon the belief that the assassination was the work of a foreign power.

Sincerely

George E. Reedy

Orville L. Freeman

Orville Freeman served as Governor of Minnesota from 1955 until 1961, when he was named U.S. Secretary of Agriculture by President Kennedy.
[45]

I was aboard Air Force Two along with other members of the cabinent and Presidential Representatives from the JFK Staff one hour out of Honolulu on our way to Tokyo for a meeting with the Japanese cabinet.

The reaction could best be expressed, I believe as "incredulous" stunned might also be a proper adjective. Mrs. Freeman and I were having breakfast, we were half way through when Secretary Rusk, Administrative Assistant informed me that the Secretary would like to see me in his compartment. I responded I would be there in a few minutes after I had finished breakfast. He responded somewhat grimly that he thought the Secretary would like to see me immediately. That seemed unnecessary with a ten hour flight before us but I set my breakfast aside and went to the Secretary's compartment. It was immediately apparent that Secretary Russ was deeply disturbed about something. He looked at me with almost desperation in his eyes and said "the President has been shot." I was stunned. My first thought was where was he hit. Dean Rusk responded to that question by saying apparently he was hit in the head. My odd response to that was "maybe he will be all right, I have been shot in the head and came through it ok. Funny, what one thinks of under such extraordinary circumstances. My mind flashed back for an instant to the battle on Bougainville in the Solomon Islands where I was seriously wounded.

The story of our doubt based on the lack of information as to what we should do; continue on, turn back, go to Texas, go to Washington, I'm sure has been reported by many others.

The trip back was a grim one. Quiet tears were shed by a many of us. There was deep concern as to where the country will go now. I was surprised that so few aboard that plane had had close contact with Vice President Johnson. I had known and worked with the Vice President over many years, particularly when I was Governor of Minnesota and he was Majority Leader. I was able to reassure some of my travelling companions that I felt that he would provide strong leadership and that his public reputation as a strong conservative was miscast. I was confident that he would provide strong and liberal leadership and carry forward the Kennedy program. Happily that proved to be the case.

Sincerely yours,

Orville, L. Freeman

Orville Freeman, seen here with the President on January 23, 1962, served as Kennedy's Secretary of Agriculture. Freeman was with Secretary of State Dean Rusk enroute to Tokyo when they received word that the President had been shot in the head. Freeman's response was, "Maybe he'll be all right. I have been shot in the head and came through it ok." (John F. Kennedy Library)

Arthur J. Goldberg

Arthur Goldberg, a former Associate Justice of the U.S. Supreme Court, has also held positions as the U.S. Secretary of Labor, the U.S. Representative to the United Nations, and Ambassador-at-Large. In 1978, he received the Medal of Freedom.
[55]

ARTHUR J. GOLDBERG

I was on the Supreme Court when I first heard the news of President Kennedy's shooting.

I reacted to the news, as did all Americans -- with feelings of great sorrow.

I was of the view -- and still am -- that President Kennedy's death would have a significant impact on our nation's domestic and foreign policy.

Sincerely yours,

Arthur J. Goldberg

Secretary of Labor Arthur Goldberg confers with President Kennedy on May 25, 1961. Kennedy appointed Goldberg to the United States Supreme Court in 1962. Goldberg was on the Court when he learned of the President's death. (John F. Kennedy Library)

"Americans are free to disagree with the law, but not to disobey it. For in a government of laws and not of men, no man, however prominent and powerful, and no mob, however unruly or boisterous, is entitled to defy the commands of our court of law. If this country should ever reach the point where any man or group of men by force or threat of force could long defy the commands of our court and our Constitution, then no law would stand free from doubt, no judge would be sure of his writ, and no citizen would be safe from his neighbors."

— *Televised Address from the White House, September 30, 1962*

Nicholas Katzenbach

In addition to serving as Attorney General of the United States from 1965–66, Nicholas Katzenbach has also held positions as Assistant and Deputy Attorney General and Under Secretary of State.
[41]

    I was eating lunch with Assistant Deputy Attorney General Joe Dolan (later Bobby Kennedy's legislative assistant) at a small fish restaurant near the Department of Justice in Washington.

    My immediate reaction was one of disbelieve. We immediately left the restaurant and rushed back to Bobby Kennedy's office in the Department of Justice. Bobby Kennedy was at home at the time and not in his office. There we learned from Bobby Kennedy's secretary, Angie Novello, that the President would undoubtedly die.

    I believe at that time I was too devastated with the news, and too involved with many other matters related to it, to give any serious thought to the impact that President Kennedy's death would have on the nation.

Sincerely,

Nicholas deB. Katzenbach

Alexander M. Haig

In addition to serving as the U.S. Secretary of State from 1981–82, General Haig has also held positions as White House Chief of Staff and Commander-in-Chief of the U.S European Command.
[38]

Office of
Alexander M. Haig, Jr.

At the time of President Kennedy's shooting, I was serving as Military Assistant to the Secretary of the Army, Cyrus Vance, with specific responsibility in the area of Central America. These duties involved a close collaboration with the General Counsel of the Army who at the time was Joseph A. Califano, Jr. I was at my desk in the Pentagon when word was received of the shooting.

The reaction was, of course, one of great shock and genuine concern that the assassination itself was somehow related to the tense relationship between the Administration and Castro Cuba.

Beyond the shock and sadness shared by most Americans, I was greatly concerned that the violent tendencies which mushroomed after that tragic event were somehow a legacy of the exploitation of the historic quest for social justice by the Soviet Marxist-Leninist system. Clearly, a most sensitive outcome of the Kennedy assassination has remained the degree to which the event itself might be linked to international communism in the Soviet model. I continue to suspect that the last chapter on this issue has not been written. In any event, the proliferation of international terrorism and so-called wars of national liberation since that event suggest that the United States and the free world have yet to come to grips with the issue. This is not to suggest any particular insights on the actual motivations for the assassination but subsequent events tend to confirm that the broader problem remains a continuing and perhaps growing threat to rule of law and to international peace and stability.

Sincerely,

Daniel Patrick Moynihan

Before becoming U.S. Senator from New York in 1977, Daniel Moynihan served as Ambassador to India and as Permanent Representative to the United Nations. He also served as Assistant Secretary of Labor under President Kennedy.
[36]

DANIEL P. MOYNIHAN
NEW YORK

United States Senate

I was at a Georgetown house discussing the renovation of Pennsylvania Avenue.

I was almost thrown into shock. I knew I would never be young again.

I expected that we would think about what had happened, and not simply in terms of what it meant to us as individuals. Surely I had learned that one man's death does not bring an end to things.

Sincerely,

Daniel Patrick Moynihan

Mark Lane

Washington attorney Mark Lane is the author of Rush to Judgement, A Citizen's Dissent, *and* The Strongest Poison.
[36]

MARK LANE

I was returning to court from a noon recess in a case on trial in Foley Square in which I was serving as the defense lawyer. As I walked through Chinatown, just a short distance from the courthouse, I saw crowds of people gathered around radios. I asked what had happened and was told that President Kennedy had been shot. I ran to the press room in the courthouse and saw the local reporter from the New York Times. As he completed a telephone call, tears in his eyes, he told me that the president was dead. The contemopaneous television and radio reports were continuing to announce only that he had been wounded.

I knew, admired and had supported John Kennedy. I had worked with his brother, Bobby, in coordinating the New York City aspect of the 1960 campaign for the presidency. John Kennedy had endorsed me and his support was likely decisive in my being elected to the New York State Legislature. His death placed in power a man who opposed much of what John Kennedy had proclaimed he stood for. The sense of loss was felt both personally and politically.

I feared that President Kennedy's opposition to the war in Viet Nam and his publicly stated committment to withdraw "advisers" from that area of the world would be superceded by a contrary and dangerous program implemented by the new president. I also feared that ambitious Neanderthals would seek to twist the facts about the assassination to imperil all of us who share this planet.

I hoped that the integrity of our state and the soul of the nation would be preserved by a government and a news media willing to share with the American people the facts surrounding the death of President Kennedy. Instead the government produced an unanimated work of fiction (written by seven moral dwarfs, entirely lacking the grace of Snow White, who demonstrated an historic failiure of both nerve and intellect) entitled the Warren Commission Report.

Sincerely,

Mark Lane

Harry Reid

After serving in the U.S. House of Representatives from 1981–87, Harry Reid was elected U.S. Senator from Nevada in 1986.
[24]

United States Senate

COMMITTEE ON APPROPRIATIONS

I remember clearly the events of that day. I was a law student at that time, studying in a vacant classroom at George Washington University, here in Washington, D.C. I recall that somebody walked in and told me that the President had been shot.

My reaction was one of sadness. I felt really, truly sad. At that time, I worked for Congressman Walter Baring of Nevada. I remember that I went into the congressional office that night and Congressman Baring was there. He asked me to come into his office, where we sat and talked about John F. Kennedy's death.

At the time, I was so stunned and confused by the news. I knew then that the country was going to change, but I wasn't sure what the extent of it would be. I remember, though, that the full impact of his death did not come until the funeral of his brother, Robert Kennedy, five years later. I remember Edward Kennedy giving a heart-rendering eulogy of his brothers. I'll always remember that. I cried when I heard it.

HARRY REID
United States Senator

Michael N. Castle

Mike Castle served as Delaware's Attorney General and Lieutenant Governor before he was elected Governor of Delaware in 1984.
[24]

STATE OF DELAWARE
OFFICE OF THE GOVERNOR

MICHAEL N. CASTLE
GOVERNOR

At the time of President Kennedy's assassination, I was a third-year law student at Georgetown University Law Center. I was in the law school library when I first heard the news.

My initial reaction was the same shock and dismay probably felt by all Americans. My reaction immediately after that was one of astonishment that a person as inconsequential as this assassin could -- by the simple act of firing a rifle -- take the life of what may have been the most important person in the world, and totally change the future course of human events.

The routine events of my life during the days that followed are forgotten. But I remember driving past the White House; I remember standing on Connecticut Avenue to watch the funeral procession go by; and I

remember stepping outside the house in which we were
living in Arlington, Virginia, to watch as jets flew
overhead in a formation from which one plane was
missing -- the traditional tribute to a fallen
comrade. And I was struck by the great sadness that
had befallen a single family, as well an entire nation.

The event and the following days marked such a sad time
in the history of the country that it was hard to judge
the impact of President Kennedy's death at that time.
To one living in Washington it was clear that the
youthful spirit embodied by President Kennedy and his
family would not be continued in President Johnson's
Administration. This was a personal loss felt by many,
regardless of whether they agreed or disagreed with
President Kennedy's policies. Fortunately, our
constitutional process of succession is such that no
gap in leadership was felt, although it became evident
that a change in direction would occur under a new
president. Because this proceeded in increments rather
than in a rush, however, I had no feeling of impact on
the policy or the overall future of the nation, until
the policy became clear and the nation started to take
a new direction under a new leader.

Sincerely yours,

Michael N. Castle
Governor

Art Buchwald

Art Buchwald's syndicated column won the Pulitzer Prize for Outstanding Commentary in 1982. His books include Paris after Dark, While Reagan Slept, Great Society, *and* I Am Not a Crook.
[38]

ART BUCHWALD

I was in a taxi coming from National Airport. I arrived at the National Press Building and saw guys dashing out as if there was a bomb scare. I stopped one of the newspapermen and asked what had happened and he said, "Kennedy's been shot."

I think I cried a couple of times. I know I was in a daze. I finally went to my typewriter and wrote a column about Kennedy. It wasn't very good.

On that date I was so upset I hadn't given it much thought.

Sincerely,

Art Buchwald

Art Buchwald

IV

"THE TORCH HAS BEEN PASSED...": A NEW GENERATION OF AMERICANS LOSES ITS CHAMPION

"Let the word go forth from this time and place, to friend and foe alike, that the torch has been passed to a new generation of Americans—born in this century, tempered by war, disciplined by a hard and bitter peace, proud of our ancient heritage—and unwilling to witness or permit the slow undoing of human rights to which this nation has been committed...."
— *President Kennedy's Inaugural Address, 1961*

The beginning of John Kennedy's tenure as President marked a distinct transition in American government. Not only was the oldest President, Dwight Eisenhower, relinquishing the reins of authority to the youngest man ever elected to that office, but Kennedy himself recognized that there was a new generation in America. In his inaugural address, President Kennedy challenged that generation of young Americans to join him in service to our country. Promising them that "the energy, the faith, the devotion which we bring to this endeavor will light our country and all who serve it—and the glow from that fire can truly light the world," thousands responded to his challenge.

More than twenty-seven years after President Kennedy issued his challenge, many of America's political leaders credit John Kennedy as the inspiration for their involvement in our political system. Many of them were standing on the threshold of their careers when they answered Kennedy's call to service. For some, that meant seeking public office. But many others chose to become politically involved through the private sector.

Now these men and women reflect upon the influence of John Kennedy in their lives, and recall the tragedy of his death. When those shots rang out in Dallas, the torch—accepted by John Kennedy on behalf of a new generation—faded, but it did not fail. For these Americans, that light first ignited by John Kennedy continues to shine.

James J. Blanchard

*After three terms in the U.S. House of Representatives,
James Blanchard was elected Governor of Michigan in
1982.*
[21]

JAMES J. BLANCHARD
GOVERNOR

STATE OF MICHIGAN
OFFICE OF THE GOVERNOR

I think that everyone who was alive remembers where they were
when President Kennedy was assassinated....

I was at Michigan State University as a senior and active in politics,
a young Democrat, president of my class, and I think the person I most
admired was John Kennedy. I remember going to class on Friday,
November 22 and upon learning of the shooting, racing back home to
watch the reports on television. I was shocked and very saddened to
learn that he in fact was dead. President Kennedy was truly, at that
time, president for young America, people who were 18, 19, 30 or 40.
He brought to government something we had not seen for years, the
notion that politics was honorable service, that people should be involved in politics and public life, and that there was a role for young
people with fresh new ideas.

Since that point politics has never been the same in America. I personally think that we have gone through a steady stream of setbacks
that have given to our political system almost a nervous breakdown,
beginning with his assassination and others...Martin Luther King,
Robert Kennedy, the attempts on George Wallace and Ronald Reagan.
The Vietnam War, a terrible recession and then Watergate...have all
led to a loss of confidence in our government institutions.

James J. Blanchard
James J. Blanchard
Governor

Geraldine A. Ferraro

Geraldine Ferraro, a former Member of the U.S. Congress from New York, was the first woman ever nominated for national office by a major political party when she became the 1984 Democratic Candidate for Vice President.
[28]

Geraldine A. Ferraro

I was walking with my mother-in-law along Austin Street in Forest Hills. (Austin Street is a strip of stores in my neighborhood.) I was pushing my eldest daughter Donna (who celebrated her second birthday three days later on the same day as John Kennedy Jr. celebrated his third) in her stroller. Shop keepers ran out into the street shouting the news in disbelief.

I was horrified and frightened and rushed home to hear the news reports.

I felt it would be an irreparable loss. He was the first President with whom I could identify. His hopes and plans for the future of this country were those of a father with young children. His dreams were mine - and I had confidence he would achieve them. On that day, besides the sense of deep loss, there was a fear that perhaps there was a conspiracy to undermine our government.

Very truly yours,

Geraldine A. Ferraro

Neil Goldschmidt

Neil Goldschmidt, one-time U.S. Secretary of Transportation, was elected Governor of Oregon in 1986.
[23]

NEIL GOLDSCHMIDT
GOVERNOR

OFFICE OF THE GOVERNOR
STATE CAPITOL
SALEM, OREGON 97310-1347

     ... I was a Senate Intern to United States Senator Maureen Neuberger. I had begun this job at about the time of Martin Luther King's march on Washington, following my graduation from the University of Oregon the previous Spring. I had just been in the Senate Chambers and, if my memory serves me correctly, President Kennedy's brother Ted was in the presiding Chair of the Senate. Someone had come to get him and he had left the floor. I was showing some friends of mine, who were guests, the Senate Chamber. We left not knowing why Senator Kennedy had left the Chair, and didn't realize until a few minutes later about what was then a rumor about President Kennedy being shot in Dallas. I went back to the Senate Chamber, to the location where the Senators gather in an anteroom off the chambers where people were checking, what my memory tells me was, a wire service machine or some kind of an information machine which was feeding the scattered information of the moment. We, of course, learned a short time later what had happened or at least that he had died at Parkland Hospital. Nothing in my life, before or since, hit me so hard. Like the rest of the country I was stunned that it could happen, absolutely turned inside out by the unfairness of it all. Through the following days I joined the country at T.V. sets and radios to listen and to try to understand it without success.

... I had first heard John Kennedy at the Lane County Courthouse in Eugene, Oregon, during his campaign for President. It's a moment mentioned in Teddy White's "Making of a President". This limited exposure to Kennedy gave me great hope about our political process and about the process of change, that I believed and lots of other people believed our country needed. When I heard the news I was empty and at the same time angry and afraid; worried for his family, worried it could happen so easily, worried that there didn't have to be a reason and unable to accept that; and very discouraged for my country, that it was going to have to live through something so difficult.

... There were so many ruumors about the reason for the murder; some people believing that it was right-wing fanatics, others believing that Castro's agents had done it. Before we recovered from the shock of the President's death, we witnessed the film of Jack Ruby's murder following that of the President. It was a sense that things were getting out of control: it wasn't so much that I could predict the impact that it would have on the nation; as that we all knew that the Vice President was now going to lead the government. We knew we had to support him in order to maintain our responsibilities in the world, but we also knew that most of us wouldn't have elected him in the first place, and now that one bullet had changed the course of history so cruelly.

Sincerely,

Neil Goldschmidt
Governor

"It ought to be possible for American consumers of any color to receive equal service in places of public accommodation, such as hotels and restaurants and theatres and retail stores, without being forced to demonstrate in the street, and it ought to be possible for American citizens of any color to register to vote in a free election without interference or fear of reprisal."

— *Televised Address from the White House, June 11, 1963*

Joseph A. Califano, Jr.

Joseph Califano served as U.S. Secretary of Health, Education and Welfare from 1977 to 1979. He is the author of The Student Revolution: A Global Confrontation, *and* A Presidential Nation.
[32]

I first heard the news of President John Kennedy's shooting while I was in the bottom of a dam in West Virginia. I was inspecting it in my role as General Counsel of the Army and Special Assistant to the Secretary of the Army for Civil Functions with responsibility to supervise the Corps of Engineers.

I was stunned by the news and immediately rushed back to Washington. It was a particularly trying time for me, because it was John Kennedy who had inspired my interest in government and politics and whose New Frontier I had left my practice in New York to join as a young lawyer.

Sincerely

Joseph A. Califano, Jr.

Richard D. Lamm

Richard Lamm served in the U.S. House of Representatives from 1966 until 1974, when he was elected Governor of Colorado. He held that position until 1987.

[28]

STATE OF COLORADO

Richard D. Lamm
Governor

I heard of the news of John F. Kennedy's shooting when I was before a hearing of the Public Utilities Commission of the State of Colorado. I was a young lawyer sitting at the council table when someone came in with the horrible news that stunned everyone in the room.

I was stunned and incredulous. That soon turned into a sense of deep grief and loss. John F. Kennedy had been a very influential person in getting me interested in public policy, and like so many others in my generation, I owed him a great debt.

On that date, I realized that America had lost a great president.

Sincerely,

Richard D. Lamm
Governor

Emmy Award winning actress Jessica Walter has appeared on television in "Mission Impossible," and "Trapper John, M.D.," and on film in Play Misty for Me *and* Lilith.
[19]

I remember the day-moment I heard the news and the ensuing period vividly.

To be specific, at about 2P.M. or so, I was heading west on 46th street in New York City, having left an audition for a Broadway show and encountered Marian Seldes, a fine actress and friend and we decided to have a quick bite of lunch together before I went uptown to a singing lesson and she went back to the rehearsal she'd left. As we walked up the block we noticed a large crowd standing in front of a television store. Some of them were crying and we joined the group to see what had happened. It was there that we learned the the President had been shot.

I was shocked, frightened and scared for my country and myself.

I had not been old enough to vote in 1960, but John F. Kennedy had captured my heart and was the first politician I'd ever felt strongly about.I marched in the candlelit parade during his campaign and eagerly helped as best I could during that campaign. I looked to him as a potentially great leader of our country and especially as someone who would be inspiring to the young Americans that desperately needed that inspiration.

Then I saw Jack Ruby kill Oswald on television and I thought that the world had gone crazy.

I believe that anyone who was old enough to remember that day, that time, will never forget it.

Sincerely, .

Jessica Walter

Jessica Walter

Richard W. Riley

Richard Riley was elected Governor of South Carolina in 1978, after serving in the state legislature for four years.
[30]

State of South Carolina

Office of the Governor

RICHARD W. RILEY
GOVERNOR

When I heard about President Kennedy's shooting, I was at my home in Greenville for lunch with my wife.

My reaction to the news was that I was stunned.

On that date, I felt that the impact of the assassination would be that the hopes for the future for excellence and for higher expectations that President Kennedy represented to my generation were shattered.

Yours sincerely,

Richard W. Riley

Larry Pressler

Following one term as a Member of the U.S. House of Representatives, Larry Pressler was elected U.S. Senator from South Dakota in 1978.
[21]

United States Senate

COMMITTEE ON FOREIGN RELATIONS

I was a student at the University of South Dakota in Vermillion, South Dakota when I heard the news of the assassination of President Kennedy. I was on my way to logic class and my reaction was mixed with feelings of shock and disbelief. I believe that I was too stunned at the time to assess the impact this tragedy would have on our nation.

I greatly admired President Kennedy and felt a sense of personal loss. In 1963 I was selected to present the 4-H "Report to the President" and it was one of the highlights of my young life to have had the opportunity to personally meet with him in the White House Oval Office.

While our nation was reeling from this tragic loss and in a state of shock, it was reassuring to witness the transfer of authority to President Lyndon Johnson and to know that we could continue to function in times of crisis just as the framers of our constitution intended.

Rona Barrett

Rona Barrett's columns have appeared in numerous movie magazines, newspapers, and monthlies, including Photoplay *and* Rona Barrett's Hollywood.
[29]

Rona Barrett
Communications
Inc.

I was in Palm Springs when I heard the news. I was
spending the weekend at a famous Palm Springs racquet
club. People came running out of the clubhouse
screaming that someone had shot Jack Kennedy. An
instant calm came over the people sitting at the pool
and those in the hotel. I've never seen so many
people immediately affected by one man's death. The
grief I saw on people's faces was as if someone had
just killed a memeber of their immediate family. The
grief I felt was like nothing I had ever experienced.
I had only experienced one death up to that time --
the death of one of my grandparents, and my distress
over Kennedy's death seemed far greater.

Nobody slept that day or for 72 hours after that. I,
like everyone else, sat glued to the TV set watching
Kennedy's body go from the hospital to the airplane,
seeing Lyndon Johnson being sworn in as President, and
finally, the funeral of JFK.

Having been one of the primary organizers of the Young
Democrats for Kennedy in 1960, I only had an immediate
reaction to what the future held in store for this
country. My instinct was that it would take a very
long time for the young people to ever believe and
trust in anyone or anything, including the political
process.

Sincerely,
Rona Barrett

Julia Child

*Julia Child, the former hostess of the public television
program, "The French Chef," is the author of* Mastering the Art of French Cooking *and* French Chef.
[51]

We were having lunch and a friend called up, "Turn on the TV, President Kennedy has been shot." We turned it on, and stayed by it.

Disbelief, sadness, anger, desolation.

I had had such hope for us; he was the only young and vigorous head of state at that time anywhere, and he had the enthusiastic support of the young of the nation. I still feel things would have been far different here had he lived, and I can't believe we would have gotten ourselves so embroiled in Viet Nam, or that we would have had such troubles with our young people later on. I don't think we have ever recovered from that loss!

Julia Child

Rudy Boschwitz

Rudy Boschwitz was elected U.S. Senator from Minnesota in 1978.
[33]

I started my own retail warehousing business in 10/63 and was loading plywood on a customer's car when I heard the news. I had a real sense of loss because JFK was the first politician on the national level I really identified with due to his youth.

I wasn't into politics in those days.

> "...while maintaining our readiness for war, let us exhaust every avenue for peace. Let us always make clear our willingness to talk, if talk will help, and our readiness to fight, if fight we must. Let us resolve to be the masters, not the victims, of our history, controlling our own destiny without giving way to blind suspicion and emotion...."
> —*At the University of Maine, 1963*

Donald W. Riegle, Jr.

After ten years in the U.S. House of Representatives, Donald Riegle was elected U.S. Senator from Michigan in 1976.
[25]

When I left Michigan State, I took a job with IBM in White Plains, New York, and I began my daily commute up and down the Saw Mill River Parkway. My first assignment was in something called Plant and Lab Accounting Co-ordination. After several months of that I was transferred to Pricing.... I was on the telephone when word rippled through the building that President Kennedy had been shot. People dashed out of their cubicles, but nobody could get any information. There were no radios or TV sets in the building and the IBM intercom hadn't said a thing.

I ran out to the parking lot and turned on the radio in my car. I was facing this long, low, modern building with all the windows on one side and I could see people continuing to work inside. What struck me was how few of them left the building to find out what was happening. I was dumbfounded and I thought: "Why aren't more people concerned enough to turn on their car radios? Why doesn't the need to know just shove them out that door? How can they be content with fragments of information?"

The horrifying details kept spilling from my radio. The President had indeed been shot. Half his head was blown away. He was in critical condition and there was some question as to whether Lyndon Johnson had been shot too. I was stunned – it didn't seem possible. After a few minutes of this I went back to my office. Just then the intercom reported the news of the shooting. Nobody knew the circumstances, the voice kept repeating; he would have another report when there was something further to say.

I felt my deepest kind of personal shock and I just had to go back to my car. Minutes later the word came through: Kennedy was dead. I

Reprinted with permission from O, Congress *by Donald W. Riegle, Jr. and Trevor Armbrister, Doubleday and Company, Garden City, New York, 1972.*

didn't want to believe it. I looked back at the building and it was business as usual. In my division a presentation was going on in the comptroller's office. I could see guys with flip charts talking and gesturing as though nothing at all had happened, and I was never more struck by the meaninglessness of what they were doing....

I returned to my office. Thirty or forty minutes passed and then the man on the intercom said the President was dead. But IBM continued to shuffle papers. Nobody missed a stroke. I finally telephoned one of the company's executives and said I thought it was inappropriate for us to continue to work–that out of respect for the late President we ought to close for the rest of the day.

"Well, you know," he replied, "we've checked the precedents on this. Franklin Roosevelt also died on a Friday and there was a national day of mourning the following Monday. So, we'll have a holiday next Monday; you'll have that day off."...

That experience made me realize that I was not cut out to be that kind of organization man....In the fall of 1964, I left IBM and went to Harvard Business School to earn my doctorate in business-government relations....As you can see, for me, it was truly a life changing experience.

Sincerely

Donald W. Riegle, Jr.

"It may be said now that I have the best of both worlds, a Harvard education and a Yale degree."
—*Upon receiving an Honorary Degree from Yale University,*
1962

Charles S. Robb

Charles Robb married President Lyndon Johnson's elder daughter, Lynda Bird, in December, 1967, and served as Governor of Virginia from 1982–86.
[24]

COMMONWEALTH of VIRGINIA
Office of the Governor

Charles S. Robb
   Governor

I was a First Lieutenant in the U. S. Marine Corps stationed at Camp Lejeune, North Carolina, serving as aide-de-camp to the Commanding General of the Second Marine Division. The General and I were just boarding his helicopter at the rifle range for a flight back to Division Headquarters when the pilots informed us that President Kennedy had been shot in Dallas and was being rushed to the hospital.

We both had the same sense of shock and disbelief shared by all Americans when we first heard the news. I asked the pilots to patch us in to a civilian radio frequency on our headsets and we listened silently on the flight back. When we got back to our offices, I obtained a portable radio to try to find out how the President was doing and when it was reported that President Kennedy was dead, I walked in to the General's office and gave him the sad news. Neither of us said a word thereafter. Like most Americans we then spent the next few days glued to our television sets trying to make sense or come to grips with the tremendous loss all of us felt.

I'm not sure that I tried immediately to assess the impact Presi-
Kennedy's death would have on the nation. I did think about our
potential vulnerability in terms of national defense, but for the
most part I thought about and prayed for the Kennedy family, as well
as the man I had no way of knowing would one day become my father-in-
law.

Sincerely,

Charles S. Robb

Mike Sullivan

*Mike Sullivan was elected Governor of Wyoming in
1986.*
[24]

STATE OF WYOMING
OFFICE OF THE GOVERNOR

MIKE SULLIVAN
GOVERNOR

... I
remember the beautiful November day in Wyoming which
contrasted so to the gloom cast by the news of the
assassination.

I was a junior in law school at the University of Wyoming in Laramie. We had just been dismissed from a morning class, and I can remember the step which my foot hit as the news hit like a tidal wave. John Kennedy had campaigned at the University, and he was a symbol of all that was strong and good about our country. I remember the heartache of those next few days and cannot, even today, consider the subject without that same feeling of sadness and despair returning.

On that day, I had a substantial concern for the stability of our country and our system. I soon learned that, notwithstanding the greatness of one individual, the wisdom of our form of government and the resilience of the American people are much more permanent and lasting than the contribution of each of us as indivuals. Nevertheless, the impact of President Kennedy's death was, and continues to be, a most significant event in my life and, I am sure, most Americans who experienced the tragedy.

With kind regards, I am

Very truly yours,

Mike Sullivan

"Prosperity is the real way to balance our budget. Our tax rates are so high today that the growth of profits and pay checks in this country has been stunted. Our tax revenues have been depressed and our books for seven out of the last ten years have been in the red. By lowering tax rates, by increasing jobs and income, we can expand tax revenues and finally bring our budget into balance..."
— *Televised Address from the White House, September 18, 1963*

Barbara A. Mikulski

After representing Maryland in the U.S. House of Representatives from 1979–87, Barbara Mikulski was elected to the Senate in 1986.
[27]

UNITED STATES SENATE

BARBARA A. MIKULSKI
MARYLAND

I was a graduate student in Social Work. On November 22, 1963, I was working at a family counselling service office in York, PA. A client came into my office and told me of the shooting. I couldn't believe it. I turned on the radio. The DJ had just announced the President's death and began playing the National Anthem.

I was shocked, horrified, grief stricken and disbelieving. We closed the counselling office and a black graduate student and I drove the 60 miles back to Baltimore. We drove with our headlights on and we listened to classical dirge music. It was the longest hour of my life.

I knew President Kennedy's life and the impact of his death would be felt for generations of Americans to come. We missed his youth, vigor and ideas in 1963 -- just as we miss them now, 25 years later.

Sincerely,

Barbara A. Mikulski
U.S. Senator

George S. Mickelson

George Mickelson served five years in the South Dakota legislature before he was elected Governor in 1986.
[22]

STATE OF SOUTH DAKOTA

GEORGE S. MICKELSON
GOVERNOR

On November 22, 1963, I was a law student at the University of South Dakota and enroute to attend a Constitutional Law Class when I heard the news the President had been shot. My initial reaction was one of disbelief. Particularly so because, during that particular era in our country's history, President Kennedy represented a very positive image for the United States. I found myself needing to stay in close touch with current information by following all of the proceedings on television and through other media sources.

Very truly yours,

GEORGE S. MICKELSON

Richard G. Lugar

Richard Lugar, a former mayor of Indianapolis, began his first term as U.S. Senator from Indiana in 1977.
[31]

RICHARD G. LUGAR
INDIANA

United States Senate

I first heard the news of President Kennedy's death over my car radio as I pulled into the parking lot of a bank on West Washington Street in Indianapolis, Indiana. I was serving as Vice President and Treasurer of a small manufacturing business and made the daily deposits of checks to a local branch. I rushed back to the factory to turn on the television with the hopes that the initial news would turn better in subsequent reports.

From the first reports, I had a sickening feeling that the unthinkable was going to happen. I left work to be at home with my wife, Charlene, and my three young sons, Mark, Bob and John. For the next three days we stayed very close to each other thinking about our country and praying for strong leadership and continuity of the idealism which President Kennedy expressed so dramatically.

On that fateful day in November 22, 1963, I was confident that the general thrust of President Kennedy's leadership would be carried forward. I had certainty in the continuity of all of our government institutions and great pride that our nation could sustain such a blow with compassion and resiliency. Nevertheless, I felt an immediate sense of great personal loss. It was never my privilege to meet President Kennedy, but I had felt many strong ties to his personality and his style of leadership. I admired his press conferences and I enjoyed his humor. I have been fascinated ever since in all of the dramatic accountings of the days of his presidential campaign and the days of his presidency....

Sincerely,

Richard G. Lugar
United States Senator

"No man can fully grasp how far and how fast we have come, but condense, if you will, the fifty thousand years of man's recorded history in a time span of but a half century. Stated in these terms, we know very little about the first forty years, except that at the end of them advanced man had learned to use the skins of animals to cover himself. Then about ten years ago, under this standard, man emerged from his caves to construct other kinds of shelter. Only five years ago man learned to write and use a cart with wheels....The printing press came this year, and then less than two months ago, during this whole fifty-year span of human history, the steam engine provided a new source of power....Last month electric lights and telephones and automobiles and airplanes were available. Only last week did we develop penicillin and television and nuclear power, and now if America's new spacecraft succeeds in reaching Venus, we will have literally reached the stars before midnight tonight."

—*At Rice University, September 12, 1962*

Carl Levin

Carl Levin was President of the Detroit City Council prior to his election to the U.S. Senate from Michigan in 1978.
[29]

CARL LEVIN
MICHIGAN

United States Senate

I first heard the news of President Kennedy's shooting as I was driving to my neighborhood law office in Detroit. I was stunned at the news and prayed for a miraculous recovery.

I remember my wife and I holding our <u>five month</u> old daughter up to the television that night with tears in our eyes, telling her to look at the horrors people could perpetrate. We knew she couldn't understand but we wanted her somehow to be affected the way we were.

We felt that his death meant more than the loss of a President who gave us optimism and hope. It also meant that violence against public figures would surface again and again because of the notirety it gives sick people.

Sincerely,

Carl Levin

109

Robert W. Kasten, Jr.

After serving two terms in the U.S. House of Representatives, in 1980 Robert Kasten was elected U.S. Senator from Wisconsin.
[21]

ROBERT W. KASTEN, JR.
WISCONSIN

United States Senate

I was on the campus of the University of Arizona at the time I first learned of the attempt on President Kennedy's life. I was shocked and saddened by the news. Frankly, I just couldn't believe it.

I knew immediately that President Kennedy's death would represent a great loss of leadership for our country. The strength of his personality was apparent in all sectors of American life and the loss of Jack Kennedy was extraordinary for us all.

Vice President Johnson was an experienced public servant and, frankly, I think it helped a lot to have a very seasoned individual in the position under these circumstances.

Best regards,

Robert W. Kasten, Jr.

Gary Hart

Gary Hart served as U.S. Senator from Colorado from 1975–87. He is the author of Right from the Start, The Double Man, *and* America Can Win.
[26]

GARY HART

I was leaving my student apartment in New Haven on November 22, 1963, for an interview with a Denver law firm when I heard the radio report that President Kennedy had been shot. Walter Cronkite announced minutes later that the President was dead.

It seemed impossible -- except for all that has happened since, I would say it still does. I went ahead with the interview, largely a brief period given to shock and silence.

That weekend was spent with my wife's family and it was a period of great grief, as if a vibrant member of our family, or a close personal friend, had been insanely murdered.

On that date, America lost both her youth and her innocence.

Twelve years later, as a member of the Church Committee in the United States Senate, I participated in an investigation of the connection between President Kennedy's death and efforts by the CIA and the Mafia to assassinate foreign leaders. I believe such a connection does exist.

Sincerely,

Gary Hart

Stephen J. Cannell

Stephen J. Cannell has written and produced such TV series as "The Rockford Files," "The Greatest American Hero," and "Baretta." He won Emmy Awards in 1979, 1980, and 1981.
[22]

THE CANNELL STUDIOS

STEPHEN J. CANNELL
CHAIRMAN OF THE BOARD
CHIEF EXECUTIVE OFFICER

When President Kennedy was shot, I was attending the University of Oregon in Eugene. It was a rainy day and the news of the President's assination spread across the campus in a wave of pale faces and shocked expressions.

I remember going to a coffee shop where we all hung out and sitting with my friends in stunned silence wondering how this could happen in our country...wondering how somebody who had become a part of my life through the media could be snatched away by an assassin's bullet.

This wonder turned to anger and I suppose, within days, it turned to a deep sense of patriotism. It made me stop thinking about next week's beer bust and begin to feel much more protective of my country and its leaders.

The impact of Kennedy's death on the nation was very hard for me to gauge at that time in my life. I think I had a sense more of the deterioration of the values I had grown up with...values that allowed us to leave our front doors unlocked and our cars parked with the keys in the ignition. It seemed this was physical proof of our slipping into a more vigilent age where new protections would be needed to assure our freedoms.

Sincerely,

Stephen J. Cannell

Bill Clinton

Bill Clinton served as Arkansas Attorney General, and was then elected Governor in 1978, 1982, and in 1986.
[17]

STATE OF ARKANSAS
OFFICE OF THE GOVERNOR

Bill Clinton
Governor

I was a high school senior in 4th period calculus class.

I was devastated, I had met President Kennedy only a few months before when I went to the White House as a Boys Nation delegate and I was very supportive of him.

I felt that it filled the nation with grief and determination and that President Johnson would be able to carry on effectively. Still I was afraid that Kennedy's potential to benefit our nation and the world would never be realized. My feelings were best captured by what Abba Eban of Isreal said in his speech to the United Nations: "Tragedy is the difference between what is and what might have been".

Sincerely,

Bill Clinton

David L. Boren

David Boren was elected U.S. Senator from Oklahoma in 1978, after serving one term as Governor of Oklahoma.
[22]

DAVID BOREN
OKLAHOMA

United States Senate

                    ... In the fall of 1963, I left
the United States to begin studies at Oxford University in
Oxford, England, as a Rhodes Scholar. It was an exciting
period for young Americans inspired by the goals set for us by
our young idealistic President John F. Kennedy. It was the
time of the Peace Corps and many other initiatives in which
Americans hoped to change the world in a positive way.

        I was walking down a street in Oxford on November 22,
1963, when I saw a large crowd gathered around the television
sets in the window of an appliance store. The crowd was
standing in stunned silence as the announcer read a bulletin
that John Kennedy had been killed. Men and women in the crowd
began to weep, strangers embraced each other in consolation. I
realized as I shared my grief with English men and women that
John Kennedy belonged to all of humankind. He was a symbol of
our hope, of the dreams that seem to burn most brightly in the
young, an encouragement to the older generation all around the
world that their successors were committed to high and noble
ideals.

        Not just Americans, but an entire generation lost a part
of its innocence on that November day. What shocked me most
was that a man who was committed to such worthy goals could be
destroyed by such a dark and senseless act of violence. After
the shock had passed, we all were left with a deeper commitment
to work for those unselfish goals that had been placed before
us.

                            Sincerely,

                            David L. Boren
                            United States Senator

114

V

TODAY'S POLITICAL LEADERS RECALL NOVEMBER 22, 1963

"Let every public servant know, whether his post is high or low, that a man's rank and reputation...will be determined by the size of the job he does, and not by the size of his staff, his office or his budget....Let public service be a proud and lively career."
—The State of the Union Message, 1961

"I tell you the new frontier is here, whether we seek it or not. Beyond that frontier are uncharted areas of science and space, unsolved problems of peace and war, unconquered pockets of ignorance and prejudice, and unanswered questions of poverty and surplus. I believe the times demand invention, innovation, imagination, decision. I am asking you to be new pioneers on the New Frontier. My call is to the young in heart, regardless of age--to the stout in spirit, regardless of party..."
—Nomination Acceptance Speech, 1960

To John Kennedy, public service was the most noble profession to which anyone could accede. He once confessed, "The political world is stimulating. It's the most interesting thing you can do. It beats following the dollar." From his first day as President, he encouraged every American to seek a means by which they could best serve their country.

Now dozens of men and women—who have contributed at least a portion of their lives to "lead the land we love"—recall where they were when they heard the tragic news from Dallas, and share their feelings toward John Kennedy. Many of them were in office at the time. Many more have since entered public service seeking a "proud and lively career."

Former Presidents and would-be presidents join governors, senators, congressmen, and other public officials to remember John Kennedy in a unique tribute to the 35th President.

James Abdnor

Following four terms as a member of the U.S. House of Representatives from South Dakota, James Abdnor served one term as a U.S. Senator.
[40]

JAMES ABDNOR
SOUTH DAKOTA

United States Senate

This day stands out in my memory as I suspect it does for most Americans who realized what was happening then.

It was noon hour in Kennebec, South Dakota, and I had just come in from the field to have lunch with friends who had a radio playing. The regular programming was interrupted for the awful news from Dallas.

My reaction was shock, disbelief that such a thing could happen.

I do not recall thinking about the impact on the nation specifically, but later did pause to reflect on what a wonderful commentary it was on our system that under such circumstances the transition could be so orderly and government could go on without disruption. What a tremendous example for other nations!

Sincerely,

JAMES ABDNOR
United States Senator

Lamar Alexander

Lamar Alexander was the Governor of Tennessee for twelve years.
[23]

State of Tennessee

LAMAR ALEXANDER GOVERNOR

I was attending class at New York University Law School in New York City when I first heard the news of President Kennedy's shooting.

I could not believe the news.

I was not sure what would happen. I remember being greatly reassured by President Eisenhower's statement that, despite our shock, the business of the nation would continue.

Very best regards.

Sincerely,

Lamar Alexander

Bill Allain

Following four years as Mississippi's Attorney General,
Bill Allain served one term as Governor.
[23]

STATE OF MISSISSIPPI
OFFICE OF THE GOVERNOR

BILL ALLAIN
GOVERNOR

                             ... I was trying a law suit in Clarksdale, Mississippi, brought by the then Attorney General, Robert Kennedy, brother of the President.

My immediate reaction to the news that the President had been shot was one of shock and disbelief that this type thing could happen in our country.

At that time, it was difficult to assess the impact of President Kennedy's death on the nation. Although President Johnson had been in politics for a number of years, no one was sure at that particular time what course he would set for our nation.

Respectfully,

Bill all.

BILL ALLAIN,
GOVERNOR

118

Victor Atiyeh

Following stints in both the Oregon House of Representatives and the State Senate, Victor Atiyeh served two terms as the Governor of Oregon.
[40]

VICTOR ATIYEH
GOVERNOR

OFFICE OF THE GOVERNOR

... It does not come as any surprise that everyone would remember that moment precisely because of the enormity and drama of the event. I am not an exception.

Our Oregon Legislature was in special session for the purpose of rebalancing our budget. I can remember vividly getting the word that "the President has been shot" as I stood by my desk on the floor of the House of Representative chambers. Quickly I went downstairs to the press room and there learned that the President was dead.

My reaction was deep sorrow for the President, his family and our country, mixed with intense anger that anyone was insane enough to think that anything could be settled by murder. There was a very quiet emotional pall that settled over the entire Capitol Building that day. Our special session recessed following the assassination.

At that moment I did not calculate the impact on the nation other than transition which I knew was in order. As a proud believer in this system of government I knew that we would quickly and safely have continuity.

Very truly yours,

Victor Atiyeh
Governor of Oregon

James A. Baker III

After serving as White House Chief of Staff for four years, James A. Baker III was named Secretary of the U.S. Treasury in 1985.
[33]

THE SECRETARY OF THE TREASURY
WASHINGTON

I was in the cafeteria of the Exxon Building in downtown Houston when I heard the news. The shock of what had happened in my home state was overwhelming. I was initially concerned about the transition of political power. Fortunately, President Johnson promptly reassured the whole nation and the world by his actions.

In the following days, events confirmed our deepest faith in American institutions and character. Americans of every social, political, economic and philosophical group came together into one immense grieving family.

Sincerely,

James A. Baker, III

Norman H. Bangerter

Norman Bangerter was elected Governor of Utah in 1985, after three years as Speaker of the Utah House of Representatives.
[30]

STATE OF UTAH
OFFICE OF THE GOVERNOR

NORMAN H. BANGERTER
GOVERNOR

I was in my pick-up truck driving across town.

I was shocked at the news and stunned with the rest of the nation.

I felt that President Kennedy's assassination was a sad day for the future of our nation, because of my confidence in the people and our system of government.

Sincerely,

Norman H. Bangerter
Governor

Abraham D. Beame

Abraham Beame was Mayor of New York City from 1974–1977.
[57]

ABRAHAM D. BEAME

I was in my office at the Municipal Building of the City of New York, of which I was Comptroller.

As to my reaction - I was stunned and shocked.

It is difficult for me to recall my immediate feeling other than we lost an inspiring leader. Events moved so fast with the swearing-in of President Johnson.

Sincerely,

Abraham D. Beame

Henry Bellmon

Henry Bellmon, a former U.S. Senator, has twice served as Governor of Oklahoma.
[42]

HENRY BELLMON
GOVERNOR

STATE OF OKLAHOMA
OFFICE OF THE GOVERNOR
OKLAHOMA CITY

The morning President Kennedy was assassinated, I was in my office in Oklahoma City. I was Governor of the state at that time. I had just finished meeting with a visitor when my Administrative Assistant came in to tell me the President had been shot.

I expect my reaction was fairly typical. Absolute shock; questions; a need for more information; talk about the successor; more questions. I don't recall thinking beyond the moment, about the impact his death would have on the nation. I was saddened by the assault on the President and on the political system. In spite of all our advances and sophistication, barbarism seems always to be close at hand.

Sincerely,

Henry Bellmon

Lloyd Bentsen

Lloyd Bentsen began his first term as U.S. Senator from Texas in 1971. In 1988, Senator Bentsen was the Democratic nominee for Vice President.
[42]

LLOYD BENTSEN
TEXAS

United States Senate

I was on my company plane flying from Lincoln, Nebraska to Houston, Texas and stepped off the airplane in Houston to be told of the assassination of President Kennedy and the wounding of Governor John Connally.

My reaction was one of horror.

My hope was that the country would rally around President Johnson and help him bring the nation together after such a tragic event.

Sincerely,

Lloyd Bentsen

Jeff Bingaman

Following a term as New Mexico's Attorney General, Jeff Bingaman was elected U.S. Senator from New Mexico in 1982.
[20]

JEFF BINGAMAN
NEW MEXICO

United States Senate

     I was working in the freshman dining hall at Harvard where I held a part-time job while attending school. I was in total shock when I heard the news, and I really didn't have any idea of the impact it would have on the nation.

            Sincerely,

Jeff Bingaman
United States Senator

William F. Bolger

William Bolger was Postmaster General of the United States in 1978.
[40]

Air Transport Association OF AMERICA

WILLIAM F. BOLGER
President

I was in my office in Boston.

It was a shock to me and at first not believable. The next reaction was anger that such a thing could happen in the United States.

The possible impact on the nation did not receive much of my attention that day. My thoughts were mainly with the Kennedy family.

Sincerely,

William F. Bolger

Christopher S. Bond

Prior to becoming U.S. Senator from Missouri in 1987, Kit Bond served two terms as Governor of Missouri.
[24]

CHRISTOPHER S. BOND
MISSOURI

United States Senate

I was also in Fort Worth on that day as a clerk for a United States Appellate Judge who was sitting in official session in Fort Worth on that day. In addition to the horrible shock that we all felt from the news, we were also concerned as to whether there might at that time be some concerted effort to attack other federal officials, particularly judges who had recently made rulings unfavorable to certain people in Texas.

I was, on that date, very unsure as to the impact that President Kennedy's death would have other than to feel that the people of the United States would rally behind Vice President Lyndon Johnson and would assure his re-election in 1964 in order to be certain of the continuity of government in the United States.

Sincerely,

Christopher S. Bond

Julian Bond

After ten years as a Member of the Georgia House of Representatives, Julian Bond was elected to the State Senate in 1975.
[23]

JULIAN BOND

The State Senate

I heard of President Kennedy's shooting while at lunch at Paschal's Resturant in Atlanta. His death was confirmed later.

My first thoughts were repulsion at the act and fear that Lyndon Johnson would be hostile to civil rights.

I can remember little wonder about who did it or why - just a cold fear that Kennedy's moderate policies would be replaced with Johnson's conservative views. Johnson, of course, surpassed Kennedy's civil rights efforts.

Sincerely,

Julian Bond

128

Bill Bradley

Prior to becoming a U.S. Senator from New Jersey in 1979, Bill Bradley played professional basketball with the New York Knicks.
[20]

BILL BRADLEY
NEW JERSEY

United States Senate

I was studying in my carrel at Princeton University's library when I heard a student shouting, "The President's been shot. The President's been shot." My first thought went to Princeton's President, but by the time I reached the student center, I knew it was President John F. Kennedy. The eating room was filled wall to wall with professors, students, kitchen workers, secretaries. All were listening to the PA system--to the radio announcers describing the scene at the hospital and the tragic events earlier in the day. The levels and hierarchies of Princeton disappeared. We were all citizens-- bewildered, shocked, fearful for the worst. No one spoke. The announcer closed his report by confirming that President Kennedy had just died. People looked down, glanced at each other--tears in eyes. The national anthem followed. At first, a few stood. Then others. Soon the whole room was standing in the silence of sadness, in outreach to each other, and with concern for that larger national community which many before us had served.

Sincerely,

Bill Bradley
United States Senator

Terry E. Branstad

Terry Branstad was elected Governor of Iowa in 1983, after serving as Lieutenant Governor for four years.
[17]

OFFICE OF THE GOVERNOR

TERRY E. BRANSTAD
GOVERNOR

When President Kennedy was shot, I was a junior at Forest City High School in Forest City, Iowa. I was sitting in class when the announcement came over the P.A. system.

I remember feeling shock and disbelief. Presidential assassinations were something you read about in the history books. It seemed like something this tragic could not have occurred in our modern times.

After the announcement of President Kennedy's assassination, I remember the atmosphere in our high school. As the students passed between classes, there was dead silence in the air. No words were spoken, everyone was numb with shock.

When the President was assassinated, I wasn't sure of the impact it would have on the nation. But, I did realize this was a major historical event and I kept the newspaper from that day and for the days that followed all the way through the funeral.

Sincerely,

Terry E. Branstad
Governor of Iowa

John Breaux

John Breaux was elected U.S. Senator from Louisiana in 1987, following sixteen years as a Member of the House of Representatives.
[19]

𝔘nited 𝔖tates 𝔖enate

COMMITTEE ON ENVIRONMENT AND PUBLIC WORKS

At the time of the assassination, I was attending the University of Southwestern Louisiana as a political science major and I distinctly remember walking into the student union and hearing about the news on television. Of course, everyone had gathered immediately around the TV to watch the events as they unfolded. My political science class, the next period, was in such a state of shock that the Professor simply brought us all together and promptly dismissed the class.

My reaction of shock and real despair was typical of most Americans in the sense that something so tragic could happen. I had read and studied about the assassinations of other Presidents, but it seemed so far in the distant past that it was hard to believe such a tragedy could happen in modern America.

With regard to the effect, I really did not think of any long term effects except for the fact that the transition and change of power to Lyndon B. Johnson was accomplished very smoothly. My thoughts were that other countries, in many cases, would not have had such a smooth transition and that it spoke well for the system and showed that it did, in fact, work.

Sincerely,

JOHN BREAUX
United States Senator

Edward W. Brooke

Edward Brooke was Massachussetts Attorney General when he was elected to the U.S. Senate in 1966 where he served for twelve years.
[44]

I was delivering an address to the student body at the Catholic University in Utah. One of the sisters scurried to the stage to let me know the President had been shot. I then made the announcement to the students and concluded my remarks with a prayer, before dismissing the assembly.

As my travel arrangements were being made to return to Massachusetts, I sat with the Mother Superior and the President of the Student body in shock and disbelief as we watched the news unfold. I still feel a sense of sharing of our grief with those two individuals.

Since I was not in Washington, DC at the time (being Attorney General for the Commonwealth of Massachusetts), I do not recall what my immediate reaction was as to the effect the assination would have on the nation.

Sincerely,

Edward W. Brooke

Edward W. Brooke

Richard H. Bryan

Richard Bryan was elected Governor of Nevada in 1982 after serving as that state's Attorney General. [26]

THE STATE OF NEVADA

RICHARD H. BRYAN
Governor

EXECUTIVE CHAMBER

I first heard the news of the assassination in Las Vegas shortly before noon, Pacific Standard Time. Two days before I had been sworn in as a new member of the Nevada Bar. On that Friday I was in the law offices of the Foley Brothers, with whom I had associated.

Because of the early, garbled news accounts, it was not immediately clear that the President had been hit. My first thought was of Adlai Stevenson, who had been in Dallas a few weeks before and had been struck by right-wing pickets protesting, if I recall correctly, the United Nations.

There was so much confusion initially that it was not until hours later that I realized the magnitude of the tragedy. By then, like most Americans, I was so stunned that I couldn't comprehend what the implications were for the nation.

Sincerely,

RICHARD H. BRYAN
Governor

Yvonne Brathwaite Burke

Yvonne Burke served six years in the California House of Representatives and six years in the U.S. House of Representatives.
[31]

I was practicing law in 1963 and was in the midst of a jury trial in Los Angeles when I heard the news that the President had been shot. I was in the process of selecting a jury at the time the news first came to the attention of the judge.

Judge Dalsimer recessed the trial and the jury and all of the parties sat quietly in the courtroom while the radio was brought in for us to listen to the events and were ultimately told that the President had been killed.

On November 22, 1963, when I first heard news of the the President's death, I was not certain what was going to happen to the nation and whether or not the nation would be able to continue in an orderly way. I felt more secure when I was aware that President Johnson had been sworn in and that the Vice-President had taken over the reigns of government.

Yours very truly,

Yvonne B. Burke

George Bush

Prior to becoming Vice President of the United States in 1981, George Bush held positions as U.S. Ambassador to the United Nations and Director of Central Intelligence. He was nominated for President by the Republican Party in 1988.
[39]

THE VICE PRESIDENT

WASHINGTON

I was in East Texas speaking at a Kiwanis Club luncheon when I heard of the Kennedy assassination. I was making a political speech as part of my campaign for the U.S. Senate.

My reaction to the news was one of shock and disbelief.

I don't recall that I considered immediately the impact on the nation. President Johnson moved so fast--properly so--to take over that there was never any question of continuity.

Sincerely,

George Bush

Carroll A. Campbell, Jr.

Carroll Campbell, a former Member of the U.S. House of Representatives, was elected Governor of South Carolina in 1987.
[23]

State of South Carolina

CARROLL A. CAMPBELL, JR.
GOVERNOR

Office of the Governor

On November 22, 1963, I was the owner of Handy Park Company in my hometown of Greenville, South Carolina. That day, I had gone to one of the parking lots to see an attendant and, while there, the news of the assassination came over the radio. I could not believe what I had heard and sat there in shock and disbelief. It was hard for me to believe that such a tragedy could happen in our lifetime and why anyone would commit such an act on our President. It was a day that everyone in this country mourned together and will never forget.

Sincerely,

Carroll A. Campbell, Jr.
Governor

136

Jimmy Carter

Prior to his inauguration as the 39th President of the United States, Jimmy Carter served as a Georgia State Senator and Governor of Georgia.
[39]

On that November day,...I remember that I climbed down from the seat of a tractor, unhooked a farm trailer, and walked into my warehouse to weigh a load of grain. I was told by a group of farmers that the President had been shot. I went outside, knelt on the steps, and began to pray. In a few minutes, I learned that he had not lived. It was a grievous personal loss—my President. I wept openly for the first time in more than 10 years—for the first time since the day my own father died.

...To our loss, we will never read the books he would have written about his own Presidency. His death impoverished not only statecraft but literature as well....

President Kennedy understood the past and respected its shaping of the future. Yet he was very much a man of his own time. The first President born in this century, he embodied the ideals of a generation as few public figures have ever done in the history of the Earth. He summoned our Nation out of complacency, and he set it on a path of excitement and hope.

The accomplishments of this thousand days, as you well know, are notable, though his Presidency was too short for him to finish all the tasks that he set for himself. We honor him not just for the things he completed but for the things he set in motion, the energies that he released, and the ideas and the ideals which he espoused.

Reprinted with permission from remarks made by President Carter at the Dedication Ceremonies for the John F. Kennedy Library in Boston, Massachusetts on October 20, 1979.

William J. Casey

The late William Casey was chief of the Central Intelligence Agency from 1981–87.
[50]

The Director of Central Intelligence

I had just landed at Kennedy Airport in New York, flying in from Indianapolis, and as I walked through the terminal I learned that President Kennedy had been shot in Dallas.

My reaction was one of great shock. Some minutes later, I learned that the President had died. I don't recall considering immediately the impact on the nation. I do recall that that evening my wife and I got together with half a dozen friends for dinner and had a very somber discussion wondering how this tragedy could have occurred, appreciating the fact that our Constitution gave us a sure mechanism for the swift transfer of authority in so tragic a circumstance, and assuring each other that our nation would carry on and meet its responsibilities.

Sincerely,

William J. Casey

John H. Chafee

Before becoming a U.S. Senator from Rhode Island in 1977, John Chafee held positions as Governor of Rhode Island and U.S. Secretary of the Navy.
[41]

JOHN H. CHAFEE
RHODE ISLAND

United States Senate

At the time I was Governor of Rhode Island and was in my office at the State House when a secretary rushed in and said President Kennedy had been shot.

My reactions were a jumble of emotions: disbelief and hope that the reports were wrong; confusion because the initial reports indicated that the Vice President had also been shot and for a time it seemed like there was a conspiracy to eliminate our top leaders; sadness that such a thing could happen to one so young and with such promise and that it could happen in our country.

At the time I do not recall analyzing what impact President Kennedy's death would have on the nation. Everything was in such a turmoil.

Sincerely,

John Chafee

Lawton Chiles

Following twelve years in the Florida House of Representatives and the Florida State Senate, Lawton Chiles was elected to the U.S. Senate in 1970.
[33]

LAWTON CHILES
FLORIDA

United States Senate

I was in my hometown of Lakeland, Florida and had stopped in a filling station when I first heard the news.

I was utterly shocked and stunned: it was as if time had stopped for a moment. I could hardly believe the tragic death our President had met.

I did not immediately consider the impact this would have on our nation, but I recall President Johnson's moving words spoken at Andrews Air Force Base on return from Dallas, this was indeed a "sad time for all people".

With best wishes, I am

Most sincerely,

LAWTON CHILES

William S. Cohen

William Cohen was elected U.S. Senator from Maine in 1978. He has also served six years in the U.S. House of Representatives.
[23]

WILLIAM S. COHEN
MAINE

𝔘𝔫𝔦𝔱𝔢𝔡 𝔖𝔱𝔞𝔱𝔢𝔰 𝔖𝔢𝔫𝔞𝔱𝔢

        I first learned of the President's shooting while in a car on Commonwealth Avenue in Boston and my reaction was of shock and sadness.

        Of course, I had no way of knowing at that time what the full impact would be on the nation. I experienced a profound sense of loss and assumed that political differences notwithstanding, all Americans felt the pain of a deep and irreparable wound. History has proven that the pain has not diminished over the years.

                          Sincerely,

                          William S. Cohen
                          United States Senator

Martha Layne Collins

Martha Layne Collins was Lieutenant Governor of Kentucky, and then served as Governor from 1983–87.
[27]

OFFICE OF THE GOVERNOR

MARTHA LAYNE COLLINS
    GOVERNOR

... I was at home in Versailles, Kentucky, in the den when I heard the news of the assassination. Like every American, I was shocked and outraged that such a violent act could happen in this country. It's difficult to remember how I thought the assassination would affect the county; I know I felt the country would certainly survive this horrible tragedy, although the course of our history was changed forever. It has always been my belief that when faced with adversity, Americans tend to come together and the resolve to keep going gets stronger. I think every American felt a certain bond throughout those difficult days in November, 1963.

Sincerely,

Martha Layne Collins

Kent Conrad

Kent Conrad was elected U.S. Senator from North Dakota in 1986.
[15]

KENT CONRAD
NORTH DAKOTA

United States Senate

I was in Exeter, New Hampshire on my way to the gym when I first heard of the shooting of President Kennedy.

My reaction was one of disbelief, anger, concern and questioning of why and who.

I believed that President Kennedy's death would be a traumatic shock for the country and that it would take away some of our optimism and confidence.

Sincerely,

KENT CONRAD
United States Senator

143

Steve Cowper

Steve Cowper was elected Governor of Alaska in 1986.
[25]

STEVE COWPER
GOVERNOR

STATE OF ALASKA
OFFICE OF THE GOVERNOR
JUNEAU

Just like most people in the country, I remember exactly what I was doing when I heard President Kennedy had been shot. I had recently graduated from law school and was in the law library in Norfolk, Virginia studying to take the bar examination and doing legal research. I called my office to speak to my secretary and she told me about the President.

As you can imagine, my reaction was one of shock and dismay. President Kennedy had given great vitality and optimism to the country and his death brought a dark cloud down on everyone. Afterwards, I found it very hard to concentrate on my studies and my job.

To this day, I often think of that day and wonder how the country would be different had President Kennedy been able to fill out his term of office. I think he would have done great things for all of us.

Sincerely,

Steve Cowper
Governor

144

Mario M. Cuomo

Mario Cuomo was elected Governor of New York in 1982. He had previously served as Secretary of State and Lieutenant Governor.
[31]

STATE OF NEW YORK

EXECUTIVE CHAMBER

MARIO M. CUOMO
GOVERNOR

I was in my law office in Queens, New York.

I did not believe the news. I was shocked.

I felt that President Kennedy's death would leave a void in our nation. I was right.

Sincerely,

Mario M. Cuomo

Dennis DeConcini

Arizonan Dennis DeConcini was elected to the U.S. Senate in 1976.
[26]

DENNIS DeCONCINI
ARIZONA

𝔘𝔫𝔦𝔱𝔢𝔡 𝔖𝔱𝔞𝔱𝔢𝔰 𝔖𝔢𝔫𝔞𝔱𝔢

I was in my office working on real estate files in Tucson, Arizona at the time the assignation took place.

My reaction was one of shock and disbelief. I literally did not believe it for several minutes, and had to hear it again before I was really convinced that he had been killed.

On the date of the assassination, I cannot recall accurately what my assessment was of the impact of the assassination. I was not fearful of a threat to our constitutional government and was assured that Vice President Johnson would take over the office as he appropriately did. My feelings about the impact was of great sadness for the country and his family.

Sincerely,

DENNIS DeCONCINI
United States Senator

146

George Deukmejian

After three years as California Attorney General, George Deukmejian was elected Governor in 1983.
[35]

State of California

GOVERNOR'S OFFICE

GEORGE DEUKMEJIAN
GOVERNOR

At that time I was a member of the State Assembly of the State of California and was in my district office in Long Beach, California. I first heard about the shooting from another person in the office. We turned on a radio to learn if it was true and to obtain as much information as possible.

I couldn't believe that anyone could accomplish such an act, especially with the Secret Service and other law enforcement protection that surrounds the President. I wanted to keep listening to the radio to find out who did it, how it was done, and to learn how seriously the President was wounded.

I thought the death of President Kennedy would be a great personal loss to our nation because he was a popular president; but with our laws of succession, I did not feel that it would result in a major shift of public policy.

Most cordially,

George Deukmejian

George Deukmejian

Pete V. Domenici

A former mayor of Albuquerque, Pete Domenici began his first term as U.S. Senator from New Mexico in 1972.
[31]

PETE V. DOMENICI
NEW MEXICO

United States Senate

As is the case with everyone of an age to remember that day, the memory is indelibly etched in my mind.

I was in a car returning from quail hunting near Deming, New Mexico, with six friends when we heard that President Kennedy had been assasinated. The shooting had occurred earlier in the day but we were unaware because we had been hunting.

We listened to the reports in utter shock and disbelief. There was dead silence in the car; the only sound was the radio broadcasters repeating their incredible story.

We were incredulous at the report. I don't think there was anything more than our questioning 'why' and 'how' could this kind of thing have happened. I don't believe we expressed any deep thoughts about the our government or the future of the country. Our questions were more philosophical, "what's going on", and "what's the world turning into?". We were extremely sorrowful as we watched the repeats of the news. Our hearts went out to his young family.

Sincerely,

PETE V. DOMENICI
U.S. Senator

Michael S. Dukakis

Following eight years in the Massachusetts House of Representatives, Michael Dukakis served two terms as Governor of Massachusetts. In 1988, he became the Democratic nominee for President of the United States.
[30]

THE COMMONWEALTH OF MASSACHUSETTS
EXECUTIVE DEPARTMENT

MICHAEL S. DUKAKIS
GOVERNOR

On November 22, 1983, I was returning to my law office from lunch when I heard of the assassination of our President.

I remember that my immediate reaction was one of disbelief and shock, followed by an overwhelming feeling of grief for the family of our President, and the people of our great nation. To this day, it is painful for me to recollect the tragic event which ended the life of this exceptional American President.

On the day of the assassination of President John F. Kennedy, I expected that his death would have a serious effect on the future political course of our country, and it did.

Sincerely,

Michael S. Dukakis

David Durenberger

David Durenberger began his first term as U.S. Senator from Minnesota in 1979.
[29]

United States Senate

COMMITTEE ON FINANCE

My memories of JFK's assassination are vivid.

I was at Nick's Broiler on Concord Street in South St. Paul eating lunch.

I reacted with shock, disbelief, and prayer. I remembered how I felt at age ten when FDR died and, later, when Pope Pius XII died.

At the moment all I could think about was the impact of the loss of a loved one.

Sincerely,

Dave Durenberger
United States Senate

Anthony S. Earl

Anthony Earl served for five years in the Wisconsin legislature prior to his election as Governor in 1982 where he served until 1987.
[27]

State of Wisconsin
Office of the Governor

Anthony S. Earl

I was visiting Fort Monroe, Virginia with colleagues of mine who were Navy men stationed in the Norfolk area.

My reaction to the news:

Disbelief; Hoping it wasn't serious; Confusion and anger; great sadness.

On that date, my reaction to the impact this would have on the nation was, as I recall:

The end of a promising era; "loss of innocence;" felt it portended very poorly for the nation.

(It is difficult to realize it is twenty-five years since President Kennedy's untimely and tragic death.)

Sincerely,

Anthony S. Earl
Governor

James Exon

Before taking office as U.S. Senator from Nebraska in 1979, James Exon served two terms as Governor of Nebraska.
[42]

J. JAMES EXON
NEBRASKA

United States Senate

I was in my office in Lincoln, Nebraska when I first heard the news that President Kennedy had been shot. Initial reports did not indicate that the shooting was fatal.

My first reaction was the hope and prayer that the wounds were not serious. Later, when I learned that the President was dead, I had such a sense of loss for the country because this young man had lifted the sights of the nation. He had instilled a new vigor in the American spirit. I hoped that this new spirit wouldn't die with him.

I knew that the country would come together, just as we always do in time of crisis, but there was no way of knowing at the time what would happen to the programs that President Kennedy was proposing.

Cordially,

J. James Exon
United States Senator

Jake Garn

Jake Garn began his first term as U.S. Senator from Utah in 1974. In 1985, he became the first private American citizen in space as a member of the Shuttle Discovery crew.
[31]

JAKE GARN
UTAH

United States Senate
WASHINGTON, D. C.

When I first heard of the President's assassination, I was on a dock in San Francisco taking delivery of a new 1963 Volkswagen Beatle.

I was informed by a dockworker and simply did not believe it to be true. After hearing the news myself on the car radio, I still found it difficult to believe or accept.

President Kennedy's death was such a surprise and shock I did not even consider the national impact on that day.

Sincerely,

Jake Garn
United States Senator

John Glenn

John Glenn, one of the original seven astronauts in the U.S. space program, was the first American to orbit the Earth. He was first elected to the U.S. Senate from Ohio in 1974.
[42]

United States Senate

COMMITTEE ON
GOVERNMENTAL AFFAIRS

I was still in the Mercury Space Program then, and I heard the news on my car radio as I drove through Dallas. I was deeply shocked and saddened, and when I learned that America had lost a President, I knew that I had also lost a friend. After November 22, 1963 I felt that America had lost her innocence, and that in some ways we would never be quite so young again.

Best regards.

Sincerely,

John Glenn
United States Senator

Now a U.S. Senator, John Glenn was still an astronaut when JFK escorted him to the White House on February 26, 1962, shortly after Glenn became the first American to orbit the Earth. When America lost a President, Glenn commented, "I knew that I had also lost a friend." (John F. Kennedy Library)

"Those who came before us made certain that this country rode the first waves of the industrial revolution, the first waves of modern invention and the first wave of nuclear power, and this generation does not intend to founder in the backwash of the coming age of space. We mean to be a part of it. We mean to lead it, for the eyes of the world now look into space, to the moon and to the planets beyond; and we have vowed that we shall not see it governed by a hostile flag of conquest, but a banner of freedom and peace. We have vowed that we shall not see space filled with weapons of mass destruction, but with instruments of knowledge and understanding."

—At Rice University, September 12, 1962

Albert Gore, Jr.

Al Gore was elected U.S. Senator from Tennessee in 1984 after serving four terms in the House of Representatives.
[15]

ALBERT GORE, JR.
TENNESSEE

United States Senate

When I heard of the assassination I was on my way to high school basketball practice here in Washington. Practice was immediately canceled and those of us on the team quickly returned home.

I was totally stunned by the news.

Though I was only a high school junior at the time, I nevertheless gave a great deal of thought to the impact of the assassination on our country. We were fortunate that President Johnson moved quickly to maintain continuity and leadership.

Sincerely,

Albert Gore, Jr.
United States Senator

Bob Graham

After two terms as Governor of Florida, Bob Graham was elected to the U.S. Senate in 1986.
[27]

STATE OF FLORIDA

OFFICE OF GOVERNOR BOB GRAHAM

At the time of the assassination, I was in Coral Gables attending a banquet for the Allen Morris Legislative· Awards. Lieutenant Colonel John Powers, the featured speaker, was in the middle of his remarks when someone handed him a piece of paper. He blanched, and then announced that the President had been shot in Dallas. There was no report on his condition. The master of ceremonies stated that the event was over.

As I was driving back to Miami Lakes, I heard the report that announced President Kennedy's death. I was very shaken. I pulled the car over to the side of the road. I sat there, stunned.

Sincerely,

Governor

Fred Grandy

Prior to becoming a U.S. Congressman from Iowa in 1987, Fred Grandy had a successful TV and screen career. Among his acting credits are "The Love Boat," "Welcome Back Kotter," and the movie, Close Encounters of the Third Kind.
[15]

FRED GRANDY
6TH DISTRICT, IOWA

Congress of the United States
House of Representatives

On November 22, 1963, I was attending Phillips Exeter Academy in Exeter, New Hampshire. On that afternoon, I was rehearsing a school play when I was first told of Kennedy's assassination. The sad news was followed by the announcement that our performance of the play that night would be cancelled.

The most striking recollection I have of the news was that it was the first time in my life that I realized that our leaders were vulnerable. When you're 15, the leader of your country seems immortal. The news of Kennedy's death shattered that perception.

Charles E. Grassley

Charles Grassley spent three terms in the U.S. House of Representatives before he was elected U.S. Senator from Iowa in 1980.
[30]

𝔘nited 𝔖tates 𝔖enate

I was at my punch press on the assembly line of the Waterloo Register Company in Cedar Rapids, Iowa when I heard the news of President Kennedy's assassination. My immediate reaction was one of disbelief. After a period of a few hours and for the next several days, I felt bewilderment. I didn't believe that much change in the nation would come at first. Now I look back and see considerable change resulting from LBJ's different approach to governing.

"The fact people are peacefully protesting the denial of their rights is not something to be lamented. It is a good sign....It is in the American tradition to stand up for one's rights – even if the new way to stand up for one's rights is to sit down."
—*During the 1960 campaign*

Joe Frank Harris

Joe Frank Harris took office as the Governor of Georgia in 1983, after sixteen years in the Georgia House of Representatives.
[27]

STATE OF GEORGIA
OFFICE OF THE GOVERNOR

Joe Frank Harris
GOVERNOR

As I recall, I was driving onto a job site where employees of my concrete products business were at work. The first report over the radio indicated that both President Kennedy and Vice President Johnson had been shot, and immediately my fear was that the United States was being made a victim of a terrible conspiracy. Soon, those radio reports corrected my impression, and I knew that only President Kennedy lay badly wounded in Dallas.

At the time, my wife and I were expecting our first child, and my thoughts, of course, focused on what this terrible tragedy would mean to the future my child could anticipate. The next few days were long, sad ones for my family and me, and even today, it pains me to recall that point in our history.

With kindest regards, I remain

Sincerely,

Joe Frank Harris

160

Orrin G. Hatch

Orrin Hatch was elected to the U.S. Senate from Utah in 1976.
[29]

ORRIN G. HATCH
UTAH

𝔘nited 𝔖tates 𝔖enate

When I first heard of John F. Kennedy's death, I was at the morgue in Pittsburg, Pennsylvania, investigating a legal case. I reacted as most people did at the time. I was stunned, shocked, and very saddened by the news. I was very concerned about the impact of President Kennedy's death on the nation. I was not sure what would happen. It seemed to be one of the most numbing experiences I have ever had. However, I felt that the country would experience an orderly succession and that Lyndon Johnson would immediately take over the reins of government. Nevertheless, I was very concerned at the time about the transition of power from John F. Kennedy, who many of us trusted, to Lyndon Johnson, who many of us distrusted.

Sincerely,

Orrin G. Hatch
United States Senator

Mark O. Hatfield

Prior to becoming U.S. Senator from Oregon in 1977, Mark Hatfield served two terms as Governor of Oregon. His books include Conflict and Conscience *and* Between a Rock and a Hard Place.
[41]

MARK O. HATFIELD
OREGON

United States Senate

On the day that I heard the news I was in my office as Governor of the State of Oregon.

When I first heard the news from a staff member I did not believe it as I thought it was an attempt at sick humor.

Once the impact of the news sunk in, I had no analytical reactions as I was so completely overwhelmed by the emotional impact of the assassination.

Sincerely,

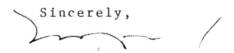

Mike Hayden

Mike Hayden, a former Speaker of the Kansas House of Representatives, was elected Governor of Kansas in 1986.
[19]

STATE OF KANSAS

OFFICE OF THE GOVERNOR

Mike Hayden *Governor*

... I was attending college at Kansas State University in Manhattan, Kansas.

With shock and disbelief.

On that date, what impact did you feel President Kennedy's death would have on the nation? I don't recall that I even took time to consider the impact it would have on the nation.

Sincerely,

MIKE HAYDEN
Governor

Chic Hecht

Chic Hecht was a member of the Nevada State Senate before he was elected U.S. Senator from Nevada in 1982.
[34]

CHIC HECHT
NEVADA

UNITED STATES SENATE

I was running my clothing business in Las Vegas at that point in time, and my reaction was one of utter shock and disbelief. After it was confirmed, I sensed that there would be a change in direction for our Country.

Sincerely,

Chic Hecht

164

Howell Heflin

Howell Heflin was elected U.S. Senator from Alabama in 1979. He was formerly Chief Justice of the Alabama Supreme Court.
[42]

United States Senate

COMMITTEE ON
AGRICULTURE, NUTRITION, AND FORESTRY

I was practicing law in Tuscumbia, Alabama on November 22, 1963 when President John F. Kennedy was assassinated. I had planned to be in Dallas, Texas that day to take a deposition in a case; but the case got settled the first of the week and, therefore, I cancelled my plans to be there.

My first reaction to the news of the shooting was that I hoped that it was not serious and that he would recover. I began to listen for all news pertaining to the matter, hoping that he would survive. When his death was announced, I realized that we had lost one of our finest Presidents and the nation was indeed the victim of this horrible assassination.

I anticipated the impact on the nation would be tragic and the nation as a whole would be terribly saddened. My anticipations came true. But I also realized that in its history America has overcome great obstacles and that America's resilience to bounce back would again be exhibited. It did.

Sincerely yours,

Howell Heflin

Jesse Helms

Jesse Helms was elected U.S. Senator from North Carolina in 1972 after eight years on the Raleigh City Council.
[42]

JESSE HELMS
NORTH CAROLINA

United States Senate

... I was returning to the television station in Raleigh following a luncheon downtown. A radio station interrupted its programming for a bulletin stating that the President had been shot. It was not disclosed at that time that Mr. Kennedy was dead.

I was about five minutes from the television station when I heard the news. I proceeded directly to the station and took charge of our coverage from that point on.

At the time I was executive vice president of the station (WRAL-TV, Raleigh).

I reacted precisely as everyone else did-- with shock and disbelief.

As for the "impact" I'm not sure anyone was giving thought to that. I do recall wondering what kind of President we would have in Lyndon Johnson. I wrote an editorial for that evening's news giving my personal assessment of the tragedy and my recollection of my relationship with Mr. Kennedy.

It was a time of sadness for the nation and the American people, including me.

Sincerely,

[signature: Jesse Helms]

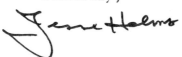

Ernest F. Hollings

"Fritz" Hollings, a former Governor of South Carolina, was first elected to the U.S. Senate in 1966.
[41]

ERNEST F. HOLLINGS
SOUTH CAROLINA

𝔘𝔫𝔦𝔱𝔢𝔡 𝔖𝔱𝔞𝔱𝔢𝔰 𝔖𝔢𝔫𝔞𝔱𝔢

... My reaction to the news of President Kennedy's assassination was not only of a friend lost but a tragedy for the nation. President Kennedy brought to government a sense of excellence and of the elevation of politics that has seldom been seen in our nation. He truly brought with him the best and the brightest, and his young Administration was on the road to what I am convinced would have been a record of tremendous accomplishment for the United States. As someone who had worked closely with President Kennedy on the personal level, I felt a tremendous sense of loss. You asked for my reactions on that date: I think because of my closeness to him, I felt the impact on the nation would be tremendously adverse. The standards John Fitzgerald Kennedy brought to public life not only graced his Administration, but provide a sterling example of what public service is all about.

With kindest regards, I am

Sincerely,

[signature: Fritz Hollings]

Ernest F. Hollings

167

Harry Hughes served two terms as Governor of Maryland, after serving twenty-two years in various state offices.
[27]

STATE OF MARYLAND

EXECUTIVE DEPARTMENT

HARRY HUGHES

GOVERNOR

        When I first heard the news of President Kennedy's fatal shooting, I was sitting in my law office in Denton, Maryland.

        I reacted to the news with disbelief and shock. I immediately went out onto the street to confirm the news and to communicate my feelings with someone.

        I have no clear recollection of my thoughts about possible impact of this terrible event on the future of our nation.

Sincerely,

Governor

Nancy Landon Kassebaum

Nancy Kasssebaum was elected U.S. Senator from Kansas in 1978.
[31]

NANCY LANDON KASSEBAUM
KANSAS

United States Senate
WASHINGTON, D. C.

I had just held a coffee meeting for the Institute of Logopedics and was alone in the kitchen when I heard the announcement. I will never forget the keen sense of sadness, loneliness, and disbelief. It was a day that indelibly touched the heart and soul.

Warmest regards,

Nancy Landon Kassebaum
United States Senator

Thomas H. Kean

Thomas Kean was elected Governor of New Jersey in 1980 after eight years in the New Jersey House of Representatives.
[28]

STATE OF NEW JERSEY
OFFICE OF THE GOVERNOR

THOMAS H. KEAN
GOVERNOR

On the day of the President's assassination, I was a graduate student at Columbia University. I was working on a paper when I heard the news of the assassination. I remember feeling angry, numb, and helpless. I forgot my work and went home. The assassination made me worry about the future of a democracy in which such violence against our elected leadership could happen.

Sincerely,

Thomas H. Kean
Governor

170

Jack Kemp

Prior to becoming a Member of the U.S. House of Representatives in 1971, New Yorker Jack Kemp played professional football for thirteen years, ending his career with the Buffalo Bills.
[28]

JACK KEMP
THIRTY-FIRST DISTRICT
NEW YORK

HOUSE OF REPRESENTATIVES

When I first heard the news of President Kennedy's death, I was practicing with the Buffalo Bills for our upcoming game with the Boston Patriots. I reacted to the news with tears and knew that the impact on our nation would be a shock, but one that this great democracy could withstand.

Sincerely,

171

Jeane J. Kirkpatrick

Jeane Kirkpatrick was United Nations Ambassador for the United States from 1981–85.
[37]

JEANE J. KIRKPATRICK

I was driving one of my sons to an appointment.

I was stunned. It seemed incredible. He was so alive, so young, so vital.

I thought everyone would be grieved, as I was, and also that Lyndon Johnson would be an effective president.

Sincerely,

Jeane J. Kirkpatrick

Paul Laxalt

Paul Laxalt has held positions as Governor of Nevada and U.S. Senator from Nevada.
[41]

PAUL LAXALT
NEVADA

𝔘nited 𝔖tates 𝔖enate

Truly, November 22, 1963, was one of the saddest
days in our history.

On that date I was travelling by car in a
rural area in Nevada. I heard the news by
car radio.

My reaction was one of disbelief -- the
assassination was beyond my comprehension
or belief.

I felt the nation would react with indignation
and grief. That is what eventually occurred.

Sincerely,

PAUL LAXALT
U. S. SENATOR

173

James G. Martin

James Martin, a former Member of the U.S. House of Representatives, was elected Governor of North Carolina in 1984.
[27]

STATE OF NORTH CAROLINA
OFFICE OF THE GOVERNOR

On November 22, 1963, at the time of President Kennedy's assassination, I was an Associate Professor of Chemistry at Davidson College in Davidson, North Carolina.

When I received word that President Kennedy had been assassinated while riding in a motorcade in Dallas, I was shocked and stunned.

As a nation, we were appalled; and the world mourned his death. I prayed that love would find its way into the hearts of the family and give them comfort and strength.

Sincerely,

James G. Martin

Ned McWherter

Ned McWherter was elected Governor of Tennessee in 1986. He previously served for eighteen years in the Tennessee House of Representatives.
[33]

State of Tennessee

NED McWHERTER
GOVERNOR

I was working in the back of the Martin Shoe Company in Martin, Tennessee. I remember I was packing shoes when a man we called "Uncle" Jack Vincent came running back and said he had just heard on the radio that President Kennedy had been shot. I will remember that moment as long as I live.

I felt just like a bee had stung me. It was that sharp a feeling.

I don't remember thinking much at that moment about the impact on the nation. I just felt sad and depressed that our President had been shot on a main street in Dallas, Texas.

Sincerely,

Ned McWherter

Ned McWherter

Howard Metzenbaum was elected U.S. Senator from Ohio in 1976.
[46]

HOWARD M. METZENBAUM
OHIO

𝔘nited 𝔖tates 𝔖enate

I was in a restaurant having lunch with some friends of mine.

I couldn't believe it and kept praying and hoping that he had not been fatally shot.

I felt a great sense of loss and let down. President Kennedy represented something higher than usual on the American political scene. His dreams for the future and his concepts for the present (as of that time) were different from the rest. Seldom has there been one individual who had the capacity to cause so many throughout the world to believe not only in the present but the future as well.

Yours very truly

Howard M. Metzenbaum
United States Senator

William G. Milliken

William Milliken served as Governor of Michigan from 1969–82. He had previously been that state's Lieutenant Governor.
[41]

WILLIAM G. MILLIKEN

I was in Muskegon, Michigan testing the waters for a possible campaign for Congress-a schedule for the day which I promptly cancelled.

I was stunned and deeply moved.

I felt it would have a profound and lasting impact--which it has.

Sincerely,

William G. Milliken

Frank H. Murkowski

Frank Murkowski was elected U.S. Senator from Alaska in 1980.

[30]

FRANK H. MURKOWSKI
ALASKA

United States Senate

WASHINGTON, D.C.

I'm sure all Americans remember vividly where they were at the time they first heard about President Kennedy's assassination. In 1963 I was a banker in Wrangell, Alaska (pop. 2,500). The morning of November 22nd, about 9:00 A.M. Alaska time, I was sitting in the Bakery Coffee Shop when we heard the news on the radio. I was shocked and extremely saddened. Like Americans throughout our nation, I said a silent prayer for our President and his family. As I recall, I had questions at the time if the assassination and subsequent events were part of a conspiracy. To this day, those questions have not been satisfactorily answered.

With best wishes,

Sincerely,

Frank H. Murkowski
United States Senator

George Nigh

George Nigh was Governor of Oklahoma from 1963–66, and again from 1979–87.
[36]

GEORGE NIGH
GOVERNOR

STATE OF OKLAHOMA
OFFICE OF THE GOVERNOR

I was on my honeymoon and also attending the World JCI (Junior Chamber of Commerce International) convention in Tel Aviv, Israel.

I was told by a cab driver that President Kennedy was shot. I thought he was trying to tell me another Kennedy joke. (They were going around in those days.) I told him that I didn't travel half way around the world to hear a Kennedy joke. Then, the doorman at our hotel told me that it was true, that indeed the President had been shot.

I felt it would immediately slow down our efforts to rebuild pride in our country–something that Kennedy was doing. Of course, there was also a tremendous shock to the country.

Sam Nunn

Sam Nunn served four years in the Georgia House of Representatives before he was elected to the U.S. Senate in 1972.
[25]

United States Senate

COMMITTEE ON ARMED SERVICES

      I was checking a real estate title in the Crisp County, Georgia, Courthouse on Friday when I heard the news of the shooting.

      I was shocked and deeply saddened.

      It was impossible to assess the impact of the assassination on the country. I knew we had lost a brilliant young leader and I offered my prayers for his family, the new president and for our nation.

                         Sincerely,

                         Sam Nunn

Robert D. Orr

Robert Orr was elected Lieutenant Governor of Indiana in 1972, and then became Governor in 1980.
[46]

OFFICE OF THE GOVERNOR

ROBERT D. ORR
GOVERNOR

Mrs. Orr and I were between Indianapolis and Columbus, Ohio, on a commercial flight to New York. The pilot announced an unconfirmed report that President Kennedy had been shot in Texas. On landing for the stopover in Columbus, we heard the confirmation of Kennedy's wounding and later death from Walter Cronkite on television. We were in the middle of the terminal with a large crowd who stood stunned at the news. Cronkite was at a big meeting place in Dallas where a huge crowd had been waiting for the Kennedys to arrive for an after-luncheon address. They stood stunned like all of us at the Columbus Airport.

Mrs. Orr and I went to a small coffee shop in the terminal and sat in disbelief, making little conversation before we went to re-board our plane to New York. The plane was full of stunned passengers saying nothing.

I made no effort to assess the impact until late that evening in a gathering of old friends. We discussed what might now happen. I don't remember that any of us anticipated the overwhelming impact on the world, the instant martyrdom that would be accorded Kennedy, or the political reaction in Congress in the quick enactment of Kennedy's social programs which had been without much support prior to the assassination. These programs became Johnson's Great Society and were enacted as a memorial to the martyred young president. On November 22, 1963, few could look beyond the disbelief that the assassination could have happened and the real concern that some conspiracy might be afoot to murder others in the government.

Sincerely,

ROBERT D. ORR
Governor

Charles H. Percy

Charles Percy served as Chairman of the Board of the Bell & Howell Corporation before serving as U.S. Senator from Illinois from 1967–85.
[44]

CHARLES H. PERCY
ILLINOIS

𝔘nited 𝔖tates 𝔖enate

I was at the podium at a luncheon being given at the Conrad Hilton Hotel in Chicago, listening to a speech being given by Robert Taft, Jr. His subject was the Constitution of the United States and the continuity of government that it has provided, making the United States, a young nation, the oldest government that has lived under a single Constitution. The news of President Kennedy's assassination began spreading through the room and was finally announced from the podium. As I recall, Bob Taft, Jr. expressed thoughts about the confidence all of us could have, and the world could have, that the continuity of government in the United States would be preserved regardless of this tragedy.

I reacted with shock and dismay. My mind immediately flashed to my first meeting with John F. Kennedy and his family at a party in New York. I was introduced by his longtime friends Mr. and Mrs. Tom Watson, Jr. and through that introduction began a friendship that resulted in a number of exchanges of views. The friendship extended through the years to virtually every member of the family, some of whom I still see regularly.

I knew the nation would suffer a great loss, but John F. Kennedy would provide an inspiration not only to citizens of the United States but citizens of the world for years to come. His impact perhaps was deeper in Latin America than anyplace else on earth, though his impact was a great and lasting one in many more remote parts of the world. In visiting homes in Latin America, whether they be in wealthy districts of Buenes Aires or shantytowns in the outskirts of metropolitan areas, inevitably a color picture of John F. Kennedy would adorn the wall, even those of tin huts. He was truly a hero and inspiration to millions

of people. He embodied the spirit of a young nation; high
in hopes, aspirations and expectations, and gifted with an
eloquence of expression that contributed greatly to his
leadership abilities.

Warmest personal regards,

Pat Robertson

*Pat Robertson founded the Christian Broadcasting
Network in 1960 and served as the television host of
the "700 Club" from 1968–87. He was a candidate for
President of the United States in 1988.*
[33]

**The
Christian
Broadcasting
Network
Inc.**

Pat Robertson
PRESIDENT

On November 22, 1963 I was in the studio of our
television station, WYAH-TV, in Portsmouth, Virginia
when I was interrupted by a telephone call from my
wife, who had just seen the news flash on television
of the shooting of President Kennedy. I ran to our
news room as the Associated Press ticker was beginning
to send out the details. From then until the President's
funeral, I was covering the event along with our news
director on our radio station WXRI and on our television
station, Channel 27 in Portsmouth.

My reaction to the event was obviously stunned disbelief, but the need to communicate the tragedy to
our audience overcame any of my own personal feelings.
The disbelief turned to some dismay, when I began
hearing and reading other commentaries calling Lee
Harvey Oswald a "right-wing extremist" when most of
us knew or were learning that Lee Harvey Oswald was
a convinced communist who had connections in Cuba
and the Soviet Union.

I did not fear for the safety of the United States
because Lyndon Johnson, who was a very strong capable
figure, was standing by immediately to take the reins
of power. My primary thought, besides that of grief
and amazement, was the question, "Who did it and why?"
Seeing the expression on Oswald's face when he con-
fronted Jack Ruby, heightened in me a feeling that
something had happened here that reflected a group
of conspirators, not just a lone gunman. Obviously,
as a newsman, my thought was to determine the extent
of any conspiracy and whether it went beyond Dallas,
Texas into Cuba or into the Soviet Union.

Sincerely,

Pat Robertson
President

"I believe in an America where religious intolerance will
someday end—where all men and all churches are treated
equal—where every man has the same right to attend or not
to attend the church of his choice—where there is no Catholic
vote, no antiCatholic vote, no bloc voting of any kind - and
where Catholics, Protestants, and Jews, both the lay and the
pastoral level, will refrain from those attitudes of disdain
and division which have so often marred their works in the
past, and promote instead the American ideal of brotherhood."
—Before the Greater Houston Ministerial Association, 1960

George Romney

George Romney has held positions as Chairman of the Board of the American Motors Corporation, Governor of Michigan, and U.S. Secretary of Housing and Urban Development.
[56]

GEORGE ROMNEY

I was at a Midwest Governor's Council luncheon at the Strategic Air Defense Center outside Omaha, Nebraska.

We first heard the President had been shot and hoped it would not be fatal. Our hopes were shattered and with sorrow all those present immediately returned to their respective states.

What followed was a period of uncertainty about President Johnson's policies because of the differences in their background and methods.

Sincerely,

George Romney

185

Terry Sanford

Prior to his 1986 election as U.S. Senator from North Carolina, Terry Sanford served as Governor of North Carolina and as President of Duke University.
[46]

𝕰nited 𝕾tates 𝕾enate

The President's death came on the eve of the annual Duke-Carolina football game. Thirty-one floats were forming for the pre-game parade in front of Woolen Gymnasium when the news of the assassination became known in Chapel Hill. The parade dissolved even before the student organizers formally called it off. The game itself was postponed. Crowds of people in shock gathered on the campus and downtown. Many instructors called off classes. Church services were held as early as three hours after the announcement was made. ROTC buglers played taps at the campus flag pole. The South Building bell tolled for the President, and for all of us....

The shock cannot be exaggerated. Our country was paralyzed with grief. Nearly all of us can remember precisely what we were doing when we heard the news. We are permanently imprinted with that moment. The effect on the world was disbelief and despair. One of the unforgettable images of the funeral was the long line of world leaders who walked somberly behind his casket....

John Kennedy mobilized the American spirit and sent it looking for a proud peace.

We believed him because he made it possible to believe in ourselves. He quickened our spirits....It is impossible to recall, for those who did not experience it, the raw excitement of the Kennedy years. Never mind his flaws or the fact that his programs may have been headed into major problems with Congress. He was the kind of inspiration we had nearly forgotten.

We Americans were not alone in our response to him. I saw his picture recently on the wall of the Foreign Minister of Costa Rica. Similar pictures became in many countries a kind of American icon. All the more devastating, then, when Kennedy was ripped out of our lives.

Sincerely,

[signature: Terry Sanford]

TERRY SANFORD
United States Senator

Senator Terry Sanford of North Carolina—seen here with JFK at a campaign rally in 1960 while Sanford was Governor—remembers that Kennedy "quickened our spirits. It is impossible to recall, for those who did not experience it, the raw excitement of the Kennedy years."

Ted Schwinden

Ted Schwinden served in the Montana House of Representatives and as Lieutenant Governor before he was elected Governor of Montana in 1980.
[38]

$\mathfrak{State\ of\ Montana}$
$\mathfrak{Office\ of\ the\ Governor}$

TED SCHWINDEN
GOVERNOR

I had just come into our farm house for lunch when my mother-in-law called and said, "Turn on your radio, the President has been shot."

I hurt.

I didn't think about impact. Like most Americans, I suppose, I assumed -- correctly -- that the nation would continue.

Sincerely,

TED SCHWINDEN
Governor

Paul Simon

Paul Simon, one-time Lieutenant Governor of Illinois, served ten years in the U.S. House of Representatives before his election to the U.S. Senate in 1984.
[34]

PAUL SIMON
ILLINOIS

United States Senate

I was in Chicago having lunch with a man who was then a state representative, Anthony Scariano, now an apellate court justice. Someone came over saying "The President's been shot," and we thought it was one of those "sick jokes." But it was clear in an instant it was not. We went to a neighboring bar where they had a television set on and watched it for a moment. I was scheduled to be at a state legislative committee meeting that afternoon in Chicago, but I knew it would not proceed. I got in my car and listened to the radio as I drove from Chicago down to Southern Illinois.

I remember the whole thing having a tremendous emotional impact on me.

Cordially,

Paul Simon
U.S. Senator

189

Alan K. Simpson

Alan Simpson began his first term as U.S. Senator from Wyoming in 1979. Prior to that he served in the Wyoming House of Representatives.
[32]

AL SIMPSON
WYOMING

United States Senate
Assistant Republican Leader

When I learned of President Kennedy being shot, I was practicing law in Cody, Wyoming. I was heavily involved as a young lawyer in the community and raising three beautiful children who were born in 1957, 1959 and 1962. I was going home to join them for lunch when a friend of mine -- Mel Fillerup, a fellow attorney -- came right up to me at the entrance of the Shoshone First National Bank where I officed and said to me that John Kennedy had been shot in Dallas. I really actually almost reeled against the door. I said, "Well, what happened?" He said, "I don't know, he's alive and I guess everything is O.K."

I remember walking on home. When I got home, I went into the kitchen and my wife, Ann, was crying. The kids seemed quite bestirred and moved. She said, "The President is dead." We were awed, stunned and numbed. I recall eating lunch -- and yet I also hardly recalled what I was doing.

It was one of those beautiful November days in Wyoming. I just said to Ann, "You know, I just need to go away and think. I'm going to scrub the things I have at the office." I just drove out of town with my fishing pole. I remember hiking into an area several miles from town in the late afternoon sun and I thought about life; family; my country; and sacrifices -- yes, even the supreme one -- that a person can make for his country. It was a very moving and unforgettable day.

It was a day that robbed us of the luster and pagentry of the presidency. I knew it would be a great loss, but I also knew that this country responds in times of tragedy, and trial and tribulation.

Within hours, President Johnson was our new president with the transition beginning and the healing starting. This is a remarkable country and it will prevail for centuries yet to come. When it was all said and done, the impact on our nation was actually quite minimal -- as far as the continuation of governmental operations was affected. That is the brilliance of our system.

It is a government of laws and not men. Yet, we sometimes think of it otherwise because there are some very vital personalities that simply command the view within the entire nation. But, that is not what makes us unique. It is that marvelous Constitution that we celebrate this year and the "system" that makes it so extraordinary. The three branches of government -- regardless of the personalities present on the scene in each branch. It is our reverence towards those three branches of government -- even in their rather extraordinary imperfections -- that is what it is about in America.

Most sincerely,

Alan K. Simpson
United States Senator

George A. Sinner

George Sinner was elected Governor of North Dakota in 1984 after six years in the state legislature.
[35]

State of North Dakota

OFFICE OF THE GOVERNOR

GEORGE A. SINNER
GOVERNOR

I was at my farm in North Dakota when I learned of President Kennedy's assassination.

My reaction was utter disbelief and anger at many possibly responsible groups.

I feared many things as a result of Kennedy's death, including the violence of the far right – as well as the Mafia. I was also not enthused about Lyndon Johnson and feared increased militarism.

Sincerely,

George A. Sinner
Governor

Arlen Specter

Arlen Specter served as Assistant Counsel for the Warren Commission. In 1981, he began his first term as U.S. Senator from Pennsylvania.
[33]

ARLEN SPECTER
PENNSYLVANIA

United States Senate

As you may know, I have a very keen interest in the historical accounts of the assassination of President John F. Kennedy since I served as assistant counsel to the Warren Commission.

I was riding up in the elevator in Philadelphia City Hall at about 1:40 p.m. when I heard the first report that the President had been shot in Dallas. At that time, I was on my way to a hearing on the death penalty in the case of *Commonwealth v. Anthony Scoleri.* Scoleri had been sentenced to death in the electric chair and the final date for reconsideration was Friday, November 22, 1963, and the court had set 2:00 p.m. as the hearing time. One of the principal lawyers, former Pennsylvania Supreme Court Justice Thomas D. McBride, was unable to participate because he was overcome with grief on hearing the news.

My own reaction was disbelief at the initial report that the President had been shot, and when I arrived at my desk in the District Attorney's office and later found that he had been murdered, I found it hard to believe.

I felt that President Kennedy's death would have a very severe impact on the nation because it deprived us of a great leader in midstream and it showed that even the most powerful man in the most powerful nation in the world was fragile and susceptible to being extinguished by the single act of a single deranged man.

Sincerely,

Arlen Specter

193

Robert T. Stafford

Robert Stafford served in the U.S. House of Representatives from Vermont from 1961–71. In 1971, he was appointed to fill a vacancy in the U.S. Senate.
[50]

ROBERT T. STAFFORD
VERMONT

United States Senate

I was at the then Cape Canaveral, later called the Kennedy Space Center, standing under one of our large rockets with a Congressman from Montauk Point, Long Island, when an Air Force Brigadier General came running up to us and said President Kennedy had been shot and badly wounded.

I remember feeling a profound sense of shock and dismay, and within a few minutes additional word reached us that the President was dead.

Congressman Otis Pike and I had stopped at Cape Canaveral enroute to a Naval facility in Puerto Rico. On learning of the President's death, we cancelled the trip and returned to Andrews Air Force Base. Our plane was kept in the air for a while in the vicinity of Andrews while Air Force One, with Lyndon Johnson, already sworn in as President, was landing. Then we were allowed to land.

Congressman Pike and I were accompanied by Colonel Arnold, the son of a famous World War II General, Hap Arnold.

At the time of these events, I did not give much thought to the impact on the nation beyond the deep sense of sorrow which I think all Americans felt at the loss of the President and the outrage at the way it occurred.

Sincerely yours,

Robert T. Stafford
United States Senator

194

James R. Thompson

Jim Thompson, a former U.S. District Attorney, began his tenure as Governor of Illinois in 1977. [27]

STATE OF ILLINOIS

OFFICE OF THE GOVERNOR

JAMES R. THOMPSON
GOVERNOR

When I first heard the news of President Kennedy's shooting I was in a judge's chamber in Chicago pre-trying a criminal case. I was overcome by a feeling of disbelief. It was a confusing time.

Directly following the event I truthfully did not know what kind of impact President Kennedy's death would have on the nation. I don't think anyone really knew.

Sincerely

James R. Thompson
GOVERNOR

Richard Thornburgh

Dick Thornburgh served as Assistant U.S. Attorney General from 1975–77 and as Governor of Pennsylvania from 1979–87. He was appointed U.S. Attorney General in 1988 by President Ronald Reagan.
[31]

THE GOVERNOR

COMMONWEALTH OF PENNSYLVANIA
GOVERNOR'S OFFICE

On that day I was attending a continuing legal education seminar at the William Penn Hotel in Pittsburgh. The speaker at the afternoon session had just begun his presentation when he was interrupted with the news that the President had been shot. After about two or three minutes, many of us felt that it was inappropriate to continue the session, so we adjourned.

My initial reaction to the news that President Kennedy had been shot was utter disbelief and shock, coupled with the hope that the shooting was not fatal -- a hope that, in a very short time, proved to be fruitless.

When it was announced that the president was dead, I was at first very concerned about the possible destabilizing effects of such a tragedy on the nation. However, it soon became clear that we could weather such an event, however deep our sorrow, as we had been obliged to do in the past.

Sincerely,

Dick Thornburgh
Governor

Paul Trible

Paul Trible, a former Member of the U.S. House of Representatives, was elected U.S. Senator from Virginia in 1982.
[16]

PAUL TRIBLE
VIRGINIA

𝔘nited 𝔖tates 𝔖enate

When I first heard the news of President Kennedy's shooting, I was attending my 11th grade biology class at Abington High School, Clarks Summit, Pennsylvania. My reaction, as well as fellow school mates, was one of shock and disbelief -- kids were crying in the halls. I was too young to assess the impact President Kennedy's death would have on our nation.

Sincerely,

Paul Trible

197

George Wallace

George Wallace served as Governor of Alabama from 1963–66, from 1971–79, and again from 1983–87. In 1968, while campaigning for President as the American Independent Party's nominee, he was himself the target of an assassination attempt.
[44]

STATE OF ALABAMA

GOVERNOR'S OFFICE

GEORGE C. WALLACE
GOVERNOR

      ... I was in Haleyville, Alabama, dedicating a high school. While I was making a talk about the high school at a luncheon, the message came in that the President had been shot. We stopped the meeting at that point and sent someone to find out for us if it were fatal. Later it came through that it was fatal, and we went out to dedicate the new high school with several hundred people present. We gave a silent prayer for our President and his family and then we dedicated that moment that we were there to him and adjourned the proceedings immediately.

      My reaction was one of stunned disbelief that this fine young President, who I had supported for President and the people of Alabama had supported, had been shot down like a common criminal. I asked the question, What is happening in this country to see this bright young President shot in the prime of life?

      ... I was so stunned and shocked at that time that I did not even think about what effect it would have upon the nation although later going back to Montgomery I felt that there was going to be a great reaction in the sense that people felt that they had lost one of the greatest leaders who had been elected to the Presidency. It was one of the saddest days of our national history.

With kind regards, I am

Sincerely yours,

George C. Wallace

"We preach freedom around the world, and we mean it, and we cherish freedom here at home; but are we to say to the world and, much more importantly, to each other that this is a land of the free except for the Negroes; that we have no second-class citizens except for the Negroes?...It is not enough to pin the blame on others, to say this is a problem of one section of the country or another, or deplore the facts that we face. A great change is at hand, and our task, our obligation, is to make that revolution, that change peaceful and constructive for all."

—*Televised Address from the White House, June 11, 1963*

Caspar Weinberger

Caspar Weinberger served as the U.S. Secretary of Health, Education and Welfare from 1973–75 and as the U.S. Secretary of Defense from 1981–87.
[46]

THE SECRETARY OF DEFENSE

WASHINGTON, THE DISTRICT OF COLUMBIA

I was in my law office in San Francisco when I heard the first report of the Kennedy assassination. My first reaction was that I could not believe he had actually been killed, because the first radio reports offered some hope.

My general reaction was one of shock and anger, and a feeling that the assassination attempt (as I then thought it was) was another example of our growing propensity to apply violence to deal with every issue.

I do not think I considered immediately the impact on the nation. However, that came later, particularly when I talked with my young son that night, who had been very deeply affected by watching the whole terrible tragedy unfold on television. His reaction seemed to me to mirror that of the state of shock into which everyone of all ages had been plunged. I had known President Kennedy in college, and this was a source of additional shock and personal horror.

Sincerely,

Caspar W. Weinberger

Mark White

After six years as Texas Secretary of State, Mark White served three years as state Attorney General and then was Governor of Texas from 1983–87.
[23]

OFFICE OF THE GOVERNOR

MARK WHITE
GOVERNOR

I first heard about the assassination as I was preparing for fall exams at Baylor University Law School. I was at my apartment gathering my books when a neighbor came by to tell me that the President had been shot in Dallas. I immediately turned on the television set and left it on continuously for the next three or four days. I was watching when Jack Ruby shot Lee Harvey Oswald.

The President's death resulted from a shocking act of violence that left me feeling ill and sick at my stomach. The event convinced me of the need for a responsive criminal justice system to punish those who commit acts of such senseless violence....

Mark White

Mark White
Governor of Texas

Ronald L. Ziegler

Ron Ziegler was White House Press Secretary to President Richard Nixon from 1969–74.
[24]

National Association of Truck Stop Operators

I was working in my office at J. Walter Thompson in Los Angeles, California, when I heard the first news flash that the President had been shot in Dallas. Shortly thereafter, the news came that the President was dead.

Like most Americans, I was stunned, saddened and dismayed over the death of such a bright and dynamic leader, and that such an unthinkable tragedy could occur in the United States. Our office was immediately closed and I spent the next days following developments and sharing in the sadness of our Nation.

The U. S. moved through a number of searing tragedies in the '60's and early '70's. We can all be thankful that the resiliency of our system and the wisdom of the writers of our Constitution allows for calm and effective transfer of power when our leaders fall. Our history as a people is brightened by the memory of the presidency of John F. Kennedy.

Sincerely,

RONALD L. ZIEGLER
President

VI

JOURNALISTS AND WRITERS REMEMBER THE END OF A POLITICAL ERA

"You may remember in 1851, the New York Herald Tribune, ...included as its London correspondent an obscure journalist by the name of Karl Marx. We are told that the foreign correspondent Marx, stone broke and with a family ill and undernourished, constantly appealed...for an increase in his munificent salary of $5 per installment....

But when all his financial appeals were refused, Marx looked around for other means of livelihood and fame, and eventually terminated his relationship with the Tribune and devoted his talents full time to the cause that would bequeath to the world the seeds of Leninism, Stalinism, revolution and the Cold War.

If only this capitalistic New York newspaper had treated him more kindly, if only Marx had remained a foreign correspondent, history might have been different, and I hope all publishers will bear this lesson in mind the next time they receive a poverty-stricken appeal for a small increase in the expense account from an obscure newspaperman."

– Before the American Newspaper Publishers Association, 1961

John Kennedy averaged twenty-one news conferences a year, about one every two-and-a-half weeks. He enjoyed wrestling with the press, and often used the opportunity to not only display his grasp of issues, but his sense of humor as well.

President Kennedy was also an insatiable reader who possessed a great deal of respect for writers and their work. He too was an author, having written two best-selling books--one of which earned him a Pulizter Prize.

Several reporters who covered Kennedy's Administration now join other writers, columnists, reporters, and broadcast journalists to reflect on John Kennedy, and on what effect his death had on the nation.

Cleveland Amory

Columnist Cleveland Amory has been the television critic for TV Guide *for over thirteen years. He is the author of* The Cat That Came Home for Christmas, *among other books.*
[46]

THE FUND FOR ANIMALS INC.

... The death of JFK came as a particular shock to me, as Jack Kennedy had been a student at Harvard two years behind me, and I had known him then. And, as I continued to do through the intervening years, had admired his grace and wit and great good humor--even as a young man. To this day, I am a close friend of his sister, Patricia Kennedy Lawford, and an admirer of the grace, wit and great good humor of the entire family, including the most attractive younger generation.

On that awful day, I was on the telephone with Betty Beale, at that time a television commentator on a Washington news program. Betty was talking to me about the imminent publication of my Celebrity Register , while keeping one eye on the news ticker. I can still remember the sudden pause in our light conversation, and then the change in her voice as she said, "My God, the President's been shot." It was a little while before we knew for sure that he was dead, but I remember feeling at that moment that something special in American life had been very brutally crushed. My secretary tells me that I cried.

Cleveland Amory

204

Jack Anderson

*Investigative Reporter Jack Anderson is a nationally
syndicated columnist. His books include* McCarthy
the Man–the Senator–the Ism, The Kefauver Story,
and Fiasco.
[41]

JACK ANDERSON

When I first heard the news of President Kennedy's shooting,
I was in a hotel room with the then-editor of Parade
Magazine, Jess Gorkin, attending a story conference.

My first reaction to the news was disbelief, shock and anger --
in that order. My immediate reaction was to vent epithets
at the right-wing nuts in Dallas whom I immediately suspected, without any evidence whatsoever, to be guilty. It was
an impulsive and angry reaction.

My first impression was being appalled at the violence and
feeling that something had to be done to curb it in this
country. But since it had happened, and couldn't be undone,
I hoped it would shock the nation into coming to its senses.

Sincerely,

Jack Anderson

205

Isaac Asimov

Isaac Asimov is the author of more than 300 books. Among his best known works are Fantastic Voyage *and the novels in his* Foundation *series.*
[43]

ISAAC ASIMOV

I was in the Metropolitan Museum of Art, looking at the small replica of the Parthenon when I overheard someone else saying something about President Kennedy being shot.

In great agitation, I went to him and said, "What the hell are you talking about?"

He told me and I went straight back to the hotel room to cancel a talk I was slated to give that evening. I wasn't able to. I had to give that talk to a standing-room-only crowd all trying to get away from what had happened.

All I could feel at the time was that I didn't want Johnson. ---But I got him.

Jules Bergman

Jules Bergman was Science Editor for ABC News *from 1961 until his death in 1987. His books included* 90 Seconds to Space *and* Anyone Can Fly. [34]

Jules Bergman
Science Editor

I was on duty in our New York Newsroom at the time of the shooting. Most people had gone to lunch; I was and am curious—curious as to the sound of the Flash bells on the wire service teletypes. So I went and read in shocked disbelief.

I clearly remember crying at the time, something I hadn't done over my own father's death: I so strongly identified with JFK as a potentially great leader who could unify the nation....

I began to call local restaurants to round up our ABC News executives...to get the story on the air....

I wasn't sure [what impact it would have on the nation], at that first blush of shock and grief, but I recall balancing in my mind was it a political assassination by the Russians? I have long since concluded that it wasn't.

I have concluded that the Challenger disaster—killing 6 of my friends—is the only comparative I have to the JFK assassination.

For shock and immediate impact, the "Throttle-up" command at 1 minute and 11 seconds after liftoff of the Challenger, is the only counterpart in human drama I have to the shocking, brutal events of November 22, 1963.

As one of my astronaut friends put it, "In my book, when the simulator tells me 'throttle-up' at 1 minute, 11 seconds, my heart stops...."

And my heart stopped that day in November, 1963.

Jim Bishop

The late Jim Bishop was the author of The Day Kennedy Was Shot, F.D.R's Last Year, *and* A Day in the Life of President Kennedy.
[56]

My wife, Kelly,and I were aboard our boat The Away We Go IV, docked at West Palm, gasing up, when a dockhand gave us the news. We were unbelieving and immediately turned on the radio. We had just returned from Aruba where I had written a slender volume to be called A Day in the Life of President Kennedy. He had a copy of the manuscript with him in Dallas.

With shock, horror and a distinct physical feeling of being sick. We had so recently touched him.

I do not recall thinking of the impact on the nation. I do remember praying for the president and then for President Johnson that those close to Mr. Kennedy would not make the transition difficult.

Sincerely,

Jim Bishop

JIM BISHOP

208

Ed Bradley

Emmy Award winning broadcaster Ed Bradley has been a correspondent for "CBS News" since 1971 and an anchorman for "60 Minutes" since 1981.
[22]

CBS
NEWS

I was in Philadelphia teaching a class of sixth graders. My reaction was shock and sadness. At that time, with a roomful of youngsters I didn't give much thought to the impact it would have on the nation. We didn't really know.

Sincerely,

Ed Bradley
Correspondent
60 Minutes

James Brady

In addition to writing a weekly column for Parade
Magazine, *James Brady is an Editor-at-Large for* Ad-
vertising Age. *His books include* Superchic, *and*
Paris One.
[35]

Advertising Age

We were living in Paris where I was a foreign correspondent and
my wife and I had been out to dinner or a movie or something and
when we got home shortly after nine the babysitter said the cable company had called. The cable company was always calling with queries
from New York and I called back. The man at the other end, whose
voice I knew very well, said, "Your president was shot. I have a message from New York."

I was very angry and confused. I thought he meant the president of
my company. Why would he be shot? When I got it straight that it was
Kennedy, I took the message. They wanted French reaction for the
Monday paper.

We turned on the French radio and now they were saying Kennedy
was dead and that Johnson had been shot as well.

I didn't know what to do so I decided to go over to the American Embassy. I took a cab and it was there I got filled in on the details. There
were some other newsmen there and we all stood around talking.
Maybe I was the only one who knew Kennedy, from my three years of
covering Capitol Hill.

At that point, I can't recall coming to any conclusions about what
the assassination would mean to the nation. I only knew how stunned
I was, how bad I felt.

When I left the Embassy around midnight it had begun to rain. A
couple of French cops stood on the sidewalk, a few curious civilians. I
remember when I got into the cab the driver said, infinitely more gentle

and courteous than Paris cabbies usually were: *"Monsieur, le petit peuple de France sont avec vous ce soir."*

I realize it sounds corny, but that was what he said: "Mister, the little people of France are with you tonight."

I went home and my wife and I talked for a long time about Kennedy before we slept.

Jim Brady

"I sometimes think that we are too much impressed by the clamor of daily events. The newspaper headlines and the television screens give us a short view. They so flood us with the stop-press details of daily stories that we lose sight of one of the great movements of history. Yet it is the profound tendencies of history, and not the passing excitements, that will shape our future....Wisdom requires the long view. And the long view shows us that the revolution of national independence is a fundamental fact of our era....As new nations emerge from the oblivion of centuries, their first aspiration is to affirm their national identity."
—*At the University of California at Berkeley, March 23, 1962*

David Brinkley

David Brinkley has hosted "The Huntley-Brinkley Report" and "This Week with David Brinkley." Since 1956, he has anchored TV coverage of every presidential nominating convention, first with NBC, then with ABC.
[43]

ABC News

David Brinkley
Correspondent

I was in my office at NBC in Washington preparing for that night's news program, the Huntley-Brinkley Report, when a young staff member ran in and said, "Kennedy's been shot."

My first reaction was to see exactly what had happened -- was he seriously hurt? Was he alive? And my second was to rush into the NBC studio and put the news on the air. Huntley and I then stayed on almost continuously for three days, around the clock.

I thought the impact on the American people, since it happened in a time of social disturbance and disorder, would be profound. And I believe it was.

Sincerely,

David Brinkley

Tom Brokaw

Tom Brokaw, anchorman of the "NBC Nightly News," was White House Correspondent for NBC during the Nixon administration.
[23]

NBC News

Tom Brokaw

           ... As I'm sure it is with everyone, that moment is seared in my memory.

      I was the editor on duty at KMTV in Omaha when the news first came clattering across UPI.

      My immediate reaction was a mixture of personal grief and professional urgency. I had to get the story on the air as the network was down at the time to allow for local programming.

      I remember thinking this is a new time in our lives. We just don't shoot Presidents. As a child of the Fifties, I had a loss of innocence.

                Sincerely,

                Tom Brokaw

Helen Gurley Brown

Helen Gurley Brown became Editor-in-Chief of Cosmopolitan *in 1965. Among her many books are* Sex and the Single Girl *and* Having It All.
[41]

COSMOPOLITAN

I was in my flat on Park Avenue working on a book when a friend called to tell me of President Kennedy's assassination. My reaction was less a feeling of loss for the country as it was the insanity of someone doing this. I mostly thought of the President in his relative youth and ebullience being struck down by a maniac. I'm afraid I wasn't thinking very much about the country or even the President's family... I was simply horrified that some madman should be able to snuff out the life of someone arriving at the peak of his powers and lust for life.

All my best wishes,

Helen Brown

Hugh Downs

Hugh Downs began his TV career as announcer for such programs as "Sid Caesar's Hour," and the "Jack Paar Show Tonight." He has since hosted a variety of television shows, including "Concentration" and "20/20."
[42]

ABC News

Hugh Downs

I had come back from lunch on November 22, 1963 in the RCA Bldg. (30 Rockefeller Plaza) on my way to my office but stopped on the fifth floor at the NBC News Room. A staffer came out of the News Room and tore down the hall past me with a long piece of teletype paper streaming out behind him. I remember saying something inane like "Where's the fire" and he shouted, "They shot Kennedy".

My immediate reaction to such a statement was that it was a bad-taste joke of some sort, but after about a second-and-a-half I realized that this man really believed that the President had been shot. And, of course, subsequent events in the News Room itself bore out the reality.

The impact I felt this event would have if Kennedy died (remember that for a time we thought he might survive the assassination attempt) was that the nation might be paralyzed and become vulnerable to a number of things: an attack from outside, a crumbling of the economy, a panic and subsequent damage to civil law. The fact that none of these fears was justified produced in me a new faith in the stability of American culture.

Sincerely,

Hugh Downs

Richard Eberhart

Richard Eberhart, Poet Laureate of New Hampshire, is the recipient of such prestigious awards as the Pulitzer Prize (1966) and the Robert Frost Medal. Among his books are A Bravery of Earth, Brotherhood of Men, *and* Survivors.
[59]

My reaction to the President's assassination was one of shock, disbelief, incredulity but rapid assessment of the terrible news as we saw the events on TV and President Johnson's swift movements.

The Warren Commission's report was an attempt at truth, perhaps too much an attempt to calm the population. Perhaps the total truth will never be known as in the case of Lincoln. We learned later that a number of persons in the assassination area mysteriously disappeared and were never accounted for.

Yours sincerely,

Richard Eberhart

Ray Gandolf

Ray Gandolf, a correspondent for ABC News/Sports, hosted the television series, "Our World." He has received several journalism awards, including the Peabody and the Dupont.
[33]

ABC NEWS

Ray Gandolf
"Our World"

When President Kennedy was shot, I was writing a documentary for Eye On New York, a weekly series on WCBS-TV. I was glued to the set and Walter Cronkite from the first bulletin through the funeral, absorbing one incredible detail after another. Oswald shoots Officer Tippett, he's captured in a movie house, Ruby kills him. It was beyond understanding, like being hit repeatedly by Marvin Hagler.

It was numbing. My reaction was that of a person under anesthetic, with the feeling that somebody was trying to turn out all the lights.

Whatever thought I was able to give to the future of the country was a confidence that the transfer of power would be orderly. The exemplary behavior of Lyndon Johnson and the Kennedy family had much to do with this confidence, but there was also an unquestioning faith that this country can absorb a blow like that without crumbling. We lost a lot that day, but not our balance.

Sincerely,

Ray Gandolf

Ellen Goodman

Ellen Goodman, a columnist for The Boston Globe *and the* Washington Post Writers Group, *won the Pulitzer Prize for Commentary in 1980. She has also appeared as a Broadcast Commentator on* "Spectrum" *and the* "Today Show."
[22]

The Boston Globe

I was 22 years old and working in my first job, in the wire room of Newsweek magazine. I was ripping copy off the old machines when suddenly they started making all the noises that tell you there's a bulletin. I remember reading, upside down, at the back of the machine, that Kennedy had been shot in the hand--or so I read it--and then in the head. We wandered around the office shellshocked, crying quietly, and then in the bizarre way of journalism, got to work. Even the lowliest of us and I was the lowliest. Like most people from Mass. I knew Kennedy. My father had worked in his campaign for the Senate. He'd been in our house. My parents had been to their wedding. It was one of those moments when you know that everything has changed.

Best,

Ellen Goodman

Ellen Goodman

Alex Haley

Alex Haley's bestsellers include The Autobiography of Malcolm X *and* Roots. *The latter was the basis for ABC TV's 1976 miniseries of the same name and drew the largest audience in television history.*
[42]

Alex Haley

I was in line in a bank in Rome, N.Y.
when I became aware of sundry other
people suddenly moving about briskly,
whispering to others urgently; finally
I asked someone, who told me "President
Kennedy's shot!"

I felt numbed, dazed; I didn't want to
believe it--and then I heard the news
bulletin on a radio someone had turned up.

I felt it would have a subduing effect
 upon the nation, that hopefully so much
of the extant divisiveness would subside,
 you know?

Yours sincerely,

Alex Haley

FIND THE GOOD — AND PRAISE IT

Floyd Kalber

Floyd Kalber has worked as a newscaster and reporter for "The Today Show," "NBC News," and WLS-TV, Chicago. He covered the national political conventions in 1960, 1964, 1968, and 1972.
[38]

WLS-TV

        ... I was in my office in Chicago preparing a newscast I was to air on the NBC Television network in the early afternoon of November 22, 1963. I walked to the wire room to check the latest copy when the bells on the UPI machine started ringing. I checked in response to the bells and saw the bulletin move on the Dallas shooting and the wounding of John Kennedy.

My first reaction was the get on the air with the news but that was already being handled by the local NBC station, WMAQ-TV. I had to wait and watch the wires and get my own program on the air. It did not go on. Chet Huntley and David Brinkley handled the continuous coverage for three days in New York and Washington.

The impact of all this: At the time I felt a great sadness. It was so senseless . . so unnecessary . . such a waste. There was also the question of how the public would react. As it turned out there was no need for concern.

        Sincerely,

        Floyd Kalber

Jim Lehrer

Jim Lehrer, of the "MacNeil/Lehrer Newshour," has received numerous awards for his broadcast journalism, including an Emmy and a Peabody Award. [29]

The MacNeil/Lehrer
NEWSHOUR

JIM LEHRER
ASSOCIATE EDITOR

I was having lunch in the restaurant at Dallas Love Field, having just covered the arrival of President and Mrs. Kennedy in Dallas. I was a reporter for the Dallas Times Herald at the time.

My first reaction was one of anger. My second reaction was to call the city desk to confirm it had happened and to get orders. I was told to go to the Dallas police station, where I stayed for the next 24 hours.

I felt it would change our country in some kind of deep and everlasting way but I had no idea of how.

My best,

Jim Lehrer

James A. Michener

James Michener's books include The Bridges at Toko Ri, Space, Texas, *and* Alaska. *In 1948 he won the Pulitzer Prize for* Tales of the South Pacific.
[56]

UNIVERSITY OF
Miami

I was working in Haifa, Israel on my next novel <u>The Source</u>. It was Friday night, a holy day for Jews, and we were invited to an evening service in a Jewish home. I noticed that the host and other guests, all Israelis, were markedly somber, and at the close of the service one man said: 'Michener, we have bad news. Your President has been shot,' and when we turned on the television, this was confirmed. Said one man: 'My God! I hope the assassin wasn't a Jew.'

I went back to my informal office in the Dan Carmel and typed out a long memorandum to myself, which is on file in a library somewhere. Later I had two thoughts about that memo. I was amazingly accurate in some of my reactions. I am now not proud of some of my speculations.

My long long memorandum dealt with that and I believe I said quite firmly: 'The eastern seaboard clique will never accept Johnson as either their president or their leader. His gauche manners and rough speech will alienate them, and I see trouble for the Democrats. In 1964 he was elected by an enormous majority, but by 1967 my prediction had come true.

Sincerely,

James A. Michener
Distinguished Visiting Professor

222

Norman Vincent Peale

Norman Vincent Peale is the editor of Guideposts Magazine *and the host of the nationally syndicated radio program, "The Power of Positive Thinking." He was awarded the Presidential Medal of Freedom in 1984.*
[65]

Norman Vincent Peale

. . .

when I first heard the news of the shooting of President Kennedy, I was in my office at Guideposts Magazine, Carmel, New York.

My first reaction to this incredible news was to get on the communicating system and speak to the 500 employees asking them to immediately cease whatever they were doing and each in his or her own way to pray that the President's life would be spared.

On the date of his death, I think, the chief impact on the nation was to bring the people together, for there is a basic feeling about the presidency that the President, in a sense, is the person of the people; and therefore, the people themselves had been dishonored and maltreated. Of course, being a popular President, there was also a deep sense of personal grief.

Sincerely yours,

Norman Vincent Peale

223

Gayle Sierens

In 1987, Gayle Sierens, a newscaster for WXFL-TV in Tampa, became the first woman to announce a network televised NFL game.
[9]

I remember that day, the day President Kennedy was shot, rather vividly. I was in third grade at Christ the King Catholic School at the time. The principal had announced it to the school earlier in the day that President Kennedy had been shot. It wasn't until later, as I stood in line to catch the bus home that one of the nuns, Sister Marie Carl came outside to tell us the President had died. All afternoon at school we had been asked to pray for him.

I remember being very sad. I had just seen him a short time before as he toured Tampa. I liked his smile and knew he was very important. My mother adored him, and spoke of him often at home. I remember her crying.

I'm not sure I understood the impact his loss would have–I was too young. I did sense that we had lost someone very special.

God Bless,

Gayle Sierens

John Updike

John Updike's books include Rabbit, Run, Rabbit Is Rich, The Centaur, *and* The Witches of Eastwick. *He is a recipient of the National Book Award, the Pulitzer Prize, and the American Book Award.*
[31]

I was sitting in my dentist's office on Beacon Street, in Brookline, MA. The soothing music was broken into by a bulletin from Dallas, and then some more, so that by the time my appointment ended I knew that the President was dead.

I was saddened and dismayed, of course. I had voted for Kennedy and admired his style, especially in news conferences.

On that date, I thought the nation would be shocked and mourn, which it did, but I did not think that governmental policy would change to any significant degree under Johnson.

Yours sincerely,

John Updike

Abigail Van Buren

Through her syndicated column, "Dear Abby,"
Abigail Van Buren has advised thousands of
Americans on subjects ranging from sexual abuse
and health to alcoholism and self-esteem.
[45]

Dear Abby

My husband and I were in Tokyo, traveling the
Orient with then California Attorney General,
Stanley Mosk and his wife. (He is now Associate
Justice of the California State Supreme Court.)

We were awakened about 5 a.m. by a telephone
call from the States, relating the terrible news
of Kennedy's assassination. We turned on our TV
sets. (Satellite TV had been in Japan for only one
week.) Of course we saw Jack Ruby kill Oswald.

Our reaction? Shock, horror and disbelief.
We were enormously touched by the obvious sincere
sympathy extended by the Japanese people. Where-
ever we went--in the elevators, in the hotel lobby
and on the streets of Tokyo--the Japanese people
bowed their heads and said, "So sorry about your
president."

We were in no mood to continue our vacation,
so we cut our trip short and returned home.

Sincerely

Abigail Van Buren

Abigail Van Buren
(Mrs. Morton Phillips)

Besides co-anchoring the CBS news magazine "60 Minutes," Mike Wallace has also appeared on "Night Beat" and "Biography." He is the author of Close Encounters. [45]

CBS NEWS

I was working in the CBS Newsroom in New York when the first bulletins cleared.

My reaction was shock, and the hope that he'd be alright, that it was only a superficial wound.

After the bad news had sunk in, I didn't think so much of what impact his death would have on the nation. Rather I was moved and reassured by the way the machinery of government worked to assure quick continuity.

Sincerely,

Mike Wallace
Senior Correspondent
CBS News/60 MINUTES

Arthur Walworth

Arthur Walworth is the author of Black Ships Off
Japan, Cape Breton, *and* Wilson and His Peace-
makers. *In 1958, his two volume biography of Woodrow
Wilson was awarded a Pulitzer Prize.*
[60]

I heard about the shooting over a radio while walking down the
street in New Haven.

I was chilled by the obvious menace to law and order, and also by
the prospect that this flawed man, for whom I had voted only because
Nixon was impossible, and who seemed unworthy of canonization,
might come to be worshipped as a martyr and thus weaken the nation's
moral fiber.

Sincerely yours,

Arthur Walworth

Arthur Walworth

VII

THE ENTERTAINMENT WORLD RECALLS THE DEATH OF THE PRESIDENT

"Art establishes the basic human truths which must serve as the touchstones of our judgement. The artist...becomes the last champion of the individual mind and sensibility against an intrusive society and an officious state....I see little of more importance to the future of our country and our civilization than full recognition of the place of the artist. If art is to nourish the roots of our culture, society must set the artist free to follow his vision wherever it takes him."
– *President Kennedy at Amherst, Massachusetts, 1963.*

John and Jacqueline Kennedy's move into the White House ushered in a renaissance of the arts in Washington, which vicariously spread across the country. Arthur Schlesinger later wrote about Kennedy: "He saw the arts not as a distraction in the life of a nation but as something close to the heart of a nation's purpose....The arts therefore were, in his view, part of the presidential responsibility, and he looked for opportunities to demonstrate his concern." Kennedy promoted the arts by inviting artists from every field to the White House.

Once, in response to an invitation to a White House dinner, author John Steinbeck noted the change in attitude in Washington: "What a joy that literacy is no longer prima facie evidence of treason." As if to reiterate John Kennedy's commitment to the arts, the only permanent memorial to him in Washington is the John F. Kennedy Center for the Performing Arts.

Kennedy's interest in the arts earned him the respect of the entertainment world. Always conscious of image, entertainers saw in John Kennedy a certain star quality. Young, handsome, vigorous, and witty, Kennedy could command the very medium which could make or break celebrities: television. Now representatives from every sector of the entertainment world reflect on John Kennedy, remembering how they learned of his death, and sharing their feelings about him.

Edward Asner

Perhaps best known for his role as Lou Grant on "The Mary Tyler Moore Show," Edward Asner has also appeared in "Roots" and "Fort Apache, The Bronx." He has served as President of the Screen Actors Guild.
[34]

EDWARD ASNER

I was in Sacramento, in the State Capitol building, when I first heard of the Kennedy shooting...I was filming a series with Richard Crenna--SLATTERY'S PEOPLE--which dealt with lawyers and politics. We were rehearsing at the time, and everyone else had taken a break...a wardrobe person came in to adjust the suit I was wearing and said, "Isn't it horrible about President Kennedy?"

Standing in the State Capitol building, hearing the news had a profound impact on me, and I felt great sadness and loss. I feel it would be a better world today if we had not lost Jack Kennedy.

Edward Asner

Dan Aykroyd

Emmy Award winning actor Dan Aykroyd was a mainstay in the early years of NBC's "Saturday Night Live." His film credits include "Ghostbusters," and "The Blues Brothers."
[11]

D. E. AYKROYD

I was eleven years old at the time and recall now that aside from the explosion of Challenger, this event is the only one about which I can recall exact time, place, and reaction.

I was in afternoon recess at Annunciation Primary School in Hull, Quebec, Canada. The news came across the playground in a wildfire chain of children's voices. Like many there, I wept at the news and even as a Canadian felt a strange insecurity for the future.

I feared that possible invasion from Soviet aggressors might occur. The reason for this was that all of us at school had been politically aware of events like the Cuban missile crisis, as a couple of months previous to that time in history a 60-foot steel pole with a huge air raid siren had been installed in the schoolyard where I heard the news.

Burt Bacharach

Among composer Burt Bacharach's hits are "What the World Needs Now Is Love," and "Do You Know the Way to San Jose?" He received Academy Awards for his score for Butch Cassidy and the Sundance Kid, *and for the song,"Raindrops Keep Fallin' on My Head."*
[34]

BURT BACHARACH

I WAS IN THE BRILL BUILDING IN NEW YORK CITY
WRITING A SONG WITH HAL DAVID. IMMEDIATELY
LEFT THE BUILDING AND WANDERED EAST TO
P.J.CLARKES. I GOT SMASHED AND INTO A FIGHT
WITH SOME PEOPLE WHO WERE HAVING A GOOD TIME
LAUGHING ETC., TOTALLY DISRESPECTFUL OF THE
MOMENT.

I GOT UP THE NEXT MORNING AND THOUGHT I'D
DRIVE DOWN TO BUCKS COUNTY TO GET AWAY
FROM IT ALL. ON THE WAY I DROPPED MY DOG
OFF AT THE VETS OFFICE, IT WAS PLANNED
HE WOULD BE PUT TO SLEEP THAT DAY.

GOT TO THE HOTEL ROOM AND TURNED ON
THE TELEVISION. IT SEEMED LIKE I
NEVER STOPPED WATCHING AND NEVER LEFT

THE ROOM FOR TWO DAYS. EVERYTHING JUST
STOPPED, THE COUNTRY, THE SPIRIT, ALL
THE HOPES.

YEARS LATER YOU JUST KEPT THINKING
WHAT MIGHT HAVE BEEN.

Joan Baez

Folk/Rock Singer Joan Baez was widely-recognized for her stands in the antiwar and civil rights movements of the late 1960s and early 1970s. Her hit recordings include "The Night They Drove Old Dixie Down."
[22]

I was shopping for groceries early one morning, just as the coastline mist was lifting from the quiet November streets of Carmel, and the checkout man said casually but importantly, "Kennedy's been shot."

I didn't understand what he was talking about, and nodded and smiled and lugged the groceries off to the car. But his voice kept running through my mind, and with a queer sensation creeping up my spine, I turned on the radio.

Kennedy had been shot, but he was still alive and the entire country was in a sickly panic. I felt the stirrings of hysteria within me, not really knowing why. I didn't believe the myths about him so much as I wanted him to be a heroic figure.

Reprinted with permission from And a Voice to Sing With: A Memoir *by Joan Baez, Summit Books, New York, New York, 1987.*

Kaye Ballard

Actress Kaye Ballard starred in the '60s sitcom, "The Mothers-in-Law."
[37]

KAYE BALLARD

When I first heard the news of the shooting,
I was on my way home in a taxi in
Greenwich Village. The driver & I were
stunned & frightened, and began talking
as if we'd always known each other —
On that dreadful day, <u>nobody</u> was a stranger,
<u>nobody</u> was indifferent.

For the rest of the day & so many days after,
my friends & I watched the TV over & over & over,
constantly, in a state of shock & grief.
It was the beginning of the end of so many proud
hopes. It was the saddest day I can remember.

Kaye Ballard

Gene Barry

Actor Gene Barry's film credits include Purple Mask, China Gate, *and* Soldier of Fortune. *He also appeared in the TV series,* "Bat Masterson," *and in such Broadway plays as* "The Perfect Setup" *and* "La Cage Aux Folles."
[41]

G E N E   B A R R Y

On that terrible morning I was filming a segment of my television series "Burke's Law" in Los Angeles with actor Kevin McCarthy. A stagehand came in saying he thought President Kennedy had been shot. We scolded him for joking about a thing like that.

It was very shortly confirmed. Kevin and I had to stop working. We couldn't go on. Four Star Studios sent all of us home and then closed down.

I was filled with deep grieving and felt that the future of America and the world had been seriously changed and set back. To this day, I haven't gotten over it.

Why is it always the "good guys"?

Gene Barry

Ralph Bellamy

Ralph Bellamy starred in the films Sunrise at Campobello, Rosemary's Baby, *and* Oh, God!, *among others. On TV, he has appeared in "Eleventh Hour," "The Winds of War," and "Gunsmoke."*
[59]

RALPH BELLAMY

I was shooting an episode of a Tv
series(THE ELEVENTH HOUR), at MGM, when someone came
on the set with word that J.F.K. had been shot.

We were shocked.

Everyone in the cast and crew just
stood riveted and gazed sightlessly.
After a lapse of what seemed a half hour or so, the
producer said to me "What do you think? What should
we do?". I said "Well, the Theatre tradition is 'The
show must go on.'"
We tried to go back to work but the actors couldn't
remember their lines and the crew was distrait.

We went home.

My feeling about J.F.K.'s death
was that perhaps the international relations and good
will he had initiated might fade. In fact that kind of

disintegration seems to have grown since the time of his death.

Sincerely,

[signature]

Stephen Bishop

Singer/Composer Stephen Bishop was named Best New Male Vocalist at the 1977 Rock Music Awards. Among his better known albums are Red Cab to Manhattan, Bish, Careless, *and* Sleeping with Girls.
[11]

I was in beginning Music class with clarinet in hand as my teacher Mr. Hume announced, "The President has been shot."

He gave us the impression that he would live though. It was 7th grade, Horace Mann Jr. High.

I was stunned but being one of the highest ranking twerps of my grade, I didn't take it with the maturity of an adult. I was upset about missing all my regular cartoon programming. The effect it had on everyone around me made me realize the heaviness of what had happened. Everyone in my school really liked Kennedy, he was *the young* President.

At that time, things were in a whirlwind. No one would have suspected a conspiracy on my block. I was a newspaper boy in San Diego and I had sold lots of newspapers. I think people felt insecure of what our Nation would do. It was very sad and I was unsure as to what would happen but at the same time, I had trust in what would happen to our system.

[signature]

P. S. Some say the Beatles' popularity flourished from the wave of mourning Kennedy's death. That the Nation wanted to finally forget and continue life as we would never know again.

237

Erma Bombeck

Humorist Erma Bombeck's column, "Wit's End," is nationally syndicated. She is the author of the bestsellers, The Grass Is Always Greener over the Septic Tank *and* Family: The Ties that Bind and Gag. [36]

Erma Bombeck

My husband had just had back surgery. I was chairman of the church bazaar and was giving my parents an anniversary party.

My reaction to the news was absolute numbness as we moved from one event to the other. My first thought was, "What have we become?" Were we going to be like other nations who, when they didn't like their leader, simply got rid of him?

I could not possibly have foreseen what followed.

Kind regards

Erma Bombeck

Michael Caine

British film star Michael Caine has appeared in Alfie *(Academy Award),* The Ipcress File, The Man Who Would Be King, Educating Rita, *and* The Fourth Protocol, *among other motion pictures.*
[30]

MICHAEL CAINE

I was getting ready to go out for the evening and listening to music on the radio when the programme was interrupted and informed us that Kennedy had been shot.

I was stunned and did not want to go out, however, it was too late to cancel dinner. When I got to the restaurant everybody, ofcourse, was in the same state of shock. Basically, because I think we knew that it was the end of an unique and important new era. Most of the women were crying and I remember thinking quite suddenly how strange that they should be, when it wasn't even our President, but, ofcourse, they were right to cry because things would never be the same again.

Yours sincerely,

Michael Caine

Dick Clark

Dick Clark has hosted and produced numerous TV programs devoted to Rock and Roll music, including "American Bandstand," "Elvis," and "American Music Awards."
[34]

We were travelling with the Dick Clark Caravan of Stars. This was a busload of popular music artists on a tour of one-nighters. On November 22, 1963, we arrived in Dallas.

That afternoon, I was to attend a Dr. Pepper softdrink convention. In preparation for my appearance, I went to a meeting of executives. One of them mentioned the fact that President Kennedy was to be in town later that day. Someone else in the room commented on the fact that there was a great deal of security for the President; he was the center of some controversy at the moment. At that point, another person told a current joke that was going around. It was about a bystander who was observing all presidential security and quipped "oh, hell, who'd want to shoot Jack Kennedy - he ain't done nothin'".

Following the meeting, I went to my room to rest. I called a programming executive at ABC in New York. He wasn't in his office so I left word.

Later on in the afternoon, he awakened me with a call, saying, "You're in Dallas?"

I said, "Yes. It's a long way from home - not a great place to be."

He said, "You're right. What's happened?"

In my confusion, I said, "I don't know what you're talking about."

He said, "You mean to tell me you don't know President Kennedy has been shot?"

That was the first word I heard of it, an event that had happened just a few blocks from my hotel. He naturally assumed I was calling with some report or comment. Like everyone else, I was stunned.

I called the road manager of the tour. We conferred.

In those days, I kept a diary. The notation for
November 22, 1963 read: "I wonder if there'll be a show
tonight." I was so shocked at the news that I couldn't
properly focus on the President's death.

By the way, the program that night was cancelled.
Strangely enough we went on to perform the next night
and every night thereafter. In retrospect, I guess we
just went on with our lives..We did what we had to do,
which probably is the universal reaction to losing
someone. The survivors must continue on.

Sincerely,

Dick Clark

DICK CLARK

"We are underexercised as a nation. We look instead of
play. We ride instead of walk. Our existence deprives us of
the minimum of physical activity essential for healthy living.
The remedy, in my judgment, lies in one direction—that is,
in developing programs for broad participation in exercise
by all of our young men and women..."
    —Before the National Football Foundation, 1961

Rosemary Clooney

Among Rosemary Clooney's hit recordings are "Come-on-a-My-House" and "Tenderly." Her acting credits include White Christmas *and* Here Come the Girls.
[35]

Rosemary Clooney

I was rehearsing the Gary Moore Show at the Ziegfeld Theatre in New York City. The control room switched monitors to the network after the first Cronkite report.

The show was cancelled. I drove to Philadelphia to be with my husband who was working on a show. I talked to my family and stayed in front of the television set for three days.

I had worked on President Kennedy's campaign and I was devasted by his death. I felt as though it would never be the same again, and I don't believe it has. *Is . ever will be —*

Sincerely,

Rosemary Clooney

Doris Day

In addition to starring in her own TV series, Doris Day has been featured in such films as Pillow Talk *and* Please Don't Eat the Daisies. *Her hit recordings include* "Lullaby of Broadway" *and* "Que Sera, Sera."
[39]

DORIS DAY

When I think back to the day I heard the news of President Kennedy's assassination, I remember that I wasn't feeling well and was home in bed, even though I was working on a film at the time. I was watching TV, and the program was interrupted with a special news bulletin. I was in shock. I just couldn't believe it.

I picked up the phone and immediately called my husband, Marty, at the office. Then I called friends and it seemed that we all just wanted to talk and console each other. What a needless tragedy and one that this country will <u>never</u> <u>ever</u> <u>forget</u>!

Most Sincerely,

Doris Day

Doris Day

Jimmy Dean

Before becoming Chairman of the Board of the Jimmy Dean Meat Company in 1972, entertainer Jimmy Dean appeared on ABC's "The Jimmy Dean Show." He recorded "Big Bad John" in 1961.
[35]

Jimmy Dean
Chairman of the Board

I was seated in my den talking on the phone to a man named John Denny in Nashville discussing publishing rights on some material I had written and he said "My God, they have shot the President".

I dropped the phone, went immediately to the television set and never did remember to hang up the phone.

I feel it is pitiful the devastation wrought by crackpots throughout the world.

Sincerely,

Jimmy Dean

Jimmy Dean

Phyllis Diller

Phyllis Diller's film appearances include Eight on the Lam *and* The Private Navy of Sergeant O'Farrell. *She starred in the '60s TV program, "The Beautiful Phyllis Diller Show," and is the author of* Phyllis Diller Tells All about Fang.
[46]

Phyllis Diller

I was living in St. Louis and I was awakened by my New York theatrical agent with the news of President Kennedy's death.

It was one of those revelations you can't believe. You think it can't have happened.

But then, I turned on television and watched Jack Ruby shoot Lee Oswald "live" on the news.

I was appearing at a theatre in St. Louis called The Crystal Palace. I spoke with the manager of the theatre and told him I felt it would be bad taste to appear that night and do comedy. I was certainly in no mood to laugh; cry? yes.

— *Phyllis Diller*

245

Chad Everett

Actor Chad Everett starred in the TV programs "Cheyenne" and "Medical Center" and in such movies as The Impossible Years *and* The Singing Nun. [27]

Chad Everett Productions

When I first heard the news of President Kennedy's assassination, I was at home, studying—no radio or T. V. on. My close friend, Nan Moorse, came to the house to tell me, knowing how I revered the President. I campaigned for him. . . tested to portray him in *PT 109* and received a telegram from him saying he liked the test but thought I was too young.

It hit me like a chain reaction. . . having been personally consoled I hit the streets to be with other friends I knew would need someone close. I saw a man slumped over the wheel in the middle of Sunset and Highland, having just heard the news on his car radio. . . the light changed twice, no one honked or swore at him. Proof perhaps of the unifying effect JFK's Presidency and life had upon the nation.

The impact was first, one of mourning, second was that of anger and third, a bonding of patriotism, although the third probably didn't occur until later.

Without Doubt,

Chad Everett

Douglas Fairbanks, Jr.

Douglas Fairbanks, Jr. starred in the movies Dawn
Patrol, Sinbad the Sailor, Gunga Din, *and* Corsican
Brothers, *among others. He also has appeared in such
plays as* The Pleasure of His Company, My Fair
Lady, *and* Saturday's Children.
[54]

The Vicarage

        I was paying a brief visit to
London and was about to take my eldest
daughter to the theatre.

        I was unbelievably shocked, stunned -
as was virtually everyone, everywhere.

        Many of the after-thoughts follow-
ing the assassination were conjectures as to what
he would have accomplished had he lived.
Tragically, he did not have a chance to do
more than to give hopes of a brighter future.

                        Sincerely,

                        Douglas Fairbanks, Jr.

"Tennessee" Ernie Ford

Ernie Ford, a recording artist with Capitol Records from 1949–76, performed the first country music show in the Soviet Union in 1974. Perhaps the best known of his many recordings is "16 Tons."
[44]

On that unforgettable day, I was on the golf course.

A golf cart came speeding to get me, saying I had an emergency call. The call was from my dear Betty sobbing uncontrollable tears.

I began sharing her shock, and was reminded of the words we have heard so often—"We will not know the time or the place. Let us then be ready."

I then said a prayer for his family and our Nation.

Dick Gautier

Actor Dick Gautier won a Tony Award for his role in Bye Bye Birdie. *His film credits include* Divorce American Style, Ensign Pulver, *and* Fun with Dick and Jane.
[26]

When I heard about Kennedy's death I was on a motion picture set. The first thing I remember was a tremendous buzzing as the tragic news was passed from person to person in hushed whispers. Then, when everyone had been informed, an uneasy quiet settled down upon us. Everyone, from the coffee boy to the director stood impassively, drained..betrayed.

Betrayed by Kennedy's lack of perfection..he was vulnerable to harm. Betrayed like a child whose parents are thoughtless enough to die. Betrayed by the assassin (or assassins) who killed our President.

Most of my peers know exactly what they were doing at that fateful moment but to this day I can't remember the movie we were filming or the name of the studio. I guess I was too stunned and moved to be aware of the irrevelancies of place and time.

Kennedy's passing was the death of hope and trust. I pray another will someday emerge to rekindle the America spirit.

That much hope survives.

Sincerely,

Dick Gautier

249

Marla Gibbs

After appearing regularly as Florence on the long-running TV program, "The Jeffersons," actress Marla Gibbs headed the cast of "227." She has won five Image Awards for her acting and has been nominated for an Emmy five times.
[32]

MARLA GIBBS

Recalling the day of President Kennedys' assassination from my memory bank is still an emotional experience. I was working for the DSR in Dt. Michigan. As a Bus information operator when the call came in to the switch board, that the Pres. had been shot.

I was shocked and a feeling of numbness;grief came over me. I could'nt believe it. I kept praying and waiting to hear that he would pull through.

I felt the impact on the nation would be equally devastating and feared we might be thrown into civil disorder. I knew for certain that civil rights would suffer.

Sincerely,

Marla Gibbs

Robert Goulet

Singer/Actor Robert Goulet made his Broadway debut in Camelot *in 1960. He has received numerous awards for his recordings, including the Grammy, Tony, and Gold Medal Awards.*
[29]

Robert Goulet

I first heard of JFK's death on the set of a movie I was making.

We broke early and my eyes were misty listening to the radio on my drive home. My wife, Carol, greeted me at the door and we attempted to console each other but she insisted that I open a hugh box that had arrived (my birthday was but a few days later) that day. I said I really wasn't in the mood but she (I thought callously) insisted and when I inevitably gave in, my tears of pain turned to tears of joy, as out popped my (then) seven year old daughter, Nicolette.

His death was a blow to us all and for much time afterward the glimmer of hope for a better world for us all seemed to dim.

We got through it, we always do--but one can't help but wonder where this Nation would be today, had he remained at the helm.

ROBERT GOULET

James Gregory

Among James Gregory's film appearances was a role as John F. Kennedy's torpedo squadron commander in PT-109. He has starred in several TV series, including in the role of Inspector Luger on "Barney Miller," and has acted extensively on Broadway.
[51]

I was on Lasky Drive, Beverly Hills, California, just having left my business manager.

I was shocked, unbelieving, drained. . . then furious, incensed, angry!

I turned the radio off and drove rapidly but carefully to my home in Brentwood, hoping that the news on TV would correct, or alleviate the devastating news heard on the radio.

Truly,

James Gregory

Pat Harrington

Actor Pat Harrington's TV credits include "One Day at a Time," "The Steve Allen Show," and "The Danny Thomas Show."
[34]

PAT HARRINGTON

I was in Nassau, Bahamas, shooting a pilot with Carrol O'Connor and Robert Brown, called 'Yellow Bird'. Someone heard the news on the radio and as it spread through cast and crew, the shoot ground to a halt, as people peeled off in two's and three's in an attempt to understand the event.

I was poleaxed, absolutely devastated. He was my hero and I loved him, one Irish Catholic for another.

I felt that his assassination would foster a climate of vengeful retribution, which we as a people would never completely overcome. Thank God I was wrong.

Sincerely,

Helen Hayes

Helen Hayes has appeared on stage in productions of Pollyanna, A Farewell to Arms, *and* Long Day's Journey into Night, *and on film in* Anastasia, *and* Helen Hayes: Portrait of an American Actress. *She is the recipient of both the Emmy and Academy Awards.*
[63]

I well remember where I was when I heard that President Kennedy had been killed.

My party and I had just arrived in Oaxaca, Mexico, by car from Mexico City. We changed for dinner. As we came down into the lobby, we witnessed an incredible scene. A mature Mexican man was standing in front of a blaring t.v. set with tears streaming down his cheeks.

Someone told me what had occurred. From then on, we were stopped every few feet by weeping Mexicans, who expressed their sympathy to us.

We wanted to get away from the light, the noise, and the crowds, so we fled to the sidewalk tables outside the hotel.

A Mexican came to our table with a radio, which was broadcasting news in English. He put the radio down, said that we could keep it for the evening and that he would pick it up from us the next morning.

The only other occupied table accommodated two couples of weeping North Americans. One said, "We're from Texas. We feel a double horror at what has happened. Please don't hate us."

I myself felt a sense of shame before these grieving Mexicans. We fled to our room, where we waited quietly until we could leave for my home in Cuernavaca the next morning.

As I entered through my garden gateway, my housekeeper welcomed me with out-stretched arms. She, too, was crying.

I had no thoughts of the effect of the event upon the nation. I thought only of the shame and pain I was sharing with all of the caring Mexicans.

Sincerely,

Helen Hayes

Florence Henderson

Florence Henderson starred in the long-running TV series, "The Brady Bunch." Her stage appearances include roles in The Sound of Music, South Pacific, Annie Get Your Gun, *and* Oklahoma!
[29]

Florence Henderson

When I first heard of the President's death I was in Philadelphia starring in a show called "The Girl Who Came to Supper" at the Colonial Theater.

Some friends of mine, Frank and Jane Egan, had come from Detroit to see the show. We had gone to lunch and as we came back in the hotel somebody yelled, "He's been shot!" We asked, "Who's been shot?" He said "The President." I went into a state of shock. I could not believe it. Like everyone else in the nation, I guess, I truly loved President

Kennedy. I believed in him and I admired
what he stood for. He had given everyone
such tremendous hope, especially me. I said,
"I have to go somewhere. I have to pray."
I remember going into this Catholic Church
and people were pouring in. I knelt down
and cried as I prayed. I just didn't understand
what had happened. I was filled with fear
that such a thing could occur in our country.
I couldn't dream of going to the theater
to do a performance. I was like a robot and
when I got into the part about the Bill of
Rights, which was supposed to be funny, I
could hardly get through it and tears ran
down my face.

I had a baby who was born at the same time
as little Patrick Kennedy so I was very caught
up in the similarities of our lives. The
fact that my baby was alive and healthy and
their baby was dead, and now the President
was dead, was just too overwhelming for me.

I had attended a gym class with Jacqueline
Kennedy in New York at one time. I wrote
her a long letter expressing my feelings of
sorrow about President Kennedy's death. I
did receive a reply. I'm sure it was a standard
formal reply that everyone got, but I just
felt so helpless. I wanted to do something
for them. I remember that it hurt me so deeply
and scared me so that I never watched one
bit of it on the news. I couldn't read the
papers. It took me years to be able to
look at anything surrounding that event. I
can now look at it with some emotional
detatchment but at that time it just broke
my heart.

I felt that his death would have such a
tremendous impact on the nation and the world.
I felt that his murder probably was a conspiracy and that if people could commit such a
horrendous act, what would be next?

I had two children, a daughter, Barbara, who
was seven and a son, Joseph, who was three
which was Caroline's age, and I was so concerned
about the effect that it would have on them
to know that such a despicable thing could
happen in our country.

As you can tell, President Kennedy's death
had a tremendous effect on me. I don't think
that anything has ever rocked our nation
in quite that way. This is probably because
of all the media we have and the immediate
impact that the graphic coverage had on all
of us -- that we sould see it just as it
happened. It's at times like these that I
wish we didn't have such immediate news.

Most Sincerely,

Florence Henderson

"What kind of peace do I mean?...I am talking about
genuine peace, the kind of peace that makes life on earth
worth living, the kind that enables men and nations to grow
and to hope and to build a better life for their children—not
merely peace for Americans, but peace for all men and
women; not merely peace in our time, but peace for all time."
—*At the American University, 1963*

John Houseman

Perhaps best known for his role as Professor Kingsfield on "The Paper Chase," John Houseman has also appeared in "Seven Days in May," and "The Winds of War." He has directed many operas and plays, including productions of The Devil and Daniel Webster *and* Hamlet.
[61]

... One of my projects [was a film] for New York's 1964 World's Fair. ... It was to be a twelve-minute film dealing with the history of immigration in the United States over the past two hundred years. ... I was informed that it was being made at the express request of President Kennedy to help create a favorable climate for the new immigration laws he was about to submit to Congress.

... I was lunching in the Oak Room of the Plaza Hotel, discussing a point in the script with one of Kennedy's bright young men when the news came—in whispered disbelief at first, then confirmed on the ticker and spreading like wildfire—that the President had been wounded and, a moment later, that he was dead. I remember drifting, aimless and incredulous, from table to table and then out onto Fifth Avenue, where drivers sat frozen behind the wheels of their buses and taxis and pedestrians stared at one another or talked in bewildered whispers.

Reprinted with permission from Final Dress *by John Houseman, Simon & Schuster, New York, New York, 1983.*

Billy Joel

Singer/composer Billy Joel's albums include The Stranger *and* 52nd Street. *Among his best known singles are* "It's Still Rock and Roll to Me," "Just the Way You Are," *and* "Only the Good Die Young."
[14]

Billy Joel

I was in my 8th grade English class in Hicksville Junior High School and I heard the principal announce the news over the P.A. system.

I couldn't absorb the enormity of the assassination at first and I remember consoling a girl who was crying. Later that day, I took a long walk alone and felt a deep bitterness and a despair I had never before experienced in my childhood.

I worried that the energy and idealism of John Kennedy represented to the youth of our nation would loose its momentum and would be replaced by cynicism and politics-as-usual.

Sincerely,

Billy Joel

Clare Kirkconnell

Actress Clare Kirkconnell portrayed Rita Harriman in the award-winning television series, "The Paper Chase."
[6]

I was very young, in first or second grade. I remember the confusion, the teachers turning on radios, running to each other from class to class. I did understand that he was our President, but what most affected me was seeing the grief and confusion it inflicted on all of the adults. It was the first time in my life I had seen adults behave as vulnerably as children. It was both scary and enlightening.

Sincerely,

Clare Kirkconnell

Kreskin

"The Amazing Kreskin" has given demonstrations of his powers of ESP on such television programs as "The Tonight Show."
[28]

I am invariably asked if I had an premonition or feeling' that this tragedy had taken place. I was attending Seton Hall University in South Orange, New Jersey during this year, although I was already appearing and travelling as a professional mentalist. I had no classes on Nov. 22. It was a bleak dreary day and at that time I was living at home with my folks. I never turned on the television in the afternoon, I just didn't care for it, but for some peculiar reason, I thought I would turn on the TV, find some program and suggest that my mother might want to watch it. It was an action I don't ever remember doing before. But whatever the program was, I found it uninteresting but within one minute I saw across the screen on the CBS station the word bulletin, and then the announcement that the President had been shot and finally Walter Cronkite's statement that Kennedy was dead.

My immediate reaction was one of horror and then an impending gloom. It's almost as if the day and the setting became an intringic part of this tragic experience and, indeed, the gloom descended around me.

What I considered initially was more in a socialogical sense, the impact that this tragedy would have, particularly since my work deals with human behavior and the feeling and the thoughts of others. I had a sense that people would want to come closer together in this national period of berievement. I was also aware that it could have been a dangerous time because it is just such periods that a ruthless individual with a charismatic personality could

261

take control over large masses of people. At this period
using the media of television. Fortunately, and I suspect
the industry was cautious, no such ruthless individual appeared
on the scene. Instead you had the presence of figures like
Walter Cronkite who gave a cohesive almost paternal security
to the American people. In a sense a man like Cronkite
reflected the feeling of the American people but did it
professionally and in a commentary manner, but I couldn't
help from time to time thinking back to the recordings I
heard as a child of another legendary coverage of the death
of a president that has been played hundred of times in
classrooms that of Arthur Godfrey on CBS describing the
funeral of President Roosevelt and then finding himself unable to complete the coverage, breaking down sobbing on radio.

In a sense the availability of television and radio gave us in
our period of sorrow a feeling of security and I mean not only
personally but nationally. Thank God I was not outside the

United States when this happened. I know I would have felt
desolate and lost.

ESPecially,

KRESKIN

> "How much better it would be, in the turbulent sixties, to
> have a Roosevelt or a Wilson than to have another James
> Buchanan, cringing in the White House, afraid to move."
> —*Before the National Press Club during the 1960 campaign*

Michael Learned

Actress Michael Learned has appeared in the TV programs, "The Waltons," "Police Story," and "Gunsmoke."
[24]

MICHAEL LEARNED

I was in Toronto, Canada taping a show called, "Morgan" when the news was announced. Everything stopped. My first reaction was disbelief and then utter shock. In deference to President Kennedy and to that terrible event, We stopped tape and didn't film anymore that day.

Shock, disbelief and horrible numbness.

On the day of his assasination I was 24 years old and could not believe that something like this could happen in America in my lifetime. Little did I know, at that time, what was to come; that assasination and terrorism would become almost daily occurences in our troubled world.

Sincerely,

Michael Learned

Loretta Lynn

Country & Western singer Loretta Lynn is the author of the bestselling Coal Miner's Daughter.
[28]

My husband and I were in Texas going North out of Dallas to Amarillo when we heard about it on our car radio. 'Mooney', my husband stopped some other cars that were traveling with us to make sure they had heard it too.

I just couldn't believe it and started praying that he would live. I have to say it was one of the saddest days of my life. At first all of us thought about canceling our concert for that night but decided at the last minute to go on with the show.

I guess my first reaction was that I thought we would have a problem holding things together in this country. I never go to to Texas or Washington D.C. without thinking of President Kennedy.

Barbara Mandrell

*Singer Barbara Mandrell was named Country &
Western's Female Vocalist of the Year in 1978 and
1979. Her albums include* Midnight Oil *and* This
Time I Almost Made It.
[14]

I was in the 9th grade and heard the news while
at school.

I was shocked and remembered that I cried.

I was too young think of the impact his death might
have on the nation.

Lee Meriwether

Lee Meriwether was Miss America in 1955. Her television credits include "Batman," "The Man from U.N.C.L.E.," and "Barnaby Jones."
[28]

LEE•LEE•LEE•LEE•LEE•LEE•LEE•LEE•LEE•

... I was in bed nursing my second daughter, Lesley, who was born on November 11th of that year. The quiet time while nursing her was always very special for me and I would often hold her for quite a while after she finished. She had, up to that time, been in perfect health.

When I heard the news on television, she stopped nursing and started to cry. She became very irritable and, later, quite colicky. Months later, when relating that story, someone said "Well, your milk turned." I don't know if it's true or not. but I know I'd never felt that utter dispair before, and Lesley never again became ill after nursing.

As far as the effect of President Kennedy's death on the nation was concerned, my feelings then were of a much more personal nature, closer to home, so to speak. My own sense of shock was coupled with the thought of this baby in my arms, and wondering if, in her lifetime, she would ever know such a president as the one we had just lost.

Sincerely,
Lee Meriwether

Peter Nero

As one of the world's most celebrated pianists, Peter Nero has performed in the greatest concert halls around the globe.
[29]

peter nero

A few months ago, I performed in San Jose with their symphony orchestra and before the concert, was handed a note. It was from a man who, as a student at San Jose college in 1963, was a member of the committee that sponsored my appearance there and how vividly he remembered the sequence of events on that terrible day, November 22nd. His note transported me back to a point in time almost 25 years ago.

The airport in San Francisco was quieter than usual that day. Having landed from New York about noon, the normal hustle and bustle was virtually non-existent. The edge was off the voices of the skycaps and the rent-a-car agent. Just another bad day for everybody, I guessed.

While driving toward the city, I started changing stations on the radio and for the life of me, couldn't find anything other than classical or slow pop music. No jazz, no rock 'n roll. I switched from AM to FM and back and concluded that the reception outside the city must be pretty bad.

As I pulled up in front of the hotel, my drummer, who had arrived the night before, came running toward me, arms flailing, an expression on his face that was difficult to describe. "The President's been shot!" he shouted several times. Knowing that he was predisposed to practical jokes, I said, "Okay, okay, what's the punchline?"

After checking in and returning the frantic phone calls from my manager, the two of us and my bass player stayed glued to the TV set in my room. When the announcement came about the tragic finale to the life of one of our greatest leaders, I, like many others, sat there numbed in disbelief.

I jumped when the phone rang. I told my manager, not knowing that the college was already debating a postponement, that there was no way I could perform and that I was going home to be with my family. I took the next plane back to New York, doing a round trip in 24 hours. I cancelled all concerts for the next two weeks and subsequently replayed them later on that season.

On the plane to New York, the pieces began to fit: the austere mood at the airport, the strange programming on the radio stations. What I could not understand was why no announcement was made by the crew on the way to San Francisco and why no one at the airport there mentioned a word. In retrospect, however, everyone else was probably as numb as me and, like myself, didn't want to believe what had happened.

I suppose everyone has a series of dates that they want to remember, usually birthdays, anniversaries of their own and those of family and close friends; all happy occasions. November 22, 1963 is a date that is an exception but one that will forever be embedded in my memory.

Buck Owens

Country & Western singer Buck Owens joined the cast of the television show, "Hee-Haw," in 1969.
[34]

Buck Owens Production Company, Inc.

I was in Corpus Christi, Texas on
November 22, 1963.

Unbelievable event and appalling.
I kept thinking they would come back
on the radio and say it was a mistake,
but when they did come back on, they said
that President Kennedy had been shot and died.

I had no idea. That thought never entered my
mind. My only thought was, how could anyone
shoot another person, let alone the President
of the United States. I knew it was going to
create some kind of a void, but I had no idea
what kind.

Sincerely,

Buck Owens

269

Gary Owens

Gary Owens's acting credits include "Rowan and Martin's Laugh-in," The Love Bug, and "Sesame Street." In 1980, he received the Hollywood Hall of Fame Award.
[27]

GARY OWENS
Supreme High Nurgle

My three-year-old son, Scott and I were in a barber shop in the San Fernando Valley when the news came on the TV. Everyone in there was shocked.

Numbed by the news, and wanting much more information, we went home and told my wife, Arleta, and one month old son, Chris, what had occured. Being a former newscaster, I then phoned the radio station where I worked and all three network news departments to gather as much data as possible.

I don't recall thinking about the nation's impact at that point as much as the anger and depression that all of us felt because of the heinous deed.

Best personal regards,

Gary Owens

Patti Page

*Singer Patti Page's recordings include "Confess,"
"Tennessee Waltz," and "Graduation Day."*
[36]

PATTACK PRODUCTIONS, INC.

I was at my mother and fathers home in
Tulsa, Oklahoma watching the parade live
on television from Dallas. With me was
my one-year-old daughter on my left.

Incredulous. Unbelivevable. And to have
witnessed it live on television, was even
more devastating.

I had lost a friend and the spokesman of my
generation.

Best wishes,

Patti Page

Cliff Robertson

Emmy Award winning actor Cliff Robertson portrayed John F. Kennedy in the movie, PT-109. *Other film appearances include* Charly, *for which he won an Academy Award, and* Three Days of the Condor.
[38]

CLIFF ROBERTSON

... John F. Kennedy's death was not only America's loss, it was a loss of great promise to the world. We can't bring him back, but we can hold on to the memories of his ideals and purpose.

I will always be grateful to him personally - not only because he chose me to portray him in "PT-109" - but because of the impact he had upon my life as an American.

Sincerely,

Cliff Robertson

Roy Rogers

Roy Rogers starred in nearly ninety western films before establishing a chain of fast-food restaurants.
[51]

Roy Rogers — Dale Evans Museum

I was driving in my car when I heard the news over the radio, telling of the assassination of President Kennedy.

I was appalled to learn that anyone would assassinate our president, especially, when he was doing the best for our country that he possibly could. It proved to me that we have alot more subversive activists in our country than we realize.

After the initial shock of the news of the assassination, I immediately offered many prayers for Vice President Johnson, to have the guidance and the strength to become the leader that our great nation needed with the passing of President Kennedy.

Happy Trails

Roy Rogers

ROY ROGERS

Mark Russell

Political satirist Mark Russell appears regularly on TV on the "Mark Russell Comedy Specials." He is the author of Presenting Mark Russell.
[31]

MARK RUSSELL

I came out of the Keith Theatre in Washington about four in the afternoon on November 22, 1963 after seeing John Wayne in "McLinton." Already the newspapers were on the street with headlines of the shooting. A few weeks earlier, Adlai Stevenson had been hit over the head with a picket sign by right-wing kooks in Dallas and my initial reaction was that the shooting of President Kennedy must have been initiated by this same faction.

I was working in the lounge of Washington's Shoreham Hotel where many of the employees including myself were laid off for several weeks. One result of the assassination was that many conventions to be held in Wasington during 1964 were cancelled.

Sincerely,

Mark Russell

Susan Saint James

Susan Saint James has appeared in the TV shows "McMillan and Wife" and "Kate & Allie." She was awarded an Emmy in 1969.
[17]

At that time, I was modeling and staying at the Barbizon Hotel for Women. I received word that there was a last minute cancellation that day and decided to go to a movie starring James Garner. After the movie, I was walking back to the agency and, at about 6 p.m., stopped by St. Patrick's Cathedral. I remember wondering why the church was jammed with people, but decided to just leave. I continued on to my agency and got into the elevator. The elevator operator, a kind black man, said to me, 'Our President is dead.' I expressed my sorrow, thinking he was talking about the president of his union (certainly not the President of the United States!). I then walked into the agency where I finally learned what had happened. I fell totally apart – called home to talk to my Mother and Father – left the agency – got a cab and went straight to the airport to fly home to Rockford, Illinois to be with my family.

My knees went weak. I was shocked – surprised. I was a young Catholic girl of 17. I did not think this could happen in America – that anyone could shoot the President of the United States. After the assassination of JFK I left the country to live in France.

The day before John F. Kennedy died, we were still living in the 50s. Thereafter, I knew we had entered the decade of the 60s.

SUSAN SAINT JAMES

Neil Sedaka

Neil Sedaka is one of America's most successful singers and composers. His hits include "Happy Birthday Sweet Sixteen," "Calendar Girl," and "Laughter in the Rain."
[24]

NEIL SEDAKA

I was finishing a record promotion tour in Washington, D.C. with my dad. I saw the news on the T.V. at the airport.

I was in a state of limbo. Everything seemed to stand still. I felt I had lost a dear friend.

I thought JFK's death marked the end of a special era in history. People changed; times changed; attitudes as well. In some ways it was similar to the shock when FDR died.

Sincerely,

Neil Sedaka

Neil Sedaka

Artie Shaw

Artie Shaw, a popular Big Band leader in the 1930s and 40s, has produced a musical version of The Great Gatsby *on Broadway and appeared in the films* Dancing Coed *and* The Trouble with Cinderella. [53]

ARTIE SHAW

I was in New York City when I first heard the news.

My first reaction was incredulity followed by dismay, and finally a profound sense of depression.

I strongly felt that the impact of President Kennedy's assassination would be a growing sense of despair and cynicism about where our world and specifically the United States, was heading.

Cordially,

Artie Shaw

Dinah Shore

Dinah Shore was regularly featured on the Eddie Cantor radio program as a singer. She has hosted a variety of TV shows, including "The Dinah Shore Show" and "Dinah!"
[46]

Dinah Shore

I was in Palm Springs. The children were in school and I was just about to play in a tennis match. When I heard the news everything stopped, I could not - would not believe it. I sat riveted and weeping in front of the television set - changing from station to station for every crumb of news I could find, praying it wasn't so.

I was scheduled to perform that evening at a theatre-in-the-round in Anaheim. I, of course, could not do a performance nor did I think that anyone would want to be entertained on the evening of such a terrible, terrible day.

My sense of personal loss was so great and grievous I don't know if I stopped at that point to consider the profound impact the death of President Kennedy would have on our nation. My fears for our country gradually began to penetrate my grief, but the transition was so smooth it reinforced strongly my confidence in our system. But to this day I cannot help but wonder what would have happened if we had had the privilege of living a little longer in the aura of his magic and grace and compassionate wisdom.

Sincerely,

Dinah Shore

Singer Dinah Shore and her husband, George Montgomery, join President Kennedy at the White House. (John F. Kennedy Library)

> "This is one country. It has become one country because all of us and all the people who came here had an equal chance to develop their talents. We cannot say to 10 percent of the population that they can't have that right; that their children can't have the chance to develop whatever talents they have; that the only way that they are going to get their rights is to go into the streets and demonstrate. I think that we owe them and we owe ourselves a better country than that."
> — *Televised Address from the White House, June 11, 1963*

Robert Stack

Emmy Award winning actor Robert Stack has starred in many films, and has appeared on TV in "The Untouchables" and "Falcon Crest."
[44]

I first heard the news on a portable T.V. set at my duck lodge in Northern California.

My reaction was one of disbelief, horror and a sense of loss. John Kennedy was a friend of mine. In fact, at one time we were roommates. So the loss of a great president was compounded by the loss of a good friend.

... I had no idea what impact President Kennedy's death would have on the nation. I know what it had on me: first, shock, then outrage, then anger. I am not sure this country will ever fully recover from John Kennedy's assassination.

Sincerely,

Robert Stack

Elizabeth Taylor

Elizabeth Taylor has starred in such movies as National Velvet, Cat on a Hot Tin Roof, *and* The Mirror Crack'd. *She won Academy Awards for Best Actress in* Butterfield 8 *and* Who's Afraid of Virginia Woolf?, *in 1960 and 1966, respectively.*
[31]

ELIZABETH TAYLOR

A friend came over to see me and Richard Burton while we were staying in Puerta Vallarta, Mexico. I was reading when our friend walked in and said, "Kennedy's been shot."

"Oh my God, no. You don't mean he's been. . ." I couldn't say the word "killed."

"Yes. He's dead."

I just couldn't believe it. I woke Richard from a deep sleep. I shook him, "Richard, Kennedy's been shot dead!"

"Oh," said Richard, and went back to sleep.

One hour later he came downstairs and said: "Did you say what I think you said?"

We turned on and fiddled with the radio to find out any information. There were very few English channels and the transmission was awful. We kept switching channels until it was confirmed. I had a great feeling of hurt and anger and bereavement. I asked the question, why? To which of course there was no answer.

After the emotional release it was a couple of days before I thought of the affect the assassination would have on the nation. I felt very far away. I really didn't know, but knowing Americans, I presumed they would rally together and form a bond of grief. People of all parties would be united and hold a mental bond. Everyone was touched and affected. It did cause a united feeling.

John Travolta

John Travolta has starred in the films Saturday Night Fever, Grease, Staying Alive, *and* Urban Cowboy. *His television credits include* "Welcome Back Kotter."

John Travolta

We were dismissed early. My fourth grade teacher – can't remember her name. We were released at 2:00 P.M. or so. The class was shocked and somewhat amazed as though it were like a dream. The family spent most of the time in front of the television watching updates and news events, i. e. the Ruby-Oswald incident, etc., which brought more intrigue into it (as days went on). Also the kids, John Jr. and Caroline, could be identified with. But I do remember wishing a plane would have been named after me. The impression of wealth was apparent.

Robert Vaughn

Actor Robert Vaughn's TV credits include "The Man From U.N.C.L.E" and "Backstairs at the White House," while his film credits include The Young Philadelphians *and* The Magnificent 7. *In 1977, he won an Emmy Award for "Washington Behind Closed Doors."*
[31]

Robert Vaughn

Nov 22, 1963 was my birthday and the third day of filming of the pilot for "The Man From U.N.C.L.E." television series.

I was driving to the home of the U.N.C.L.E. dialogue director when the Arthur Godfrey radio show was interrupted by a bulletin that three shots had been fired at the Presidential motorcade in Dallas. It was 10:30 A.M. in Los Angeles.

I picked up my car phone to tell Bill Tynan, the dialogue director, the news; the operators were already hysterical.

I reached Tynan's home shortly before 11:00 A.M., L.A. time. The president was pronounced dead. I was traumatized and unable to work further on the pilot. I had no thoughts about the future that day, only the horrific present.

Regards,

283

Lawrence Welk

Bandleader Lawrence Welk, host of the long-running "Lawrence Welk Show," recorded many albums with his Champagne Music Makers, including Bubble in Wine *and* Sparkling Strings.
[60]

TELEKLEW PRODUCTIONS, INC.

I was playing golf at the Bel Air Country Club in Los Angeles when the news was announced. Our foursome immediately ended our game, in shock and disbelief.

I do not recall that I had any specific feelings about the future of our country as a result of the assassination. Instead, I was caught up in overwhelming sadness that our young president's life had been so cruelly terminated.

Sincerely,

Lawrence Welk

Betty White

In addition to appearing extensively on stage, Betty White has starred in such TV programs as "The Betty White Show," "The Mary Tyler Moore Show," and "The Golden Girls." She was awarded Emmys in 1975, 1976, and 1987.
[39]

Betty White

Four days before John F. Kennedy was assassinated, my father died. I was bringing my mother from California to join us for awhile in New York. In closing up the house, I called to temporarily cancel the Los Angeles Times. The girl who answered was in tears and told me what had just happened.

To this day, that whole week is a confused mixture of saying goodbye to two fine men. I loved them both in different ways, and appreciate the chance to say so.

Sincerely,

Betty

Betty White

285

David L. Wolper

David L. Wolper, Chairman of the Board of Wolper Productions, has produced such films as The Making of the President, The Journey of Robert F. Kennedy, *and* Willy Wonka and the Chocolate Factory. *His television credits include* "Welcome Back Kotter."
[35]

DAVID L.WOLPER PRODUCTIONS, INC.

OFFICE OF THE PRESIDENT

When John Kennedy was shot I was in my office in Los Angeles on Sunset Blvd. in a meeting and one of my associates ran into my office to tell me that Kennedy had been shot.

I had just finished completing a documentary based on Theodore H. White's Pulitzer Prize winning novel THE MAKING OF THE PRESIDENT 1960 which was about the election of John Kennedy vs. Richard Nixon.

Shortly after I heard that John Kennedy had been shot I received a call from Theodore H. White, the author of the book and also the author of the screenplay for the documentary. He informed me he was on his way to Washington D.C. to be with some of the family and stay at the house of Governor Averell Harriman in Washington D.C.

The documentary was set for release on American television during December. After the funeral, Theodore H. White and I discussed whether we should play the documentary in it's raw state, we decided to do so, and Teddy White decided that he would do an introduction at the beginning of the television program stating that John Kennedy was a man of politics and he would have liked to have seen the documentary released just the way it is, rough and tough, instead of being a sentimental piece. That is how we released the film THE MAKING OF THE PRESIDENT 1960 which played on the ABC Television network and which subsequently won four Emmy Awards, including the "Television Program of the Year" from the National Academy of Television Arts and Sciences.

My immediate reaction was the loss of a friend, as I had looked through so much film footage on John Kennedy for THE MAKING OF THE PRESIDENT 1960 and had hoped to meet him and screen the program for him.

I felt the impact, as I was a student of history, I believed strongly that in spite of John Kennedy that the nation would pick up, recover and continue.

I fortunately had the opportunity to produce for the 1964 Democratic Convention the film called A THOUSAND DAYS about John Kennedy's brief time in office, which was shown at the convention and over the three networks, introduced by Bobby Kennedy. It brought tears and sobs to the thousands of people who attended the 1964 Democratic Convention.

Very truly yours,

David L. Wolper

"We still need the men and women educated in the liberal traditions, willing to take the long look, undisturbed by prejudices and slogans of the moment, who attempt to make an honest judgment on difficult events....I do not suggest that our political and public life should be turned over to college-trained experts, ...nor would I adopt from the Belgian constitution a provision giving three votes instead of one to college graduates—at least not until more Democrats go to college."

—*At the University of North Carolina, 1961*

VIII

SPORTS FIGURES REMEMBER JFK, HIS LIFE AND HIS DEATH

"I'm glad to be here because I feel a sense of kinship with the Pittsburgh Pirates. Like my candidacy, they were not given much chance in the spring."
— *President Kennedy shortly after the Pirates won the pennant in 1960*

"Ladies and gentlemen, I was warned to be out of here in plenty of time to permit those who are going to the Green Bay Packers game to leave. I don't mind running against Mr. Nixon but I have the good sense not to run against the Green Bay Packers."
— *President Kennedy campaigning in Wisconsin in 1960*

John Kennedy was an avid sportsman, and an avid sports fan. As much as he enjoyed watching sporting events, he loved to participate in them even more. From his earliest days, Kennedy was taught to be a tough competitor, and when it came to sports, his competitive spirit was fierce.

In school he had been a swimmer and football player—although it was during a football game at Harvard that he suffered a back injury which plagued him for the rest of his life. He was also a skilled sailor, and often escaped from the hectic world of politics aboard his sailboat, usually off Cape Cod near his home in Hyannis Port, Massachusetts. Kennedy also loved to play golf, although he kept his golf game noticably quieter than his predecessor had.

John Kennedy often used the word vigor—although it came out sounding like "vigah"—and enjoyed it when the word was used by others to describe him. As President, he promoted physical fitness in others as well, and in a much-publicized move, challenged Americans to take fifty-mile hikes.

So it is no surprise that President Kennedy enjoyed a healthy following in the sports world. More than two dozen sports figures—many of them legends in the annals of sports—recall JFK, both as President and sportsman.

Mario Andretti

Mario Andretti has won the Daytona 500, the Indianapolis 500, and the World Grand Prix.
[23]

I first heard of the shooting on the radio when I was at work in Harmony, New Jersey at the only "job" I've held before embarking on my racing career.

My initital reaction was total shock. I had only been in this country for eight years and thought that a presidential assassination could not possibly happen in this country.

At that time, I don't think I had a clear perspective on the ultimate impact the assassination would have on the nation. The feelings of grief and disbelief shared by all seemed to unite the country.

Sincerely,

Mario Andretti

Mario Andretti

Arthur Ashe

Tennis Player Arthur Ashe rose to fame when he won the National Junior Championship at the age of 17. He has also won men's singles titles at the U.S. Open and Wimbledon.
[20]

ARTHUR R. ASHE, JR.

I was a 20 year old junior at UCLA and had just walked passed the athletic field on my way to classes when a group of co-eds came rushing out of the Student Union Building crying. I asked why everyone was crying and I heard that the President was shot. I preceded on to my Business Administration class on the other side of campus but was told that classes were canceled for the rest of the day. By the time I made my way back across campus to my dorm, the flags atop the library were flying at half-mast and the bells were ringing a song that I had not heard before.

All of the Black students at UCLA considered it a tragic loss as President Kennedy was the first such sitting president to closely identify himself with the plight of Black Americans since F.D.R. We all automatically assumed that the southern-born Vice-President Lyndon B. Johnson, would do everything in his power to return us to our segregationists days. Of course, that was not to come to past.

As an athlete I remember the photographs in the paper of President Kennedy with Wilma Rudolph after she won three Gold Medals at the 1960 Rome Olympics I considered it a tragic loss.

Sincerely,

Arthur R. Ashe, Jr.

Ben Crenshaw

Professional Golfer Ben Crenshaw has won such tournaments as the Masters, the Bing-Crosby National Pro-Am, the Hawaiian Open, and the Irish Open. [11]

BEN D. CRENSHAW

... I remember very vividly that I was being picked up from school (5th grade) by one of my friend's mother. She said, "Get in the car immediately. Something awful has happened." I was supposed to go and see the President that day in Austin after he completed his Dallas tour.

I don't think there has been a more sorrowful time for the United States than during that week of mourning our young President. He was very popular, and I remember feeling so sorry for his wife and children. I also felt sorry for many fine and upstanding citizens of Dallas which received unjust criticism from the press due to this tragic occurrence.

Sincerely,

Ben D. Crenshaw

Mike Ditka

Mike Ditka played professional football with the Chicago Bears, the Philadelphia Eagles, and the Dallas Cowboys. As Head Coach of the Chicago Bears, he lead the team to a Super Bowl Championship in 1985.
[24]

CHICAGO BEARS

I had just finished football practice with the Chicago Bears in 1963. My friend, Joe Marconi and I were driving home on the now known Kennedy Expressway when the bulletin came over the radio.

Shock, disbelief, anger, frustration and sorrow. We pulled off to the side of the expressway and cried while listening to the confusing accounts of what had transpired.

I'm not sure at that time I knew what impact his death would have. I do know that our country lost a great president, a fine leader and a person that really appealed to the masses of people in our country - old, young, rich and poor.

Sincerely,

Mike Ditka
Head Coach

Don Drysdale

After pitching for the Brooklyn and Los Angeles Dodgers from 1954 to 1969, Don Drysdale retired from professional baseball to become a sports broadcaster. He was named to the Baseball Hall of Fame in 1984. [27]

I was at my home in Van Nuys, California when I first heard the news of President Kennedy's shooting. My dad had stopped over on his lunch hour. My mom was over, and my daughter Kelly was there - at the time she was four. I was walking my dad out to the car when my mom came out to tell us the President had been shot. We went back in and watched while the reports started coming through the news.

I knew that we had lost a great leader. I immediately felt, and to this day feel, that it was a plot, a plot that has been hushed up. Too many assassinations that followed were unexplainable. I do not believe the findings of the Warren Report. The clandestine actions that take place throughout the world finally had hit the United States.

Sincerely,

Don Drysdale

Lee Elder

*Golfer Lee Elder has won the Houston Open, the PGA
Seniors Tournament, and the Westchester Classic,
among other tournaments. In 1970 he founded the
Lee Elder Celebrity Pro-Am Golf Classic.*
[29]

LEE ELDER

I was on a golf course in Los Angeles, CA at Foxhills Country
Club (now condominiums) playing with Joe Roach, Smily Quick,
John Avery and "Three Iron" Gates.

We all returned to the clubhouse to watch the news on TV,
when the announcer confirmed that the President was dead.
We were shocked and deeply sadden.

... I honestly don't remember what impact I thought
his death would have at that time. However, since that tragedy,
more recently we have lost other great leaders (e.g. Bobby
Kennedy, Malcolm X and Martin L. King). I am sure my feelings
for the loss of President Kennedy is much the same as the
aforementioned leaders - The nation, and we as a people, are
at a great loss and it is impossible to replace these kinds
of persons.

Sincerely,

Lee Elder

Lee Elder

Franco Harris

Franco Harris played professional football for the Pittsburgh Steelers. He was honored as the NFL Rookie of the Year in 1972, and as the Super Bowl Most Valuable Player in 1975.
[13]

FRANCO HARRIS

I can vividly remember the day President Kennedy died. I was in my 8th grade art class working on a project. It was right after lunch when our art instructor made the announcement that the President had been shot and taken to a hospital in Dallas. The feeling of disbelief and unreality surrounded me. I guess I was in shock as were all my classmates.

That was the first time in my young life I had to accept the unacceptable - the impossible. I really thought the world would stop in light of such ugliness. But I learned - it did not - due to the strength of our country and our people - we pulled through that dark week-end.

Sincerely,

Franco

Franco Harris

Woody Hayes

The late Woody Hayes was Head Football Coach at Ohio State University from 1951–79.
[50]

The Ohio State University

**Office of The
Head Football Coach Emeritus**

On November 22, 1963 when I first heard of President Kennedy's shooting I was in a hotel in Ypsilanti, Michigan having a meeting with our Ohio State quarterbacks. A football manager came in and told us President Kennedy had been shot. Naturally, I was shocked and so were the quarterbacks. One of them, a fine Catholic, turned absolutely white. A few minutes later, I called the entire football squad together and told them the news of the President's shooting. I did try to cushion the shock by explaining to them in a democracy there was always a follow through and that if the President did not live, that he would be succeeded by another capable man, Vice President Lyndon B. Johnson.

Regarding my immediate reaction to the impact of his death, I cannot give you an accurate answer except to say that I felt that his passing would incur an enormous period of sadness in this country.

Sincerely yours,

W.W. Hayes

Lou Holtz

Before becoming Head Football Coach at Notre Dame University in 1986, Lou Holtz coached at North Carolina State University and the University of Minnesota.
[26]

University of Notre Dame

Football Office

Lou Holtz
Head Football Coach

        ... I remember the assassination of President Kennedy as though it were yesterday.

I was in my office as an assistant football coach at the College of William and Mary when I heard it on a news bulletin. I was in a state of shock and immediately called my wife, whose reaction was very similar to mine.

The real magnitude of the death of John F. Kennedy did not hit me until later that night, and I felt like I had lost a member of my family. I, like most of the country, saw the shooting of Harvey Lee Oswald by Jack Ruby on TV the following Sunday.

I really didn't think much about the impact it would have upon the country as I had a great deal of compassion at that time for his wife and, more importantly, for his mother, father, and two little children. Since the assassination I've read everything I possibly could on the details that led up to the death of Kennedy, and to this day I'm not really satisfied with the various reports I've received.

Sincerely,

LOU HOLTZ

Hale S. Irwin

Professional Golfer Hale Irwin has won titles in the U.S. Open, the Western Open, the Hall of Fame Classic, and the Hawaiian Open.
[18]

HALE S. IRWIN

Even though it was some time ago the assassination of John F. Kennedy still has left its mark on the American scene.

I was a freshman at the University of Colorado. My mother was working there at the time as well. While waiting for her in our car I heard the news flash over the car radio.

My first impression was that someone was playing a sick joke. Then as the reports became more numerous I became shocked to realize that such a thing could really happen in our country.

As to the impact that day would have on our country, I do not feel that that thought actually passed my mind. It was as if things would continue on as they had, but with a different leader with a different style.

Sincerely,

Hale Irwin

Hale Irwin

Tom Landry

Tom Landry played professional football for the New York Giants before becoming their defensive coach. He was named Head Coach of the Dallas Cowboys in 1960.
[39]

Tom Landry

        ... I was on the practice field with the Dallas Cowboys at our former training facility on Central Expressway next to our present office building. My reaction when I heard the news was one in which I was stunned. It was only a few seconds before the news passed throughout the football team. I called practice off for the day.

My impression of the impact of President Kennedy's death was one which really saddened our nation. I don't believe anyone thought that this could happen again in America. I do know that it was a sad day for Dallas, Texas since it reflected upon our city.

                    Sincerely yours,

                    Tom Landry

                    Tom Landry

Tom Lasorda

After more than twenty years playing and coaching professional baseball, Tommy Lasorda became Manager of the Los Angeles Dodgers in 1977.
[36]

LOS ANGELES *Dodgers*

I was a scout for the Los Angeles Dodgers at that time, living at my current address in Fullerton, CA, in the Orange County suburbs of Los Angeles.

I went to the cleaners and it was there that I learned that the President had been shot. I was shocked. I couldn't believe such a thing could happen in this country.

As time went on, the feeling within me became stronger and stronger that the nation had lost a truly great President. John F. Kennedy will always be remembered as an outstanding President.

We live in the greatest country in the world and we must do everything in our power to try to prevent similar tragedies from befalling us.

Sincerely,

Tom Lasorda

Jack Nicklaus

Jack Nicklaus has won many major golf tournaments, including the U.S. Open, the PGA, the Masters, and the British Open.
[23]

Jack Nicklaus

When I heard the news, I was playing the ninth hole in a tournament in Lafayette, Louisianna--I believe it was the Cajun Classic;

I was shocked and stunned, as was everyone on the course...we just couldn't believe the news;

At that point, I wasn't giving as much thought to the impact of the tragedy on the nation as I was to the awful fact that our President had been murdered, thinking how unfair it was, and feeling a tremendous sadness and loss.

Sincerely,

JACK NICKLAUS

Arnold Palmer

Arnie Palmer has won professional golfing titles at the Masters, the U.S. Open, and the British Open.
[34]

arn●ld palmer

I had just finished playing a round of golf at Latrobe
Country Club at my home in Latrobe, Pennsylvania. I
was shocked and also very angry that something like this
could happen in our country. I found it hard to believe
that it had happened.

I didn't have a particular feeling at the time about the
impact it might have on our country. My thoughts were
more personal and I felt very badly for President Kennedy's
family and close friends. I think we all thought that he
was doing a good job as our President.

Sincerely,

Arnold Palmer

Arnold Palmer

Joseph V. Paterno

Since becoming Head Football Coach at Pennsylvania State University in 1966, Joe Paterno has been named College Football Coach of the Year four times.
[36]

PennState

Our football team was practicing getting ready to go to Pittsburgh to play Pittsburgh the next day whenever I first heard of President Kennedy's shooting. As most people, I was shocked and terribly disappointed because I had a great deal of admiration for the President and because I never believed such a thing could happen in our country. I and several others discussed what kind of an impact the shooting would have on our country and we all agreed that we were entering into a new era in American lifestyle as I think has been proven by the terrible assassinations of Dr. King and Bob Kennedy as well as the attempts on President Reagan's life.

Sincerely,

Joseph V. Paterno
Head Football Coach

Floyd Patterson

Floyd Patterson won the Golden Gloves Award in 1951 and 1952, and a Gold Medal in Boxing at the 1952 Helsinki Olympics. He held the World Champion Heavyweight Titles in 1956–59 and again in 1960–62.
[28]

FLOYD PATTERSON

When I first heard the news of President Kennedy's assassination I was at my camp in upstate New York training for an upcoming bout. After completing my roadwork early that morning I was resting before starting my afternoon workout. Just as I was dozing off one of my sparring partners came into my room and told me that President Kennedy had just been shot. I jumped out of bed in shock and disblief hoping that what I just heard was somehow only a bad dream.

After turning the T.V. on I came to grips with the reality that the president we all loved was gone. I felt terrible, not only for the nation but for his family as well.

I sensed this tragedy had left our country in a state of confusion and emptiness. I kept asking myself the same questions over and over. Who was going to lead us? Make our decisions? Guide us through rough times? Secondary to my feeling of a great loss I hoped that Vice President Johnson would assume command of our country and persue it with as much vigor and enthusiasm as that of President Kennedy.

Although many years have past since that November day in 1963, I can still recall the feeling of devastation and loss like they happened only yesterday.

Sincerely,

Floyd Patterson

305

Ray Perkins

Ray Perkins, one-time Coach of the Alabama Crimson Tide, was named Head Coach of the Tampa Bay Buccaneers in 1987.
[21]

Ray Perkins
Vice President/Head Coach

I was driving my car to class. I was on 15th Street in Tuscaloosa, Alabama. At the time, I was a sophomore at University of Alabama.

I was shocked! I could not believe that someone had actually shot our President.

I really didn't think of the impact on that day.

Sincerely,

Ray Perkins
Vice President/Head Coach

Brooks Robinson

Brooks Robinson played his entire professional baseball career for the Baltimore Orioles before he was named to the Hall of Fame. He was chosen the World Series Most Valuable Player in 1970.
[26]

CROWN CENTRAL PETROLEUM CORPORATION

PRODUCERS · REFINERS · MARKETERS OF PETROLEUM PRODUCTS AND PETROCHEMICALS

        ... I first heard the news on the radio at Memorial Stadium as I was taking treatment for a baseball injury that I had received during the 1963 season.

    My reaction, along with the trainer's, was one of disbelief and we went immediately to make some phone calls. I also felt anger and sadness that this could happen.

    I did not know what impact Jack Kennedy's death would have on our nation at that time. I did believe that it would be a time of confusion because of the great rapport he had with the people of this country.

                Sincerely,

                Brooks C. Robinson

Buddy Ryan

After coaching a number of university and professional football teams, Buddy Ryan became Head Coach of the Philadelphia Eagles in 1986.
[29]

FOOTBALL CLUB, INC

I can remember very clearly that I was at Brockport State University. I had just pulled up to the gym on a recruiting trip for the University of Buffalo where I was coaching at that time. I was making a call on Jerry DiAugustino, the head coach and I started to get out of the car when I heard the announcement on the radio. It shocked the hell out of me.

My reaction to the news was that I couldn't believe it happened in Texas, as I coached at Oklahoma and Texas high schools. If it were somewhere else I could believe it but not in Texas.

I never thought about the impact that it would have on the nation, it just left a sick feeling in my stomach. It was a very sad situation and the fact that it had happened in Dallas was just unbelieveable to me.

Sincerely,

Buddy Ryan

Buddy Ryan
Head Coach

308

Marty Schottenheimer

Marty Schottenheimer, a former professional football player for the Buffalo Bills and Boston Patriots, was named Head Coach of the Cleveland Browns in 1985. [20]

The Cleveland Browns

MARTY SCHOTTENHEIMER
HEAD COACH

I was en route to class at the University of Pittsburgh when news of the shooting of President Kennedy was broadcast. Upon arrival in class, the professor shared a moment of prayer and immediately dismissed the class. Several classmates and I gathered in the student union attempting to get further information on the shooting.

My reaction was one of shock, anger and utter disbelief that a tragedy of this nature might take place.

At that moment it was difficult to imagine what impact President Kennedy's death would have on our country. Inasmuch as the events seemed so unreal to me, it was impossible to accurately assess the implications of his death.

Sincerely,

Martin E. Schottenheimer
Head Coach

Donald F. Shula

Don Shula, a former professional football player, has coached the Detroit Lions, the Baltimore Colts, and several university football teams. In 1972 and '73, he led the Miami Dolphins to Super Bowl victories.
[33]

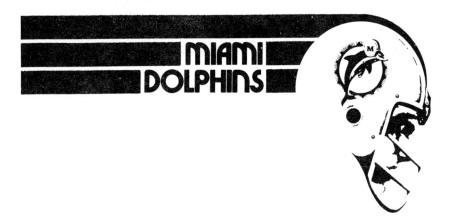

MIAMI DOLPHINS

I was on a plane on the way to play the Rams in Los Angeles and it was announced over the P.A. system.

Everybody went into total shock. It was such devastating news. At first it was hard to believe but the more you thought about it the more you realized it had happened and what a tremendous impact it would have.

Anytime you lose a man that has that kind of charisma and leadership ability it's got to be a tremendous loss to the nation. It was not only a personal loss, but also the loss of a nation.

Sincerely,

Donald F. Shula

Donald F. Shula
Vice President/Head Coach

Sam Snead

Among Sam Snead's professional golfing titles are the PGA Championship, the British Open, and the Masters.
[51]

UMi

I was at my home in Virginia at the time.

I was deeply affected by the news. It was completely shocking that so young and vital a person would be killed in such a manner. I felt just as if my country was being attacked.

As far as the impact on the country, I thought it would affect us just as if you lost your mother or father, someone you looked up to and respected being taken away suddenly and violently.

Sincerely,

SAM SNEAD

UNI·MANAGERS INTERNATIONAL

Bart Starr

Bart Starr played quarterback for the Green Bay Packers from 1956–71 and was Head Coach and General Manager of the same team from 1975–84. In 1977, he was named to the Football Hall of Fame. [29]

Walking across the stadium parking lot to our dressing room when one of our front office personnel called out the report of the shooting.

I was shocked with disbelief and ran the remaining distance to the locker room to receive more information. It was difficult to comprehend that such an inhumane act had been committed against our president.

Typically, I was more concerned with what impact this assassination would have on the Kennedy family because I confidently expected our government leaders to effect an orderly, swift transfer of power.

Sincerely,

Bart Starr

Roger Staubach

Roger Staubach, a Heisman Trophy Winner while at the Naval Academy, played quarterback for the Dallas Cowboys from 1969–79. He was named to the Football Hall of Fame in 1985.
[21]

The assassination of John F. Kennedy did have a great affect on my life at the time.

I was at the Naval Academy and in my room preparing to go to class when I first heard of the shooting.

I was in my last class when I knew that he had died and had a sick and helpless feeling. We had been preparing for the Army-Navy game to be played that weekend. But when I got to practice, we had a prayer and talked about the assassination. It did help us to put life into perspective. As big as the Army-Navy game had seemed to us, it was suddenly meaningless as we talked about this tragedy. We did play the game a week later on behalf of President Kennedy.

I felt it would have a tremendous impact on the country. But our country has such a strong democracy with a balance of power, that we were able to handle this situation. However, I still feel our country missed out on seeing a young president with great leadership qualities being able to fill his full term in our government.

Sincerely,

Roger Staubach

Johnny Unitas played quarterback for the Pittsburgh Steelers, the Baltimore Colts, and the San Diego Chargers. The AP named him "Player of the Decade" in 1970, and in 1979 he was inducted into the Football Hall of Fame.
[30]

John C. Unitas

I was flying along with my teammates to Los Angeles, California in preparation to play against the Los Angeles Rams when the announcement came over the P.A. system that the President of the United States had been assassinated. At that moment you could have heard a pin drop. I think even the engines stopped running. From that point on everyone seemed to be in a daze. To think that in our country this could happen is unreal.

The impact, I really wasn't concerned with, I knew that this country would continue to move in the direction that he had pointed. Truly time does march on.

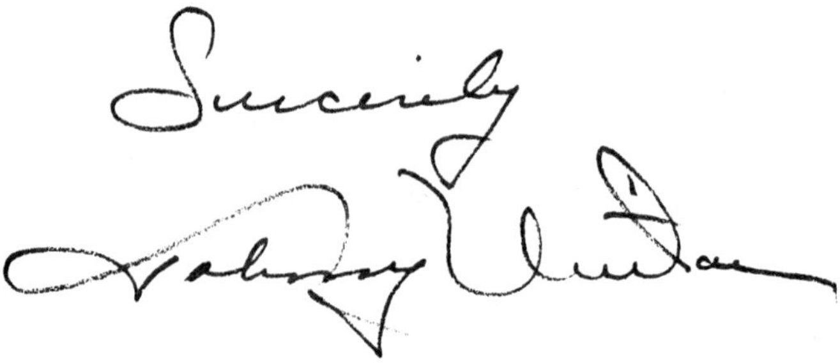

Sincerely
Johnny Unitas

Joe Walton

Joe Walton played professional football for the Washington Redskins and the New York Giants. In 1983, he was named Head Coach for the New York Jets.
[29]

JOSEPH F. WALTON
HEAD COACH

I was a player for the New York Giants in 1963 and was driving home from practice when I heard the bulletin on the radio.

I was mad as hell. How could this terrible thing happen to our President. Americans are much too trusting. When are we going to realize there are a lot of sick people in this world.

My first thoughts were of the Kennedy family. I knew the constitution enabled the government to quickly transfer authority to the Vice President. I was primarily concerned wtih the devastating impact it would have on his family.

Sincerely,

Joe Walton

Jerry West

While a member of the Los Angeles Lakers, ex-Olympian Jerry West was named to the NBA All-Star team ten times. In 1980, he was inducted into the NBA Hall of Fame, and in 1982, he became General Manager of the Lakers.
[15]

I first heard about the shooting of the President while driving in an automobile from basketball practice. My immediate feeling was one of shock and despair for he had tremendously gained the confidence of the people and had given this country a sense of direction.

My reaction was one of anger and frustration that a country of this stature could remove from our earth an important leader such as Kennedy.

The impact that I felt on this country was one of total confusion for the loss of a valued, trusted leader. Fortunately for us, America has many well qualified people and we have been blessed with fine presidents since his death.

Sincerely,

Jerry West
Vice President/General Manager

IX

OTHER PROMINENT AMERICANS REFLECT ON JOHN KENNEDY

"In the long history of the world, only a few generations have been granted the role of defending freedom in its hour of maximum danger. I do not shrink from this responsibility – I welcome it. I do not believe that any of us would exchange places with any other people or any other generation. The energy, the faith, the devotion which we bring to this endeavor will light our country and all who serve it – and the glow from that fire can truly light the world.

And so, my fellow Americans: ask not what your country can do for you – ask what you can do for your country...."

– *President Kennedy's Inaugural Address, 1961*

The American people felt that John Kennedy was often speaking directly to them, especially when he issued the challenge to "ask what you can do for your country." Unlike any President before him, John Kennedy utilized the media to reach the American people on an almost daily basis. Both the President and his wife, Jackie, presented the media with numerous stories and photographic opportunities. So the American people – always eager to learn more about the First Family – felt that they knew their President well.

Therefore, no segment of American life was left unmoved by the President's death. Citizens from every corner of the country felt the loss, regardless of race, creed, or social class. When the news of President Kennedy's death swept across the nation, men and women paused from their daily tasks – perhaps out of respect, more likely out of shock – to reflect on the death of their President. Businessmen, legal scholars and scientists, together with the leaders of religion, labor, and the military now echo the sentiments felt by millions of other Americans when they heard that their President had died.

Garner Ted Armstrong

Garner Ted Armstrong is president of the Worldwide Church of God, Church of God International, as well as the host of the radio and TV program, "The World Tomorrow."
[33]

THE CHURCH OF GOD, INTERNATIONAL

GARNER TED ARMSTRONG
PRESIDENT

I was in the midst of teaching my Systematic Theology class of about 100 students on the Ambassador College Campus in Pasadena, California, when an excited messenger came in, interrupted the class, and said, "The President has been shot in Dallas!" Shocked, startled, I turned to the class, asked them to pray (we didn't know that he had been killed instantly) that he was not seriously injured, dismissed the class, and rushed to the nearest television set.

Between the classroom building and my executive office atop the library...was one of the women's dormitories. The house mother, Mrs. Anne Mann, was a friend of twenty-some years, and I knew there would be a television set in her apartment, so together with several others who had joined me by this time, we went immediately to her apartment. Sure enough, she and several others were glued to the television set, and there we saw the chaotic media announcements of the tragedy, sketchy, repetitious, including announcements which later proved to be utterly false that the President was still alive; that a Catholic priest had said his "life was still in him"; that he had been taken to Parkland Hospital; that a hunt was underway for the assassin or assassins.

My reaction to the event was one of utter disbelief, then of a deep-seated *anger* at the monstrosity of the act; that one (or more) crazed individuals could assault the leader of the nation, and one bullet could set aside millions of ballots; it was a monstrous, bestial assault on the very roots of the nation itself. As I sat at my desk a few moments later, with the radio on, I was due in our radio studio for my daily live radio broadcast in only five minutes, and it was then that I heard the announcement from the network announcer, "Ladies and gentlemen, the President is dead. Ladies and gentlemen, our national anthem.."...As the song played, I wept. I was barely able to get my emotions under control to rush to the radio studio, and there, without notes or preparation, ad-libbed my outrage at this insane act, as if in scathing indictment of the cancer-like penchant for crime and violence that lay beneath the surface in too many millions of Americans; that the sordid tentacles of crime could reach from the gutter to strike down the highest official in the land, and therefore effectively silence an individual who stood for the hopes and dreams of millions caused *outrage* in my mind....

Knowing only very little about Lyndon Johnson..., I could only hope that he was a man of sufficient stature to step into what I felt were a very large pair of shoes. As most Americans, I was specially proud of JFK's naval blockade of Cuba; calling the Russians' hand, *forcing* the return of Russian missiles in a showdown which was to become the brightest star of his career. I felt ashamed for the nation, since, having done dozens of programs on America's incredible crime rate, I felt we had aired our filthy linen for all the world to see; that we stood with head bowed, and the torch of the Statue of Liberty bent toward the bottom of the harbor, because we had allowed lesser nations in the world to see the spectacle of the assassination of our own President.

Of course, in subsequent years, as I have seen actual attacks on both President Gerald Ford (in San Francisco, by a member of the infamous "Manson gang"), and John Hinckley's shooting of President Reagan, I have been reminded again and again of that infamous day when President Kennedy was shot.

As a minister, I see assassinations (such as those of Medgar Evers, Martin Luther King, Bobby Kennedy, etc.) and assassination *attempts* as but a symptom of a deep and underlying sickness of society itself, witness the mindless insanity of tampering with over-the-counter drugs; indiscriminate, agonizing death meted out to innocent victims by bestial murderers who, to satisfy their own tortured penchant for violence, strike out anonymously, indiscriminately.

...the criminals in our society are not necessarily a minority who lurk behind hibiscus bushes near grade schools, preying on helpless children, but who are in fact the *common man,* who, unless or until he is *converted* to the cause of Christ, remains an individual capable of wholly unacceptable acts in a civilized society.

Garner Ted Armstrong

Mary Kay Ash

Mary Kay Ash is the founder and Chairman of the Board of Mary Kay Cosmetics.
[35]

COSMETICS

Mary Kay Ash
Chairman of the Board

®

I had just come out of retirement (one month!) and opened my own direct sales business in Exchange Park Bank in Dallas, Texas. The stock market exchange was three doors down from my office. When the word came that President Kennedy had been shot, their members rushed around the mall telling everyone about it. A pall descended upon the mall, which took on a quiet and subdued air with everyone speaking in whispers.

Just as everyone else I, too, could not believe that on such a memorable occasion as President Kennedy's visit to our city that such a thing could have happened. The air had been one of celebration and festivity prior to this terrible happening. It was as if some beloved family member had had a heart attack and died in the middle of a festive occasion. I was shocked and stunned.

We all had such great hope and great expectations of our young and vibrant President Kennedy that it suddenly seemed the whole world had come to an end. We couldn't imagine that anyone could take his place or ever exhibit such vibrance, enthusiasm and great hope for our nation. We at that time felt we could only expect "second best" from his successors. Today his presence is still felt, and he is among the most remembered Presidents who have served our nation.

Cordially,

Mary Kay
Chairman Emeritus

320

Jim Bakker, President
PTL Television Network

Tammy and I were enjoying lunch in a fine Virginia Beach restaurant.

Like everyone else in the restaurant, we were numbed by the news. It was like a nightmare. The people there literally stared at each other in disbelief. Very little was said. Something that seemed impossible had just happened. We were totally shocked, as were all Americans.

At that moment, like many other people throughout the nation, I sensed such a great uncertainty concerning what might happen to the nation. However, during the next few days, as the nation was drawn together, the former Vice President Johnson and other leaders moved swiftly to keep the country moving ahead very smoothly. The actions by those leaders helped bring confidence to the people, which, at the time, was extremely important.

In warmest Christian love,

Jim Bakker
President

Melvin M. Belli, Sr.

Melvin Belli gained national attention as the defense lawyer for Jack Ruby, the man who shot Lee Harvey Oswald before a live national television audience. He is the author of Dallas Justice *and* Melvin Belli: My Life on Trial.

[56]

LAW OFFICES
Melvin M. Belli, Sr.

I was in the Superior Court, Los Angeles, trying a homicide case when the judge interrupted the proceedings to tell us of the assassination of John F. Kennedy.

He dismissed court for that day not knowing what effect the news would have on the jury and I went upstairs into the District Attorney's private office to hear the news on the radio, all the time silently praying that it wasn't a black man who had shot the President as the first report to us indicated.

Of course I was shocked and it was a feeling of unbelief but the next day when we continued the case I think everybody in the courtroom was still numb.

Jack Ruby's brother came into the courtroom to wait for a recess to see me and asked me if I wouldn't take on his brother's case and I agreed at least to go to Dallas to see him.

I became immediately embroiled in the <u>Ruby</u> case, of course long before trial, and all my thoughts were of Jack Ruby and I tried to get as much information as I could on Oswald.

Bes

Melvin M. Belli, Sr.

Henry W. Bloch

Henry Bloch became Chief Executive Officer of H & R Block in 1955.
[41]

H&R Block, Inc.

Henry W. Bloch
President and
Chief Executive Officer

I was in a meeting in the H&R Block Corporate Headquarters office in Kansas City, Missouri, with major franchise owners.

My initial reaction was shock and the room was quieted in stunned silence.

I remember wondering whether the act of violence was a one person effort or a visable piece of some broader terrorism. I wondered what it would do to affect the accessibility and availability of our president.

Very truly yours,

Henry W. Bloch

Frank Borman

Frank Borman was Flight Commander of both Gemini 7 and Apollo 8. After leaving the space program, he was Chief Executive Officer of Eastern Air Lines for ten years.
[35]

EASTERN AIR LINES INCORPORATED

CHAIRMAN AND
CHIEF EXECUTIVE OFFICER

I was flying in a helicopter between North American Rockwell's Downey, California plant and the Los Angeles International Airport. The helicopter pilot informed me of the President's death in flight.

My immediate reaction was one of disbelief.

I don't recall any thought connecting the assassination and the nation's future on the day of President Kennedy's death.

Sincerely,

Frank Borman

Cesar Chavez

Cesar Chavez is President of the United Farmworkers of America, AFL-CIO. In the 60s, his successful fight to gain unionization of California farmworkers earned him the admiration of both President Kennedy and the President's brother, Robert F. Kennedy.
[36]

UNITED FARM WORKERS of AMERICA AFL-CIO

On November 22, 1963, I had just returned to my home in Delano, California, after an errand to the post office. I remembered that I needed my appointment book before going to a meeting with farm workers in Fresno. Even though I was in a hurry because I was already late, for some strange reason -- normally it would have been the last thing I would think of doing during the day -- I flipped on the TV while looking for my book.

All of a sudden, it dawned on me what I was hearing as I searched for the book: President Kennedy had been shot...was not expected to live. I tore back to the TV and stood there watching as the incredible truth began to hit home. After a while, I slumped down in a chair to watch -- and it seems like I never moved from it until days later when the last note of "Taps" died away in Arlington Cemetery.

Like everyone else in the nation that day, my reaction was one of utter shock, but, in addition, I felt a deep sense of loss both for myself and for farm workers. A few years earlier, while I was still working with the Community Service Organization, both John and his brother Robert came out to California to visit us after they had heard about the tremendous success we were having with our voter-registration drives. They wanted to learn everything they could about our methods. It was an instant friendship. Their concern and compassion for the disenfranchised we were organizing told me right away that farm workers would have two truly compassionate and supportive friends in the future. Robert Kennedy proved that intuition right several time in the years before his assassination; sadly, John Kennedy never got the chance.

I confess I was mistaken about the catastrophic impact I
thought Kennedy's death would have on the nation. I felt
devastated because it seemed like everything he stood for and
wanted to accomplish for America -- civil rights for all
minorities, concern for human rights abroad, respect as well as
material aid for third-world countries, exciting plans for the
exploration of space -- would be lost. But it wasn't long
before I realized that President Lyndon Johnson really meant it
when he said he would do everything in his power to continue to
fight for the goals Kennedy had set for his administration.
Johnson, in spite of some glaring failures, accomplished what
he said he would. The impact of Kennedy's death, therefore,
didn't turn out to be as disastrous as I feared it would be.

Sincerely,

Cesar E. Chavez
President

"Racial discrimination in employment is especially in-
jurious both to its victims and to the national economy. It
results in a great waste of human resources and creates
serious community problems. It is, moreover, inconsistent
with the democratic principle that no man should be denied
employment commensurate with his abilities because of race
or creed or ancestry."
                    —*Special Message to Congress, February 28, 1963*

Theodore M. Hesburgh

Father Hesburgh, a recipient of the Presidential Medal of Freedom, was President of the University of Notre Dame for 25 years. His books include Thoughts for Our Times *and* God and the World of Man. [46]

University of Notre Dame

President Emeritus

The day that John Kennedy died, I was attending a meeting of the National Science Board at the University of Colorado in Boulder. We were planning to build a atmospheric research center there, having looked over the whole country for an appropriate site. This was the first center of its kind in the United States. We wanted it to be exactly right, so we held our Board meeting in Boulder and spent the morning up on the mountain walking around the snowy land where there was a plateau on which the atmospheric research center could be built.

Around noontime, we headed down the mountain in Volks wagon vans to have lunch with President Joseph Smiley and his wife at their home. As we pulled into the driveway, someone rushed out of the house and said the President has been shot. Of course, we didn't believe it until we entered the house and began to hear the reports on the radio. Since there were about 24 of us in the group, some listened to the radio in the parlor and the rest of us went into the kitchen where there was another radio. Of course, the reports got more and more dire until someone said the President has just died.

We were all in shock, I think. I felt sorry for President Smiley's wife who had to then put on a lunch for us which we endured rather than ate. Then we went back to the motel to continue our monthly Board meeting which always had a very large agenda of research items to be approved or disapproved for funding. I sat in the meeting with my mind a thousand miles away for about ten minutes and then suddenly folded up my papers and left the room, picking up my bag en route and then going to the airport in Denver.

We were supposed to have a football game with the University of Iowa in Iowa City the next day, so I called the Executive Vice President who was out there with the team. "What about the game tomorrow?," I asked Father Joyce. He answered, "I know how you feel about it, but they still want to play." My response was that football was not that important after what had just happened and in no way would we play the game. Whatever they wanted to do didn't particularly matter to me, since our team was just not going to show up for the game. I instructed him to pack up and come home on Saturday morning and to leave word that we would be willing to take whatever loss was involved in refunding tickets for those who wanted a refund. To be honest, I didn't think many people would, but, in fact, half of them did request a refund. I recall that cost us about $90,000.00. Even so, I think the principle was right and some of the other teams that were scheduled that day and intended to play had to call the games off later under public pressure. Unfortunately, one cannot say the same for the professional teams that were scheduled for that Sunday.

When I returned to the University the next morning, I had a call from Ethel Kennedy, Bobby's wife, who asked me to come down and be on the altar for the funeral at St. Matthew's Cathedral in Washington. I caught the next plane to Washington and was one of only two priests who were in the sanctuary with Cardinal Cushing and Auxiliary Bishop Hannan who gave the eulogy. The other priest was Father Fitzgerald who was Jack Kennedy's cousin.

I also recall being proud of the fact that once the Mass was finished, Cardinal Cushing went right down to the front pew and gave Jacqueline Kennedy and Rose Kennedy a big hug which I think at that point they needed.

My predecessor, Father John Cavanaugh, beat me to Washington, since he was a great friend of the Kennedys and they had sent an airplane for him. He was at the White House when the body arrived at four o'clock in the morning and offered Mass in the East Room for all of the family before the dawn.

All best wishes.

Sincerely yours,

[signature]

(Rev.) Theodore M. Hesburgh, C.S.C.
President Emeritus

In 1981, Associate Justice Sandra Day O'Connor became the first woman member of the U.S. Supreme Court.
[33]

𝕾𝖚𝖕𝖗𝖊𝖒𝖊 𝕮𝖔𝖚𝖗𝖙 𝖔𝖋 𝖙𝖍𝖊 𝖀𝖓𝖎𝖙𝖊𝖉 𝕾𝖙𝖆𝖙𝖊𝖘

CHAMBERS OF
JUSTICE SANDRA DAY O'CONNOR

When I first heard the news of President Kennedy's assassination, I was in a small pharmacy in Phoenix, Arizona, purchasing a prescription for one of my children who was ill. I was stunned by the news.

When I returned to my car, I wept because of the sense of dismay that in the twentieth century our nation's President was vulnerable to such an attack. The damage was not only to a youthful President and his family, but to all Americans who cherish their free and open society.

Sincerely,

Sandra O'Connor

Sandra D. O'Connor

Oral Roberts

Televangelist Oral Roberts founded Oral Roberts University in 1963.
[45]

ORAL ROBERTS

When the announcement came over President Kennedy's assassination I was eating lunch with my wife and two close associates. Involuntarily, we rose from the table. For some reason we walked outside without finishing the meal.

The impact was on my heart like a stabbing sensation. All I could say was "God, bless us and our nation in this hour of deepest loss."

President Kennedy had asked to see me a few months prior and we spent 20 minutes together. He was taller than I expected and the force of his personality was so strong it leaped out at me.

His first words were, "I have seen you on television and enjoyed it very much."

He seemed very knowledgeable of the works of myself and others in evangelism.

Sincerely,

Oral Roberts

Jonas Salk

*Jonas Salk developed the vaccine for Poliomyelitis in
1955. Among his many honors are the Gold Medal of
Congress, the Robert Koch Medal, and the Presidential Medal of Freedom.*
[49]

THE SALK INSTITUTE

The news that President Kennedy had been shot came to me while I
was listening to a visiting colleague presenting a seminar. I reacted with dismay and disbelief, and I imagined that this was the
work of enemies of what the President represented. I had a feeling
of great loss, for the nation and the world, of a young man who had
much to contribute. I felt that the loss of his youthful and
imaginative leadership would be difficult to replace and that we
were being deprived of great opportunity had he been able to serve
for two terms. He, and the many exceptional people with whom he was
surrounded, together could have created a new pattern for the future.

Sincerely,

Jonas Salk

Donald K. Slayton

Astronaut Donald Slayton was a member of the original Project Mercury team and also participated in the 1975 Apollo-Soyuz mission. From 1975–82, he was NASA Manager for Space Shuttle Testing. [39]

SPACE
SERVICES
INCOF AMERICA

I was in the NASA cafeteria in Houston eating my lunch,

My reaction to the news was probably identical to almost everyone else -- initial disbelief that such a thing could happen, and

I did not try to analyze the impact of President Kennedy's death on the nation either then or later. I think the transition to President Johnson was handled so rapidly and smoothly that most of us never felt things were really out of control.

Sincerely,

Donald K. Slayton
President

Mort Walker

*Mort Walker created the comic strips "Beetle Bailey,"
"Hi and Lois," and "Boner's Ark," among others.*
[40]

It seems so incongrous now that I was doing aomething so
mundane as bowling when such a momentous tragedy occured. We
were a group of New Yorker and comic strip artists enjoying
our much needed escape from our studios at the Westport, CT,
Bowling Lanes when the news began to emerge about Kennedy's
shooting. At first there was disbelief. It couldn't really be
true. We went on bowling until the news got grimmer. We
became too depressed to continue and left to see the news
on tv at a friend's home. Even when it was announced that he
was dead it was hard to comprehend.

The feeling of helplessness, fury, and frustration was
overwhelming. I wanted to turn back the clock, change his
itinerary, have him better protected, have the assassin miss...
blame someone, fill some emotional void.

I felt his death left the nation rudderless and contributed
a great deal to the racial and social disorders that followed.
The youth of our country especially felt disfranchised,
abandoned, angry, forlorn...much the same as a child feels
when a father dies. A good bit of our tranquility and trust
died with Kennedy. I am still angry. Our country may never
ever be the same again.

Sincerely,

Mort Walker

John Weitz

John Weitz has received numerous honors for his fashion designs, including the Harpers Bazaar Medallion, the Coty Award, and the Cartier Design Award. He is the author of Value of Nothing and Friends in High Places.
[40]

JOHN WEITZ

Designer Bill Blass and I were eating lunch at La Grenouille, the French restaurant on East 52nd Street in New York. We noticed that John Fairchild, the publisher of Women's Wear Daily, left his table and was called to the phone. Fairchild then came to our table and said, "Kennedy's been shot. I think it's pretty bad." The noisy restaurant slowly hushed and Bill and I broke off our lunch. We went next door to St. Patrick's Cathedral, though neither one of us is a Catholic. It was the closest place to "put in a word with the Boss" but obviously the Boss had other ideas.

The next morning, I drove to my adopted home, the old whaling port of Sag Harbor, on the tip of Long Island. The flag on the town square near the port flew at half mast and the wind had torn it in half. I stopped the car and I wept.

Sincerely,

John Weitz

Elmo R. Zumwalt, Jr.

Admiral Zumwalt was the Commander of U.S. Naval Forces in Vietnam from 1968–70 and Chief of Naval Operations from 1970–74. He and his son co-authored an autobiography, My Father – My Son.
[42]

E. R. ZUMWALT, JR.
ADMIRAL, U. S. NAVY (RET.)

I first heard the news of President Kennedy's shooting as I was standing behind the desk of the Honorable Paul H. Nitze, who was then Assistant Secretary of Defense (International Security Affairs), and who was going over an arms control analysis that I had prepared for him. The news was first reported to Paul Nitze by telephone by his secretary Margaret Martin. Paul Nitze said eight or ten times, in shock, "Oh no, Oh no." We then turned on the television to hear the news firsthand.

My reaction, as was Paul Nitze's, was one of utter horror at the shooting but one of hope based on early reports that he might live.

My view of the impact of President Kennedy's death was that it would pull the nation together in shock and grief and give a completely different man, Lyndon Johnson, time to acclimate himself to power.

Sincerely,

E. R. Zumwalt, Jr.

Afterword

"All this will not be finished in the first one hundred days. Nor will it be finished in the first one thousand days, nor in the life of this Administration, nor even perhaps in our lifetime on this planet. But let us begin."
—*President Kennedy's Inaugural Address, 1961*

Arthur Schlesinger, Jr.

Arthur Schlesinger served as Special Assistant to Presidents Kennedy and Johnson before becoming a Professor of Humanities at the City University of New York. He won Pulitzer Prizes for his books, The Age of Jackson *and* A Thousand Days.
[46]

On Friday morning I had flown to New York with Katharine Graham, whose husband Philip had died three months before, for a luncheon with the editors for her magazine *Newsweek*. Kenneth Galbraith had come down from Cambridge for the occasion. We were still sipping drinks before luncheon in an amiable mood of Friday-before-the-Harvard-Yale game relaxation when a young man in shirtsleeves entered the room and said, a little tentatively, "I am sorry to break in, but I think you should know that the President has been shot in the head in Texas." For a flash one thought this was some sort of ghastly office joke. Then we knew it could not be and huddled desperately around the nearest television. Everything was confusing and appalling. The minutes dragged along. Incomprehensible bulletins came

Reprinted with permission from A Thousand Days: John Kennedy in the White House *by Arthur M. Schlesinger, Jr., Houghton Mifflin Company, Boston, Massachussetts, 1965.*

from the hospital. Suddenly an insane surge of conviction flowed through me: I felt that the man who had survived the Solomon Islands and so much illness and agony, who so loved life, embodied it, enhanced it, could not possibly die now. He would escape the shadow as he had before. Almost immediately we received the irrevocable word.

In a few moments Galbraith and I were on Katharine Graham's plane bound for Washington. It was the saddest journey of one's life. Bitterness, shame, anguish, disbelief, emptiness mingled inextricably in one's mind. When I stumbled, almost blindly, into the East Wing, the first person I encountered was Franklin D. Roosevelt, Jr. In a short time I went with my White House colleagues to Andrews Field to await the return of Air Force One from Texas. A small crowd was waiting in the dusk, McNamara, stunned and silent, Harriman, haggard and suddenly looking very old, desolation everywhere. We watched incredulously as the casket was carefully lifted out of the plane and taken to the Naval Hospital in Bethesda. Later I went to my house in Georgetown. My weeping daughter Christina said, "Daddy, what has happened to our country? If this is the kind of country we have, I don't want to live here any more." The older children were already on their way back from college to Washington.

Still later I went back to the White House to await the last return. Around four in the morning the casket, wrapped in a flag, was brought from the Naval Hospital and placed on a stand in the East Room. Tapers were lit around the bier, and a priest said a few words. Then Jacqueline approached the bier, knelt for a moment and buried her head in the flag. Soon she walked away. The rest of us waited for a little while in the great hall. We were beyond consolation, but we clung to the comradeship he had given us. Finally, just before daybreak, we bleakly dispersed into the mild night.

We did not grieve alone....At Harvard Yard the bells tolled in Memorial Church....A. Philip Randolph said that his "place in history will be next to Abraham Lincoln." Pablo Casals mused that he had seen many great and terrible events in his lifetime—the Dreyfus case, the assassination of Gandhi—"but in recent history—and I am thinking of my own lifetime—there has never been a tragedy that has brought so much sadness and grief to as many people as this." "For a time we felt the country was ours," said Norman Mailer. "Now it's theirs again." Many were surprised by the intensity of the loss. Alistair Cooke spoke of "this sudden discovery that he was more familiar than we knew." "Is there some principle of nature," asked Richard Hofstadter, "which requires that we never know the quality of what we have had until it is gone?" Around the land people sat desperately in front of television sets watching the bitter drama of the next four days. In Washington, Daniel Patrick Moynihan, the Assistant Secretary of Labor, said, "I don't think there's any point in being Irish if you don't know that the world is going to break your heart eventually. I guess that we thought we had a little more time."...Mary McGrory said to me that we'll never laugh again. And I said, "Heavens, Mary. We'll laugh again. It's just that we'll never be young again."

...David Bruce reported from London, "Great Britain has never before mourned a foreigner as it has President Kennedy." As the news spread around London, over a thousand people assembled before the embassy in Grosvenor Square; they came in endless thousands in the next days to sign the condolence book...."Why was this feeling—this sorrow—at once so universal and so individual?" Harold Macmillan later asked. "Was it not because he seemed, in his own person, to embody all the hopes and aspirations of this new world that is struggling to emerge—to rise, Phoenix-like, from the ashes of the old?" In West Berlin people lighted candles in darkened windows. In Poland there was a spontaneous mass mourning by university students; church bells tolled for fifteen minutes on the night of the funeral. In Yugoslavia Tito, so overcome that he could hardly speak, phoned the American chief of mission; later he read a statement over the state radio and went in person to the embassy to sign the book. The national flag was flown at half-mast, and schools were instructed to devote a full hour to a discussion of the President's policies and significance. In Moscow Khrushchev was the first to sign the book, and the Soviet television carried the funeral, including the service in the church.

Latin America was devastated. Streets, schools, housing projects were named after him, shrines set up in his memory; his picture, torn from the newspaper, hung on the walls of workers' shacks and in the hovels of the *campesinos*. "For Latin America," said Lleras Camargo, "Kennedy's passing is a blackening, a tunnel, a gust of cloud and smoke." Castro was with Jean Daniel when the report came; he said, *"Es una mala noticia"* ("This is bad news"). In a few moments, with the final word, he stood and said, "Everything is changed....I'll tell you one thing: at least Kennedy was an enemy to whom we had become accustomed." In Cambodia Prince Sihanouk ordered court mourning; "a light was put out," he later said, "which may not be re-lit for many years to come." In Indonesia flags flew at half-mast. In New Delhi people cried in the streets. In Algiers Ben Bella phoned Ambassador Porter in tears and said, "I can't believe it. Believe me, I'd rather it happen to me than to him." In Guinea Séékou Tourée said, "I have lost my only true friend in the outside world." The embassy reported, "People expressed their grief without restraint, and just about everybody in Guinea seemed to have fallen under the spell of the courageous young hero of far away, the slayer of the dragons of discrimination, poverty, ignorance and war." In N'zérékoré in the back country, where one would hardly think they had heard of the United States let alone the American President, a group of natives presented a sum of money to their American pastor to buy, according to the custom of the Guerze people, a rush mat in which to bury President Kennedy. In Kampala, Ugandans crowded the residence of the American Ambassador; others sat silently for hours on the lawns and hillsides waiting. In Mali, the most left-wing of African states, President Keita came to the embassy with an honor guard and delivered a eulogy. In the Sudan a grizzled old Bisharine tribesman told an American lawyer that it was terrible Kennedy's son was so young; "it will be a long time before he can be a true leader." *Transition*, the magazine of African intellectuals, said, "In this way was murdered the first real chance in this century for an intelligent and new leadership to the world....More than any other person, he achieved the intellectual's ideal of a man in action. His death leaves us unprepared and in darkness."

In Washington grief was an agony. Somehow the long hours passed, as the new President took over with firmness and strength, but the roll of the drums, when we walked to St. Matthew's Cathedral on the frosty Monday, will sound forever in my ears, and the wildly twittering birds during the interment at Arlington while the statesmen of the world looked on. It was all so grotesque and so incredible....

It was all gone now—the life-affirming, life-enhancing zest, the brilliance, the wit, the cool commitment, the steady purpose. Richard Neustadt has suggested that two years are the period of presidential initiation. He had had so little time: it was as if Jackson had died before the nullification controversy and the Bank War, as if Lincoln had been killed six months after Gettysburg or Franklin Roosevelt at the end of 1935 or Truman before the Marshall Plan....

Yet he had accomplished so much: the new hope for peace on earth, the elimination of nuclear testing in the atmosphere and the abolition of nuclear diplomacy, the new policies toward Latin America and the third world, the reordering of American defense, the emancipation of the American Negro, the revolution of national economic policy, the concern for poverty, the stimulus to the arts, the fight for reason against extremism and mythology. Lifting us beyond our capacities, he gave his country back to its best self, wiping away the world's impression of an old nation of old men, weary, played out, fearful of ideas, change and the future; he taught mankind that the process of rediscovering America was not over. He re-established the republic as the first generation of our leaders saw it—young, brave, civilized, rational, gay, tough, questing, exultant in the excitement and potentiality of history.

Special Assistant Arthur Schlesinger stands beside President Kennedy as they join Attorney General Robert Kennedy and others to witness the televised liftoff of Mercury Astronaut Alan Shepherd on May 5, 1961. (John F. Kennedy Library)

He transformed the American spirit—and the response of his people to his murder, the absence of intolerance and hatred, was a monument to his memory. The energies he released, the standards he set, the purposes he inspired, the goals he established would guide the land he loved for years to come. Above all he gave the world for an imperishable moment the vision of a leader who greatly understood the terror and the hope, the diversity and the possibility, of life on this planet and who made people look beyond nation and race to the future of humanity. So the people of the world grieved as if they had terribly lost their own leader, friend, brother.

On December 22, a month after his death, fire from the flame burning at his grave at Arlington was carried at dusk to the Lincoln Memorial. It was fiercely cold. Thousands stood, candles in their hands; then, as the flame spread among us, one candle lighting the next, the crowd gently moved away, the torches flaring and flickering, into the darkness. The next day it snowed—almost as deep a snow as the inaugural blizzard. I went to the White House. It was lovely, ghostly and strange. It all ended, as it began, in the cold.

Credits

Photo Credits:

Cleveland Amory, p. 204, courtesy of Jerry Bauer
Jack Anderson, p. 205, courtesy of United Features Syndicate
Mario Andretti, p. 290, courtesy of Dan R. Boyd
Jules Bergman, p. 207, courtesy of ABC, Inc.
Erma Bombeck, p. 238, courtesy of ABC, Inc.
David Brinkley, p. 212, courtesy of Capital Cities/ABC, Inc.
Tom Brokaw, p. 213, courtesy of National Broadcasting Company
Art Buchwald, p. 85, courtesy of Diana Walker
Julia Child, p. 98, courtesy of James Scherer for WGBH
Hugh Downs, p. 215, courtesy of Capital Cities/ABC, Inc.
Michael Dukakis, p. 149, courtesy of Richard Sobol
Richard Eberhart, p. 216, courtesy of Hathorn/Olson Photographer, Inc.
Geraldine Ferraro, p. 89, courtesy of Rocco Galatioto
Ray Gandolf, p. 217, courtesy of Capital Cities/ABC, Inc.
Douglas Kiker, p. 40, courtesy of National Broadcasting Company
James Michener, p. 222, courtesy of Michael Lewis
Peter Nero, p. 267, courtesy of Harry Langdon Photography
Gary Owens, p. 270, courtesy of Harry Langdon Photography
Gayle Sierens, p. 224, courtesy of WXFL Tampa Television, Inc.
Sam Snead, p. 311, courtesy of U.M.I.
John Updike, p. 225, courtesy of Martha Updike

Index

Names appearing in **bold** indicate contributors to this book.

347

127; Houston, 124; San Antonio, 23, 33
Texas Book Depository Bldg., 29, 31-32
Thomas, Al, 23, 35
Thompson, James R., 195
Thornburgh, Dick, 196
Thurmond, Strom, 62
Tippett, J.D., 217
Tito, Josip, 339
Touré, Sékou, 339
TRANSITION, 340
Travolta, John, 282
Trible, Paul, 197
Truman, Harry S, 15, 340
Tunure, Pamela, 39
UCLA, 291
Udall, Morris K., 72
Unitas, Johnny, 314
United States Naval Academy, 313
Updike, John, 225
Valenti, Jack, 39, 25
Van Buren, Abigail, 226
Vance, Cyrus, 79
Vassar University, 5
Vaughn, Robert, 283
Virginia: Arlington, 84; Fort Monroe, 151; McLean, 6; Norfolk, 144; Portsmouth, 183; Virginia Beach, 321
Vogue, 5
Walker, Mort, 333
Wallace, George, 198, 88
Wallace, Mike, 227
Walton, Joe, 315
Walter, Jessica, 94
Walworth, Arthur, 228
Warren, Earl, 15
Warren Commission, 69, 81, 193, 216, 294
Washington Times-Herald, 5
Watson, Tom, Jr., 182
Wayne, John, 274
Webster, Daniel, 6
Weinberger, Caspar, 200
Weitz, John, 334
Welk, Lawrence, 284

West, Jerry, 316
West Virginia, 7, 92
White, Betty, 285
White, Mark, 201
White, Theodore H., 91, 286
Why England Slept, 2
Wicker, Tom, 41
Wilde, Oscar, 5
Wilde, Rudolpf, 20
William and Mary, College of, 298
Wolper, David L., 286
Wright, Jim, 41, 25, 26
Wyoming: Caspar, 60; Cody, 190; Kaycee, 60; Laramie, 104; Sheridan, 60
Wyoming, University of, 61, 104
Yale University, 101, 337
Yarborough, Ralph, 25, 26-27, 30, 33-34, 41
Ziegler, Ronald L., 202
Zumwalt, Elmo R., Jr., 335

About The Editor

John B. Jovich

In 1963 President John F. Kennedy visited Youngstown, Ohio as a guest of veteran Congressman Michael J. Kirwan. During that visit the President was introduced to Kirwan's neighbor, John Jovich— a meeting that was to have a lasting effect on the young man. Today, John B. Jovich is a nationally-known collector of Kennedy memorabilia and a recognized authority on John Kennedy. He has lectured throughout the United States about the 35th President. Jovich and his wife, Lisa, make their home in suburban Tampa, Florida.